P9-EEU-651

Please remember that this is a library book,
and that it belongs only temporarily to each
person who uses it. Be considerate. Do
not write in this, or any, library book.

WITHDRAWN

Beyond Disability

Also published by
SAGE Publications
in association with
The Open University

Disabling Barriers – Enabling Environments

edited by John Swain, Vic Finkelstein, Sally French and Mike Oliver

Details of the Diploma and related courses are available from
The Information Officer, Department of Health and Social Welfare,
The Open University, Walton Hall, Milton Keynes MK7 6AA, UK.

Beyond Disability

Towards an Enabling Society

edited by
Gerald Hales

The Open
University

in association with The Open University

SAGE Publications
London • Thousand Oaks • New Delhi

SAGE Publications Ltd
6 Bonhill Street
London EC2A 4PU

SAGE Publications Inc
2455 Teller Road
Thousand Oaks, California 91320

SAGE Publications India Pvt Ltd
32, M-Block Market
Greater Kailash – I
New Delhi 110 048

British Library Cataloguing in Publication Data

A catalogue record for this book is available from the British Library.

ISBN 0–8039 7956–8
ISBN 0–8039 7957–6 (pbk)

Library of Congress catalog record available

Typeset by Type Study, Scarborough
Printed in Great Britain by The Cromwell Press Ltd,
Broughton Gifford, Melksham, Wiltshire

Contents

Contributors

Colin Barnes
Lecturer/Researcher for Disability Research, School of Sociology and Social Policy, University of Leeds and British Council of Organisations of Disabled People.

Deborah Cooper
Director at Skill: National Bureau for Students with Disabilities.

Mairian Corker
Self-employed writer, researcher, trainer and consultant on all issues affecting the lives of deaf and disabled people, and qualified counsellor with own company, Deafsearch. Works for universities, local authorities and voluntary sector organisations on a contract basis.

Ken Davis
Member with Derbyshire Coalition of Disabled People.

Vic Finkelstein
Senior Lecturer, The Open University, School of Health and Social Welfare.

Sheila Ford
Lecturer and Consultant in Further Education and Disability.

Sally French
Senior Lecturer at Brunel University, Department of Health Studies and freelance writer.

Gerald Hales
Research Fellow, Institute of Educational Technology, The Open University.

Bernard Leach
Head of Department at Manchester Metropolitan University, Department of Sociology and Interdisciplinary Studies.

Dick Leaman
Independent Living Co-ordinator with Lambeth Accord.

Ann Macfarlane, M.B.E.
Director of Training and Research Consultant with Consultant Disability Services.

Sue Napolitano
Freelance writer and disabled activist.

Brenda Smith
Postgraduate Course Director and Lecturer in Disability Management at Work with City University Rehabilitation Resource Centre.

Ossie Stuart
Research Fellow with University of York, The Social Policy Research Unit.

Sian Vasey
TV Producer and Radio 4 presenter for 'Does He Take Sugar?' with Circle Pictures.

Collette Welch
Disability Consultant and freelance writer. Care Manager, London Borough of Waltham Forest.

Sallie Withers
Counsellor and Trainer in a private practice and with Herefordshire Lifestyles.

Ray Woolfe
Lecturer in Counselling Studies with Keele University, Department of Applied Social Studies.

Introduction

Much of what we all regard as 'knowledge' is heavily coloured by our individual experience; this underpins our beliefs, attitudes and constructs. The same is true of society, where the mode of practice of societally-defined aspects derives from the historical perspective. This includes components such as the expressed will of the people in democratic form, or the particular prejudices and practices of rulers; the type of education system operated and the degree to which that allows free expression or is constrained by political dogma or indoctrination; or the climate of religious and moral opinion.

Within this development of knowledge can be seen a general macroscopic trend in that over many years and centuries increasing enlightenment has suggested a passage from the feudal structure of society to the more democratic. The differences between these two which particularly concern us in this volume relate to the following. First, the feudal society has a small ruling caste which makes decisions concerning the functioning of society, the majority of the members of which have little choice but to accept the practices handed down to them. Good and beneficent practices can exist under such a system, of course, but the definition of what constitutes 'goodness' or 'beneficence' resides in the power base of the ruler(s). The aim is to retain power and decision making over the structure of life in the hands of those who 'know best'. Second, the democratic society has a small group exercising limited executive function on a short-term basis in a context which is determined by the will of the majority. The aim is to spread the ability for at least some degree of participation in decision making across a wide base of population of those affected and by providing an increasing range of opportunities (such as education) to enable every individual to be as self-determining as possible.

The progression from one state to the other will happen at varying speeds and at different times in different societies; it will also happen on a more microscopic scale at different speeds and at different times in different subsets of greater societies. Where the differential in the speed of progress between different subsets of people becomes too great there can arise a situation that some people are still being forced to work in a feudal-type structure while others have the benefit of a more free and self-determining life-style. It is this possibility in relation to people with disabilities that you should bear in mind when reading the chapters of this volume.

The idea that disability is socially-defined (also called the barriers approach) is not new: but to state it in impersonal terms does little justice to the profound effect that the details of the way society works can have on the lives of a substantial number of people. Knowledge of 'disability' (not, you will notice, the *people*, but the *condition*) is for most people limited to the occasional sight of a wheelchair or a blind person's white cane. And it is those pieces of equipment that they often remember – the hardware, not the person. The equipment, after all, is there to 'help', to 'fix things', to 'make things better'. A most common misconception is that the provision of the hardware that society has developed is a solution to any ills that may derive from disability. Thus the deaf person provided with a hearing aid has been supported by society; the blind person with a dog is perfectly mobile; and the wheelchair is the ideal means of travel for someone without the use of their legs.

Of course, when we think of the idea of 'society' providing help, support or succour we don't actually mean *us*. No, we mean the small subset of society which has been given the task of carrying out the practical jobs. This means that there is a group of people who can – and do – make provision for disabled people: they include nurses, social workers, interpreters, relatives, neighbours, paid assistants, drivers, home-helps . . . very many, in fact. But this establishment of a group which is seen by society to know the practical side of providing help for disabled people has another side: a group of people which is seen by society to *understand* the requirements of disabled people. This group can include medical personnel, advisers, counsellors, support staff, designers, planners, officers of organisations . . . another long list.

Indeed, the idea that there was a vast army of knowledgeable and competent people, some of them highly informed specialists, looking after the needs of people with disabilities, providing for their requirements large and small, would appear to many people as not only perfectly normal and natural, but generally speaking a good thing. Yet if we translate this situation back into the types of society mentioned at the beginning of this introduction, it becomes apparent that the context in which people with disabilities find themselves is not that enjoyed by many others – they are in a feudal society, not a democratic and self-determining one.

This is the major point that this book tries to develop. It is not, however, a remote treatise on the effects of life on other (disabled) individuals; it is about real people, going about their everyday life and additionally coping with the effects of

(1) a disability;
(2) the position people are placed in because of that disability.

Some of the authors discuss the effects of disability on them personally and some are concerned with the issues from the providing end of the equation. But all are concerned with the major matters of individual freedom and autonomy.

These concepts are central because a great deal of the situation in which disabled people find themselves involves some degree of intervention. Even among people who accept the social model of disability there is not always agreement as to what is acceptable in terms of intervention. For many the whole concept of 'intervention' is negative and undesirable and this is particularly so for the disabled person on the receiving end who has not been involved – or sufficiently involved – in determining what will actually take place. This can lead not only to disagreement and frustration but may also entail the personal rights of the disabled person being disregarded and the risk that they may end up worse after the intervention has taken place than they were before!

Interventions are not automatically negative, of course – indeed, they should not be. However, to make them positive, useful and fulfilling it is necessary that the wishes and goals of the disabled person are paramount and the methods of intervention, the timing of the intervention and the people involved are carefully considered and put into operation.

In this book you will meet many ideas, many concepts and many people, perhaps discussing and explaining matters that are new to you. Remember that everything here has grown up from the experience of individuals and is presented to you in the context of real lives. The ideas here may challenge you – they will certainly encourage you to think. You might well find that your ideas of what constitutes a 'professional' and the status of 'professional advice' undergo some reconsideration. You may, indeed, begin to give some thought to your own position in the scheme of things, and ask yourself 'What can I do to improve things?'

Such thoughts involve change – change in your beliefs, attitudes and ideas: and change is not always easy. If you find this difficult, first give some thought to the changes that take place in the lives of people with disabilities, especially if those changes are ones they did not request; then put the ideas in the context of the level of difficulty you have found and consider the stresses and strains which often form the backdrop to the interaction between disabled people and those who support them.

In turning this volume into a reality I have been supported by many people. The book is particularly aimed at students of the Open University and although it is of much wider use than just as part of the course, this situation means that I have worked closely with members of the Course Team in the School of Health and Social Welfare. I have also had much advice, hard work and loyalty from the individual authors. Almost every chapter in this volume has been specially written and in some cases that was not easy. My thanks go particularly to all those who slaved over a hot word-processor, not only to produce the chapters in the first place, but also to conform to the specifications I gave them. I must also record here my indebtedness to Wendy Bates, my secretary in the Open University, whose assistance in many mundane but essential organisational tasks was invaluable.

We have ended up with a book which gives a very comprehensive overview of the matter it discusses. Its primary thrust is 'enabling': I hope it enables you.

Gerald Hales
Milton Keynes
March 1995

SECTION 1: SETTING THE SCENE

We begin with a section which considers important ideas which form the foundation of any thinking in the area. Ann Macfarlane's chapter explores issues surrounding consultation, care, help, support and intervention for disabled people who have struggled and continue to struggle. She makes the point that consultation processes are not familiar experiences for disabled people and explains that this has often resulted in totally inappropriate forms of service provision. She considers Local Authorities and the processes of Assessment and includes thoughts on carers and accountability. She concludes that 'there is still a long way to go in order to break down barriers that often seem insurmountable for disabled people'.

Collette Welch contributes some detail on key issues in daily practice as they relate to the general area of Support. She explains that the key issues are not a set of rules, or even guidelines, but fulfil the role of elements that should catalyse, accompany or enhance every aspect of a working relationship or interactions between practitioner and client – elements that are often missing. The points she makes are ably illustrated with an in-depth case study.

1

Aspects of intervention: consultation, care, help and support

Ann Macfarlane

Historical perspective

For over 100 years disability has represented a culturally embedded and socially accepted form of oppression against disabled people (Barnes, 1991). In the twentieth century, following the dispersal of people from the workhouses, disabled people were either returned to village life or more systematically institutionalised in large, isolated residential establishments. Disabled children were sent away to boarding schools which were miles away from their family home. There they struggled to survive in sparse surroundings which were often poorly heated and where the food was less than adequate (Campling, 1981). The education they received comprised a basic curriculum, although – because many of these schools were established by the Church – religious education was delivered more intensively than any other subject. Disabled adults, too, found themselves separated from their families not only by distance but also by the strict regulations which were enforced. Rules often excluded visits from children, and adult visitors were often allowed in only infrequently. Much of the day would be devoted to exercising or trying to walk; because of the isolated places in which these institutions tended to be built there was very little in the way of employment or leisure stimulation. Disabled people were largely 'written off' and there were no expectations, or low expectations, of what disabled children and adults would achieve. It is only over the last 10 years or so that any real and meaningful attempts have been made to rescue disabled people from institutionalisation.

Illness and impairment

An important issue to be raised is that of the difficulties that have arisen over disabled people having been defined as 'ill'. There is often a confusion in people's minds over the distinction between 'illness' and 'impairment'. This has resulted in disabled people being caught up in the argument of whether their needs should be met by health provision (such as the community nursing service) or social service provision (such as being delivered by home care staff). When being assessed, disabled people's life-styles are broken down into segments. These segments may be labelled using such categories as 'nursing', 'personal', 'domestic' and 'social'. The debate will then focus on which authority will pay for which segment. The issue will become even more complex when a decision cannot be taken over whether a disabled person requires a bath or shower for medical or social reasons.

This chapter will explore issues surrounding consultation, care, help, support and intervention for disabled people who have struggled and continue to struggle with their ill-defined history and the difficulties which arise when illness and impairment become confused.

Introduction to the consultation process and service provision

Consultation processes are not familiar experiences for disabled people. Disabled people have survived in a society which, historically, has not included them in any form of consultation. This has resulted in totally inappropriate forms of service provision. The delivery of various forms of care, help, support and other forms of intervention are haphazard and ill thought out. Much of the service delivery experienced by disabled people has been dreamed up in offices by non-disabled people who have no understanding of what is required and certainly not had any direct experience of requiring or receiving personal assistance. For example, one of the main forms of support provided for disabled adults is that labelled 'home care'. It was formerly known as a 'home help' service but over time the service has delivered more personal support to disabled people. Decisions were often taken to discontinue routine domestic tasks and provide personal support. The difficulty with 'home care' provision is that it is designed to satisfy the needs of many disabled people and in order to do this its basis is a rota system. The rota puts disabled people into a 'queue' which means there is 'waiting time' for most of the people which quickly becomes 'wasting time' for the majority in the queue. In other words the system is designed around the staff and not the disabled person.

Local authorities and the consultation process

These issues have taken on increasing relevance since the introduction of the NHS and Community Care Act 1990, giving local authorities funding responsibilities for community care. The Act raised the issue of how consultation with disabled people would take place. Research undertaken by Glendenning and Bewley (1992) discovered that many local authorities did not involve or consult with disabled people before beginning their initial draft plans. Nevertheless, some local authorities began to make impressive and imaginative attempts at consultation processes through holding consultation

days, fora or workshops. These events have provided opportunities for
service providers from both health services and the local authority to meet
with the customers of their services to find out what is required. Experience
has shown that all too often these consultation days attract too few customers,
particularly disabled customers. The reasons why so few disabled people
become involved in these consultation processes vary. Often there is a lack of
transport, personal assistance and information in accessible formats. Many
disabled people are sceptical over whether their views will be taken seriously.
When disabled people have made the effort to attend consultation days they
have discovered that nothing has changed as a result of their attendance at
meetings. There is also the expectation that disabled people will become
involved in consultation without receiving any fee or travelling expenses. This
is unacceptable when set against a history of disabled people undertaking
unpaid labour in institutional establishments, for example, cleaning and
workshops. Their expertise is still not valued or recognised.

Suddenly to be consulted after years of struggling without any assistance, or
having received inappropriate or inadequate services, does not inspire
confidence in these consultative exercises. Some service providers are
making serious attempts to involve disabled people at all stages of service
planning and development. This is done in a variety of ways and where it
happens real results are being achieved. For example, consultation on a
one-to-one basis which involves the service provider and the disabled
customer means that a disabled person will gain confidence to carry out
self-assessment during the assessment process. This will result in a whole
range of opportunities opening up. These may include getting the local
authority to finance a personal assistance scheme to the disabled person who
can then purchase personal assistants. Perhaps for the first time a disabled
person will be able to choose who is going to provide support without having
strangers invading personal space or privacy. This self-assessment might lead
to gaining correct information for example about buying a car, getting a job,
receiving further education or participating in leisure activities. Consultation
which takes place in groups, such as disabled people being involved in a town
centre planning group alongside local authority officers, can lead to a
user-friendly environment. These meetings will also enable disabled people
to acquire new skills, such as learning how to place items on an agenda for the
meeting, how to put their views forward, and so on. It will assist disabled
people to identify their own training needs.

Assessment processes and consultation

Care in the community legislation states that an assessment should involve the
disabled person who should be able to have a say in the services that he or she
might be assessed to receive. However, assessments are usually made by a
care manager who is not only the assessor but also the fund holder. The care
manager while attempting to undertake a balanced and holistic approach will

also be making decisions about whether the disabled person's needs are of a medical or/and social nature. These decisions will not only affect how adequately the services selected will meet the disabled person's needs but will also have an influence on which budget will be debited.

Often assessments are carried out within a multidisciplinary team structure. The team may consist of many professional service providers and include a care manager, a doctor, physiotherapist, occupational therapist, a home care organiser, and so on. In the assessment process, not only is the role of the care manager extremely powerful but also the whole way in which the assessment is structured and processed can leave the disabled applicant vulnerable and unsupported. For example, assessments are often carried out in clinical surroundings to which the disabled person is invited. There can be as many as seven or eight assessors and they are likely to be people who know each other. They will have access to information but there is no check to ensure that it is accurate or well collated; it is often not shared with the applicant, in which case an obvious source of checking and verification is lost. The disabled person may be alone with all those assessors or it may be that only a 'carer' is invited to speak on behalf of the disabled person. Whatever the purpose of the assessment there needs to be some agreement about

- where it is to take place;
- why it is necessary;
- whether the disabled person requires or requests someone to assist;
- who the assistant should be if invited.

The assessment should be a form of consultation in which the disabled person can feel in control because it is that individual's life and life-style which is being considered; however, it can lead to the disabled person receiving lip service. Assessment processes should be centred on the viewpoints of disabled people. Consultation and communication with disabled people are key factors in this process but the way in which assessments are set up means there is little if any real change in the lives of disabled people. The outcome of many assessments mean that disabled people often receive fragmented and illogical support provided by the nursing service and home care staff. For example, a person providing nursing service may be able to assist the disabled person with catheterisation but his or her job description forbids the emptying of the bedpan. This means that a person from the social services department will be expected to undertake this task. It may be that only one part of a service will be provided and the boundaries will mean that a disabled person cannot get all the support and assistance required because it is not in the job description of the worker. This in turn can mean a disabled person receiving dozens of different service providers into his or her home on a frequent basis. Clear boundaries are often not worked out by the service providers themselves and many disabled people are still denied a bath or shower because a decision cannot be taken as to whether that disabled person needs a bath for medical or social reasons. Since consultation is often fragmented or non-existent between officers it is hardly likely that any meaningful consultation will occur with the disabled person.

Consultation processes and disabled people who belong to minority groups

It is important that consideration is given to how black disabled people, disabled people from other cultures, such as those from Europe, and disabled people who are lesbian or gay, find their way into and around the various consultation processes. Service providers often claim that it is difficult or impossible to discover the needs of black people, for example. Obviously, if black disabled people cannot access information in their own language then they will miss out on service provision. There is often a need to appoint an appropriate disabled development worker in a locality so that specific groups can be targeted. People from minority groups will need to have confidence in the worker and to know that their cultural issues will be understood and taken into account in service provision. Many disabled people, because of their cultural background and their sexual identity, have been denied the assistance available and every attempt should be made to include the whole disabled population, not just a section of it.

'Carers' and consultation

'Care' is often dispensed by people called 'carers'. Carers can be family members, other relatives, friends, neighbours, volunteers, or disabled people themselves, all of whom are unpaid and only some of whom *choose* to be carers. For adults who are in a partnership, the caring role can often change or spoil existing relationships. For instance, the strain of a disabled person having to rely on his or her lover for intimate personal tasks can be enormous. It can place a tremendous toll on both people and relationships can be damaged and result in the break up of the partnership. The strain is just as serious in a parental relationship where, say, an ageing father is providing care for an adult daughter. There is also the opportunity for emotional, physical and verbal abuse to occur (Macfarlane, 1994). Of course, it is not being suggested that all unpaid carers are uncaring or abusive, but it is important to recognise that relationships can change when the roles are those of 'carer' and 'cared for' and no longer 'lover' or 'family'.

There are circumstances in which the disabled person can be the manipulator or abuser and this usually comes about because the disabled person is frustrated by having no control over the situation. Often the disasbled person's life is in a complete stranglehold brought about by inappropriate housing and support. There are instances where a loving relationship can sit happily with a caring relationship but there should be the *choice* of taking on a caring role rather than having it thrust upon an individual.

It may be that the disabled person does not want to be toileted by a parent, or the parent does not want that task. Perhaps both people find it difficult to be honest and open with each other, or they may have tried desperately to receive appropriate solutions or assistance and found no one willing to respond. The disabled person and 'carer' may live in an area where there is no consultation process or service provision which can change the situation.

Paid professionals also take the label of 'carer' and this can be just as difficult or intimidating. Because a person has been trained to 'care' does not necessarily mean that they 'care' any more or less or are any more qualified for the task. Paid 'carers' are often in a system which humiliates the disabled person, leading to a loss of dignity. Paid 'carers' are seldom paid by the disabled person directly and so the control of that paid 'carer' does not remain with the disabled person. This makes it difficult to get the tasks done when and how required. Time sheets can be signed for work never carried out and so there can be just as much abuse of the disabled person whether receiving assistance from a paid or unpaid carer.

Accountability and consultation

Accountability in the consultation process is an important issue. Historically, there has been no accountability towards disabled people. For example, service providers, including doctors and paramedical staff, have used disabled people to gain knowledge by asking them to give an account of what it is like to be disabled. This has led to the expectation that disabled people will appear in front of groups of doctors or nurses and explain how they feel about themselves and how they live their life. Irrespective of the medical diagnosis a person has, whether it is that of cerebral palsy or emotional distress, there is a whole spectrum of different experiences for disabled individuals. No two people with the same diagnosis experience life in the same way and so this approach is extremely voyeuristic and dangerous. An individual disabled person talking about what it means to him or her to have cerebral palsy does not imply accountability to any other disabled person with the same medical label. What often happens in this tokenistic situation is that the professional onlooker will label the disabled presenter with some inappropriate description such as 'brave' or 'courageous' and then go on to label other people with a similar medical diagnosis in the same way. This makes it incredibly hard for disabled people to be themselves with a positive self-image. There will also be the comparison which states that 'if Mrs B who has multiple sclerosis can work then why can't Mrs A?' Tokenism does not lead to accountability. If service providers require information on a particular subject such as service planning, development or delivery, consultation needs to be undertaken with a group of disabled people which is accountable to disabled people in general.

This accountability comes through belonging to an organisation *of* disabled people who have agreed terms of reference and who understand the issues which surround being accountable to one another. Organisations *of* disabled people – that is, controlled and run by disabled people – can be contrasted with organisations *for* disabled people which are run entirely by non-disabled people or a mixture of disabled and non-disabled people. Organisations *of* disabled people may include non-disabled people but disabled members will be in the majority.

Therefore, if service providers wish to consult with disabled people, the consultation process will take into account people with different impairments. It may be that housing association providers are setting up a meeting with disabled people. That group of disabled people will possibly not have every kind of impairment between them but they will have studied the issues and will have consulted widely with people with a variety of impairments so that during the consultation period every aspect will be considered. Housing accessible to a wheelchair user also needs to be accessible to people with other mobility difficulties, sensory impairments, emotional distress, hidden impairments and learning difficulties because individuals may have multiple impairments. Consulting in this way leads to accountability with the needs of all disabled people being recognised. This process will assist in eliminating mistakes in housing and other types of provision for disabled people.

The charity issue and consultation

An area which is still under discussion by disabled people themselves concerns the many multimillion pound national organisations which have been established to provide *for* disabled people. These organisations, unlike organisations *of* disabled people, are single impairment organisations (for example, Mencap, Multiple Sclerosis Society) and do not have democratically elected executive or management committees where the majority of the members are disabled people. Over the past 40 years these organisations *for* disabled people have grown to encompass every identifiable medical condition and are in a position of great power and control. These controlling forces have done little to consult with disabled people, that is, the people they seek to serve. They join the great number of institutions which have done so much to render disabled people powerless. For example, one way in which people move forward and gain power is through being in the committee structure or by attending fora, workshops and conferences. However, many of these charity events are held in hotels which not only have inaccessible conference and syndicate rooms but which cannot provide accessible bedrooms and bathrooms either. Recently two disabled consultants whose job it was to arrange a national conference on housing and independent living for disabled people spent two months finding a hotel which could accommodate 60 disabled people. The prolific conference opportunities arising in the statutory, private and voluntary sectors seldom take into account the needs of the disabled conference-goer.

Care and disabled people

Care, for most disabled people, is a difficult word to define. Historically, disabled people have been 'cared for' in large institutional settings or within families who have had little or no support. Most of the 'care' received by disabled people has not been of their choosing or under their control. Many disabled people will define the care they have received as being oppressive, often of a custodial nature and provided in a controlled way. In large institutions disabled people have often been restricted to going to the toilet at certain times of the day and have had to accept a bath or shower on a specified day each week. One instance often quoted is that of disabled people going on to acquire kidney infections and disease as a result of restricted personal care. No formal research has been carried out but there is a body of anecdotal evidence from disabled people, and we can particularly note those who experience spinal injury and are readmitted to hospital for treatment of urinary tract and kidney infections due to limited or inappropriate personal support.

This controlled life-style also spills over into an enforced isolation whereby little stimulation is provided. This is contributed to by a lack of accessible public transport, discriminatory employment practices and inaccessible public buildings. Besides being denied care over bodily functions and personal hygiene, with little or no control over when those tasks will take place, there are other areas in a disabled person's life which can be controlled. For example, a disabled woman selected a holiday from a brochure, found out the cost and how she would travel and was assured there was good physical access which she needed. The manager of the residential establishment in which she was living told her that there was a 'home' to which she could go for two weeks and that a place had already been booked for her. The disabled woman had the total amount of money for this 'holiday' withdrawn from her account and she was forced to take this two-week vacation which was not of her choosing. Much manipulation goes on in residential establishments under the label of 'care' which seldom comes to light and over which no action is taken. Disabled people come to accept oppressive treatment. For example, a young student in a day centre who was able to communicate with an electronic alphabet board indicated that he wanted a cup of tea. The board was positioned in such a way that it was a struggle to reach and with much effort he spelled out his need for this refreshment. The person in authority to whom he was making this request and who knew the student well stated that he could not have anything to drink until he spelled out the word 'please'. Added to the disabled student's difficulty was the fact that he was sitting in a room which registered a temperature of nearly 100 degrees! Another example concerns a disabled woman lying on a trolley in an Accident and Emergency Department at the local hospital. X-rays showed she had a broken leg. Some five hours after her admission a nurse asked if she would like a drink. The woman responded by saying she would welcome a drink but would need a bedpan which would be difficult to manage. The nurse agreed and concluded that it would be inadvisable for her to have drink!

Care can be of a quality that is acceptable. However, there is anecdotal evidence that disabled people say they feel unable to state they do not receive good-quality care because they are afraid of reprisals. This anecdotal evidence of these fears particularly appears in day centres and where disabled people receive support in their own homes. Situations where the power structure leaves disabled people feeling so vulnerable makes thoughts of complaining very frightening. This is particularly evident where complaints procedures individualise the disabled person. Disabled people are fearful of reprisals either because they know what has happened to them if they have dared to complain in the past, or because they have witnessed what has happened to other disabled people who have complained. Some forms of punishment are extremely subtle and go unnoticed by all except the disabled person. For instance, a disabled person who has complained to a home care supervisor about a member of staff might then be revisited by that staff member and verbally threatened. Other similar examples include such events as staff members deliberately not going back to the disabled person so that the disabled individual is left waiting to go to the toilet for hours. Often disabled people do not know that a complaints procedure exists or how it works although some organisations are working on these procedures and consulting with disabled people's organisations so that disabled individuals can begin to gain confidence in making complaints.

Casual support and help

Over the past few years the kind of help disabled people have received on a casual basis, for example when out in the street or shopping, appears to have become less overpowering or overwhelming. The majority of non-disabled people are willing to offer assistance but the way in which the approach is made is very important. The wrong kind of assistance can result in damage to the disabled person or various kinds of abuse. Non-disabled people often say that they do not know how to approach disabled people and offer assistance. If this is the situation then they should remember that they have no responsibility for disabled individuals. There is one kind of response where the non-disabled person feels diffident over offering to help and there is the other kind where assistance can leave the disabled person feeling totally out of control. It is vital that people ask a disabled person whether help is required and how that help should be given. They should be willing to accept when a disabled person does not want assistance and immediately move away. However, there is often a difficulty with hearing the word 'no', as people feel that they are being rejected, not realising that the rejection is of the assistance offered and not of them personally. The person who is determined to do a 'good deed for the day' can be a menace. Disabled people can generally quote dozens of examples which illustrate inappropriate assistance received. They can also cite experiences where their space and privacy have been invaded. It is a fact that strangers will approach disabled people in the street and expect to receive answers to very personal or private questions. For example, it is not uncommon for disabled people to be asked whether they can have children which is not a question which would be put to non-disabled people in public. Receiving help from strangers is an important factor in the lives of most disabled people and help given which leaves the control with the disabled person is valuable. It should be remembered that disabled people are also givers.

Independent living schemes

In order to ensure that the 'care' a disabled person requires should begin to come under the control of the disabled individual a great deal of work needs to be done (Barnes, 1993). Exciting work is proceeding with the setting up of independent living schemes. In some parts of the country local authorities are beginning to understand the real benefits such schemes have for disabled people. Independent living schemes, as defined by disabled people themselves, are schemes whereby the disabled individual takes control of advertising, recruiting and interviewing for personal assistants. The local authority, together with disabled people, decides how they are to receive the money to pay their personal assistants. Because it is currently illegal for a local authority to pay money directly to the disabled individual, it is usually paid through a third party or through a trust set up by the disabled person. Therefore, if following assessment a specific number of hours and rate of payment is agreed, the local authority contribution will be paid either through a local voluntary sector organisation or directly into an established trust fund. The disabled person will then be able to have that money transferred into a private bank account.

For a disabled person to go through the process of becoming an employer who is responsible for employees can be an empowering experience. More and more disabled people are demanding independent living schemes because they have seen how such schemes can transform their lives. Usually the local authority will initially appoint a key worker to assist the disabled person in setting up his or her scheme, or it may be that a local organisation of disabled people is given the local authority budget. Their worker will then work with disabled individuals and will also encourage new applicants for independent living schemes. In some areas disabled people who have their own scheme will meet with other personal assistant users and so support each other and help to identify issues for discussion and resolution. It may be that disabled people need training on employment issues or there may be a need to establish emergency cover for personal assistants who are ill or on leave. For disabled people who do not want to become employers other more creative schemes than those which have existed for years are being worked on so that there is real choice for the disabled individual. For example, it is possible to provide rent-free living accommodation in exchange for defined assistance.

Interdependency

Interdependency is an essential element of economic and social life. This is part of a social structure which fulfils the different needs which individuals may have during a life span. Disabled people may have additional support requirements and the quantity and type of support needed will vary from person to person. How a disabled person will achieve the support required will depend on the consultation that takes place between the person offering support and the person who requires support. Initially a disabled person may require support while trying to access information. It might be that a disabled person requires support in selecting the appropriate information from a whole range of choices. It may be that physical access is denied through lack of provision to get into buildings: for example, there may be steps into the library or into the housing department. A disabled person may require different people to provide support for different aspects of his or her life: for example, the person chosen to read private correspondence may not be the person who undertakes domestic tasks. Sometimes a minor amount of support – emotional, physical, personal or practical – may enable a disabled person to be self-supporting in whatever it is he or she wishes to achieve.

Perhaps the disabled person has lacked opportunities. This often comes about due to the low expectation disabled people have of themselves and the low expectation non-disabled people have of disabled people. The common experience for the majority of disabled people is that they are told they are incapable or 'can't do' or 'shouldn't do' something and the constant repetition of such negativity often makes disabled people believe what they are being told. Disabled children often find themselves unable to make decisions or take risks, and this is also an experience for older disabled people. If a disabled person can be given positive messages, self-confidence will be gained. Once appropriate initial support has been given disabled people may soon discover their own levels of achievement. Other disabled people may need support in one area of their life only. For example, emotional support for a while might be applicable, particularly if the disabled person has been through the mental health system, or is newly disabled and needs to meet other disabled people who have had a similar experience. Some disabled people will always require support and it is how and when this is established that will be crucial to how the disabled individuals will go on and progress their lives. Support may be needed with:

- accessing information;
- personal assistance;
- domestic assistance;
- leisure and educational pursuits;
- employment;
- housing;
- financial benefits;

- transport/employing a driver;
- emotional issues.

The major support disabled people receive is that which is provided by relatives and informal support workers (Macfarlane and Hassan, 1994). It is becoming recognised that disabled people want (and in some cases are demanding) that they have choice over who provides their services. Many disabled people, whatever their age, want more control over how those services are designed and delivered. Service providers are beginning to offer more flexible services to disabled people and these new services are beginning to have an impact on the way in which disabled people can order their lives.

Becoming involved in organisations *of* disabled people

There is still a great deal of work to be done on the way in which disabled people can be at the centre of consultations and assessments, gaining appropriate support and different kinds of assistance. One important way forward is for more disabled people to become involved with organisations of disabled people. If there is no local organisation of disabled people then it may be worth getting a group of interested disabled people together to form such an organisation. In this way disabled people can empower and support each other and find ways to bring other disabled people into the network. These are exciting times for disabled people right across the world. There is a responsibility to ensure that disabled people who want to be involved in the world-wide political struggle are given the opportunity to do so in order to combat the culturally embedded and socially accepted oppression against disabled people.

Conclusion

The situations outlined in this chapter suggest that there is a need for a much stronger statutory underpinning of consultation, with enforceable legal rights for disabled people. There has been some movement – since the inception of care in the community legislation disabled people are beginning to become involved in consultation processes. However, this involvement is still on a small scale and often only relates to social services departments within local authorities. Often, these departments do not consult with disabled people prior to contracting for services within the private and voluntary sectors. Service specifications are much more likely to be inappropriate and ineffectual without consultation and can then discriminate against various sections of the population (Philpot, 1994). Further, in order to combat oppression, consultation is required on a range of wider issues such as housing, leisure, employment, education, local economic policy, access and so on. This has substantial implications in the wider society, too: if disabled people are seen to work with service purchasers and providers, who in their turn pass over some of the power, allowing disabled people to be in control of their lives, this leads to positive images of disabled people.

There is still a long way to go in order to break down barriers that often seem insurmountable for disabled people, but by examining current policies and practices – and especially by involving disabled people in a genuine and meaningful way – those barriers can be dismantled. Then change in forms of intervention, including consultation, care, help and support, will truly take place.

2
Key issues in support

Collette Welch

The evolution of the art of care management as the medium for implementing the fundamental principles of the Community Care Act with respect to disabled people is a complex and ongoing process. By describing care management as an 'art' it is intended to emphasise that a practitioner needs to exercise personal qualities and skills, particularly innovation and creativity, in order to be effective. It is particularly vital that practitioners have an unselfish attitude and approach to working with disabled people and it would not be difficult to envisage that in appropriate circumstances a successful and effective care manager could ultimately make him- or herself redundant. It is important to consider what circumstances are considered to be 'appropriate' and how a care manager can work effectively; these are issues that need to be considered in the context of actual practice.

As a starting point there are statutory and local policies, plans and guidelines, but these merely present us with a theoretical formula, structure or procedure with which to work. It is only by applying and evaluating any underlying principles in the context of actual practice and experience that we can learn which approaches and strategies are appropriate or effective in different situations. It is impossible to adhere rigidly to specific procedures or processes because of individual and circumstantial variations. As a practising care manager, most of my work is unconventional and unpredictable, because people in general are unconventional and unpredictable. This means that there is a continuous need to adopt a positive, flexible and uninhibited approach to work and relationships with disabled people.

Currently, I am practising as one of the new breed of care managers employed by a local authority. Care management and practitioners such as myself were generated by the Community Care Act which placed a statutory responsibility on the part of local authorities to implement a response to the needs of disabled people.

Essentially, care management has been defined in practice guidelines drawn up by the Department of Health Social Services Inspectorate (SSI) as 'the process of tailoring services to individual needs' by a 'cyclical process involving seven core tasks'. However, the interpretation of these definitions even in their broadest sense and meaning still leaves a considerable gap between theory and practice – or perhaps between ideal and reality. That gap is caused by lack of several components, particularly:

- information;
- continuity;
- understanding;
- experience.

Effective care management is a two-way process, involving interaction between the care manager and the disabled person. Where there is an imbalance of skills, knowledge and experience, these aspects need to be resolved, perhaps by the working out of a compromise between the practitioner and client by discussion and negotiation. It is important that a disabled person working towards independence and empowerment also acquires the ability to analyse and evaluate situations in order to make informed and appropriate decisions and choices about relevant needs and issues.

It seems that many practitioners start their working relationship with a disabled person with distinct advantages – certainly that was my experience. One such specific area is access to information on statutory and local policies and their interpretation and plans for implementation. In addition, a care manager is likely to have a clear understanding of his or her role and responsibilities as well as information on financial and other resources. It would not be difficult to come to the conclusion that care managers are selected and appointed because of qualities they possess or have acquired which of themselves could place disabled clients at a disadvantage in terms of perpetuating dependency.

It becomes obvious that there will not be one particular style or approach which is the right one. The basic philosophy and principles of care management must be seen as the foundation on which to build experience and expertise. Let us consider the base upon which this foundation is constructed.

In the practitioners' guide to care management and assessment (SSI Department of Health, 1991) seven core tasks are identified which constitute the care management process. These tasks cover responsibility for:

1 Publishing information
2 Determining the level of assessment
3 Assessing need
4 Care planning
5 Implementing the care plan
6 Monitoring
7 Reviewing.

This information is presented as a formal and structured process in order to provide guidelines for practitioners. It is the experience, knowledge and insight that result from applying those guidelines appropriately in practice that enable care managers to elaborate on the details and promote good practice.

We can identify in detail some of the elements or key issues that should be brought into daily practice when working with disabled people. To some extent these forge a link between theory and practice, sufficient at least to make the 'process' viable. These key issues do not represent guidelines or a set of rules, but rather fulfil the role of missing factors: elements that should catalyse, accompany or enhance every aspect of a working relationship or interactions between practitioner and client.

Key issues in daily practice

1 *Knowledge is power*: Knowledge and power should be shared with disabled people. They must be allowed time to assimilate information and decide what is valuable or relevant to themselves or their own life-style.

2 *Experience promotes confidence*: Disabled people must be allowed and encouraged to exercise their skills and knowledge, not just in personal or domestic interactions but in as broad a context as possible. Experience is a learning process as well as a framework of reference and this enhances self-confidence and decision making.

3 *Decision making and delegation*: Making informed choices and decisions on any issue, depends on information, knowledge and experience. A practitioner must ensure that disabled people have access to all relevant input and material which will enable them to decide what is right and best for themselves. Decisiveness will be demonstrated and developed in interactions with other people and these should be encouraged particularly in delegating tasks to carers and personal assistants.

4 *Consultation and assumptions*: Proposals, plans or developments must be discussed with disabled clients and their opinion or comments on issues relevant to them actively sought. Decisions should not be made on their behalf, nor should they be excluded from information about their own life. Assumptions of any kind should not be made.

5 *Priorities, aims and objectives*: These must be relevant to community care, care management and the relationship between practitioner and client. Priorities, aims and objectives should be discussed and clearly defined from the outset, and an agreement negotiated to determine respective roles and responsibilities in the relationship.

6 *Judgemental attitudes and bias*: Any blinkered or hidebound attitudes which might lead to a 'holier than thou' feeling, or anything that implies a sentiment of 'I know what's best for you' have no meaning or place. Indeed, they are potentially dangerous in the processes of assessment or identification of need.

7 *Respect and trust*: These are the bonuses to any worthwhile relationship, but these must be earned if they are to be accepted and understood. Respect and trust as a reciprocal process results from clarity, integrity, consistency, consideration and confidentiality in the relationship between practitioner and client.

8 *Communication and comprehension*: The quality, appropriateness and effectiveness of communication between a practitioner and a disabled

person is the bedrock of a good working relationship. Checks must always be made to ensure that any communication has been genuinely received, remembering that some people will have, for example, auditory or visual difficulties and the implications must be understood, especially if the disability is not immediately apparent, such as:

- a person with a learning difficulty;
- a person with dyslexia;
- a person for whom English is not the first language.

9 *Consideration and understanding*: An understanding and consideration of medical needs or personal care needs of a disabled person should be taken into consideration when making, for example, home visits. Discretion, tact and good timing on the part of a practitioner can assist in diminishing embarrassment or inconvenience felt by a disabled person.

10 *Perceptions and exceptions*: It should never be assumed that a disabled person has the same perceptions of his or her situation or needs as other people. This includes other disabled people, practitioners, family and friends. The management of difficulties associated with impairment or disability often involves other people, particularly carers, and in those circumstances the input or support of the carer may influence a disabled person's perception of needs and abilities. This can affect a disabled person's expectations of needs, abilities and access to support services.

11 *Perspectives and contexts*: When difficulties and need have been identified a disabled person may need assistance in establishing priorities and selecting which of these necessitate enabling interventions. This calls for considerable skill and judgement to be able to consider each difficulty or need both in isolation and in perspective against all related and relevant factors.

12 *Individual life-styles*: The uniqueness, individuality and personality of a disabled person must be reflected and respected in the response of people working with or for the disabled person, whose aspirations, expectations and needs should be understood in the context of his or her own life-style. Standards, habits and routines are the right of any individual, as facets of the person's life or personality – these must be supported or maintained wherever possible.

13 *Innovation and creative thinking*: Care management is based on two assumptions. First, that the resources available will be sufficient to provide the necessary services. Second, that the services themselves will be relatively easy to acquire. Nothing could be further from the truth. A practitioner wishing to avoid the wrath and reprisals (through the complaints procedure) of a disillusioned and disappointed client whose needs have not been met may have to change the approach. Care management is a challenge, particularly in terms of resource limitations. It offers scope and potential for the practitioner to develop an innovative and creative approach to 'meeting need' by encouraging disabled people

to consider a wide variety of solutions. This includes such examples as advertising for and employing their own support workers.

The care management connection

The unknown factors, variables and individual differences associated with the development of any new relationship are of particular significance in this context. A disabled person's personal circumstances, including individual experiences of life and people, will influence the disabled person's attitude and response to any intervention from professionals. Such intervention can easily be seen as interference. Similarly a practitioner may approach the relationship with a disabled person with preconceived ideas or a negative attitude, knowing that service options and resources are too limited to meet assessed need and that a successful outcome is unlikely. From the outset of the relationship and in any subsequent interactions it is vital that a clear understanding of roles, responsibilities and expectations is established between the practitioner and client. This may take some considerable time but nothing should be assumed or accepted within the relationship until a situation of mutual trust and respect has been established.

From the point of view of clients, the history behind their referral or connection with a care management service is particularly significant. There will be a minority group eligible for care management who have no previous history of contact with the local authority. These may be people new to the area, or people who have become recently disabled, or people whose situation or circumstances have changed to the extent that they now require services or support when they did not previously. From the first point of contact with the local authority, through self- or secondary referral, the client has 'keyed-in' to the system. Every disabled person has a statutory right to a detailed assessment of his or her needs and negotiable access to services to meet those needs. It is hoped that from the outset all clients will be provided with adequate information and advice on their eligibility for, access to and provision of services. This will assist clients in making informed choices and decisions and will enable them to enter into positive and productive discussion with, for example, service providers.

The majority of clients who are referred to a care management service, however, are already known to the local authority as established service users. The previous experiences of this client group in terms of history of their interaction with, responses to and service delivery from 'the system' may significantly, and often adversely, affect initial dealings with their care manager. Most of the difficulties encountered by these clients are undoubtedly associated with the elements of confusion, insecurity and dependency prompted by change.

Persistent and perpetual change is disabling and is a barrier to the ultimate goals of independence or empowerment. It forces people to cling to old values, systems and services, perhaps resentfully and reluctantly, even when they are outdated or inappropriate. For change to be of any value, it has to be lasting and consistent; change that is intended or perceived as only a temporary solution or measure inhibits response, cooperation and commitment.

Change resulting from statutory legislation and its implementation, together with variable interpretations at local government level, have coincided with other sweeping reforms and reorganisation. These have affected not only the statutory and voluntary sectors but also the private sector, which is now an essential and competitive area for service provision. All these events must be seen against a background of recession, which precipitated and complicated much of the change which has occurred over the past decade. In addition, departments and agencies responsible for the provision of information and advice on any changes relevant to disabled people simply cannot keep pace with new directives. Consequently, there is sporadic and disproportionate awareness and knowledge of change, not only by disabled people themselves but also by practitioners and service providers in general.

Given the complex background and the changes and confusion present in the introduction of the Community Care Act, the emergence of the new breed of care managers has met with a mixed reception from disabled clients. Many disabled clients perceive care managers to be fashionably redeployed social workers, a perception which is perhaps a symptom of chronic change. Following from this it is not necessarily surprising that the life expectancy or staying power of the care manager is viewed with some scepticism. However, irrespective of any future changes in the provision of community care the current care managers should be seen in the context of their legislative brief and essential functions. The most important principle for practice is to transfer responsibility for self-management and ultimately independence to disabled clients, by whatever means, methods or skills are possible.

Care management in practice

Practice is undoubtedly the proving ground for theory and principles as well as systems and resources. It highlights any deficiencies or grey areas which exist in the current system of accessing services, matching services to need and the coordinating services involving multi-agency input. Issues, dilemmas and situations arise daily in the lives of disabled people, as well as in case management practice, which necessitate responses neither identified by or provided for by the Community Care Act or other resources. The following example of care management in practice describes one situation involving a disabled client which illustrates some of the points and issues outlined.

Case example

An urgent message was relayed to a care management service from the relative of a severely disabled man to say that his care situation had broken down irretrievably and that urgent help was needed. The note had been annotated with the comment 'crisis intervention?' No other information was available at that time and it seemed that he was unknown in the social services department. A telephone call to the man's home met with a emotionally charged response from a relative and it took considerable diplomatic negotiations before he was allowed to take the call himself. He was clearly very distressed and repeatedly asked not to be taken into 'institutional care'. It seemed that a year previously he had been diagnosed as having an aggressive and rapidly progressive neurological condition; his care and support had been provided by and contained within the family. More recently his 'care' had been taken over exclusively by the two relatives who were now withdrawing their support. An appointment was made to visit later that same day.

Crisis intervention demands a rapid assessment of the situation as it presents itself, followed by immediate decisions about priority needs and action to meet these needs. In this case the situation presenting on arrival for the home visit was tense and highly charged. Initially, attention was divided between reassuring the client, whose express concern was that he would have to go into residential care, and defusing and containing outbursts of anger and frustration from all parties as they occurred. Once the situation was more conducive to allowing meaningful dialogue the task was to identify and prioritise the client's current needs for personal care and support in order to take appropriate action. As this could be achieved more effectively with the cooperation of the family carers present, it seemed to defuse further the conflict by encouraging some discussion and more positive interaction.

The client had expressed a clear wish to remain in his own home; that decision and choice determined all that followed. He needed 24-hour care, assistance and supervision with all activities associated with daily living. Translated into action, and to meet his considerable needs, a full-time 24-hour care package was required immediately. This would involve two main areas for negotiation, in the absence of a full assessment and conventional procedures for accessing services and resources. First, an approved agency or department had to be identified which could provide urgently a small team of experienced care staff to cope with the client's immediate situation. Second, the resources to finance the care package had to be found – also urgently. This situation called for desperate measures as it necessitated bypassing all the conventional, orthodox and approved routes by which the provision of services or resources in response to assessment are normally accessed.

With the consent of the client, the following immediate actions were taken:

1 The local authority's home care service was contacted to establish what resources were available in terms of practical and financial help. On this occasion resources could not meet the need for 24-hour care input but an agreement partly to fund the care package was made.
2 Two other emergency budgets were identified and accessed with an agreement to fund temporarily the urgent care package.
3 Having identified the client's basic care needs and drafted a simple care

plan, the search for an agency which could fulfil the brief at short notice followed. A tentative agreement was reached relatively quickly with the care coordinator of a local 'approved' care agency and this was followed up with an assessment visit to the client's home later that same day.

4 At that meeting, arranged to discuss his care needs, the client had the opportunity to meet the agency care coordinator personally at the outset. This promoted positive interaction, a sense of total involvement, and enabled the client to start thinking about his criteria for eventually choosing his own carers. The agency was made aware of the fact that it was a very difficult situation with which the client had to cope. He was unused to strangers dealing with his personal care and had no experience of identifying, delegating or directing tasks to be done. It was also essential, even for the emergency care package, that different agency carers were kept to a minimum number of experienced staff.

Subsequent meetings with the client occurred on a daily basis for the first two weeks. Not only did he require a great deal of moral support and encouragement but there was a vast backlog of information to be given to and discussed with him. This also presented an opportunity to develop a good working relationship with the client and observe and advise on his interactions with the agency care staff. A detailed assessment of his needs was completed in addition to numerous referrals and applications for support services and access to other resources.

A summary of additional and follow-up action on behalf of the client is as follows:

1 A detailed assessment of need was carried out with the client.
2 Formal application was made for long-term financial resources.
3 With the client's consent, relevant support services were requested.
4 Based on the assessment of need, a detailed care plan was drafted jointly with the care agency coordinator and the client.
5 Regular monthly review meetings were set up to monitor the care package at the client's home, involving all relevant parties.
6 The client devised his own criteria for selecting carers through the agency, which he felt was a satisfactory arrangement.
7 An application to access the Independent Living Fund was completed.
8 Referrals not only covered requests for services or resources, but were also a useful method of introducing the client to other practitioners or service providers who could be of assistance. These included: the client's General Practitioner; the district nurse; the incontinence adviser; the wheelchair services; the occupational therapy department; and the community physiotherapy department. Referrals also went to the Benefits Agency, the local authority housing department, local voluntary and independent organisations and the representative organisation for the specific disabling conditions.

When the general situation was more stable the client described something of his background and the events preceding the 'crisis'. It seemed that prior to 'losing his independence' after the 'disease and subsequent disability took over his life', he had been the mainstay and support for most of his extended family. As a result of his decline some of the family had disappeared while others continued to make demands of him and take advantage of his predicament. The two relatives who had let him down so badly had 'won him over' with the promise of providing permanent full-time care to enable him to remain in his own home. In return, and as part of the arrangement, he had shared with them his home, his vehicle and his financial resources (including benefits). This arrangement had worked reasonably well at first while his 'carers' had ample free time to live their own lives. However, when his personal and physical needs increased in proportion to his rapid deterioration, the care situation soured. The rest of his family and friends were alienated and made to feel unwelcome in his home by the carers, who began to be resentful and irritable, not only about the nature of tasks involved, but also about the amount of care required during both day and night. Over a period of three months he became increasingly isolated and depressed and withdrew inside himself. He said nothing about the 'abuse' and treatment to which he was being subjected because he was afraid that if he lost his carers the only alternative would be to go into residential care. He also felt a sense of confused loyalty to his family carers who had persuaded him that it was much better for him to be cared for by his 'nearest and dearest'. The client had never had the opportunity of discussing either how he felt about his increasing loss of independence or the fact that his life had been 'taken over' by circumstances and other people.

It was a cause for concern that his independence of body, mind and spirit had declined so dramatically over a relatively short space of time. This was not entirely the result of his progressive neurological condition but related more to the inappropriate personal care and general absence of information, advice services and support. He did not have the equipment, services or support necessary to enable him to maintain either his dignity or a reasonably independent life-style.

During the ensuing months, there were many incidents and situations, involving his family and the formal carers, where conflicts of interest or life-styles became an issue. Dependency and vulnerability are unrelated, yet that does not seem to deter some of the 'doers' and 'carers' from wanting to take over and run disabled people's lives. Family members, carers and the client reported incidents where, for example, windows were opened against his wishes, the television would be used without asking him, or he was refused cigarettes, being 'reprimanded like a child' for 'smoking too much'. The client also said that at times the inappropriate choice of language or vocabulary, including unnecessary comments, caused offence – for example, 'we are stroppy today aren't we'? or 'there's a good boy' or even referring to bodily functions or organs in coarse or infantile terms.

For the client, learning to direct his life and activities through carers and facilitators was a unique experience. Many mistakes and errors of judgement were made both by the client and by some of his carers. Ultimately he regained his self-respect, recouped much of the independence he had lost and learned to manage or delegate responsibility for running his own life. He became adept at identifying and anticipating his own care needs and deciding how and when those needs could best be met.

The care management service eventually withdrew to adopt a more passive role in monitoring the quality, consistency and appropriateness of services delivery to the client while still providing him with support and encouragement. Regular reviews and reassessment of the client's needs now ensure a rapid response to any changes that may occur in his condition or situation because of his poor prognosis.

SECTION 2: THE PRACTICALITIES

This section commences with some thoughtful insights by Sue Napolitano, who discusses the situation for mobility impaired people. She distinguishes between physical access and psychological access, making the point that the history of making access to buildings available has some unexpected negative aspects as well as helpful ones.

Colin Barnes then goes into the details relating to visual impairment. This is a chapter written from the perspective of personal experience and he expresses the hope that he can provide something of an insight into both the practical implications of his condition and his perceptions of the role of medical and/or 'rehabilitative' interventions.

Mairian Corker introduces us to the impairment of a hearing difficulty, exploring the experiences of people who have difficulty with hearing and especially considering the constraints which result as well as the possibilities that exist for rehabilitation interventions. This chapter also looks at the role of personal and professional interventions and considers differing perceptions of 'impairment' and 'disability' and the origins of those perceptions.

Section Two concludes with Sheila Ford's contribution in the area of learning difficulties. She makes the point that the concept of a learning difficulty relates to individuality and takes us through the various stages of the individual's life and development, from birth to adulthood.

3
Mobility impairment

Sue Napolitano

Mobility is a fundamental feature of human life and society. It is how, as children, we develop our spatial awareness; it is how we, literally, get what we want; and it is one of the important factors in our ability to participate in society. If societies wish to punish or disempower particular individuals or groups, one of the key ways that this can be done is through placing limitations on mobility. Prisons, pass laws, curfews and playpens are all examples of this.

When we talk about 'impairment' we refer to some limitation in the functioning of an individual's body or mental capacity. When we talk about *mobility* impairment we are usually referring to limitations that an individual has in physical functions like walking, running, climbing, and standing. Often, when someone has this kind of impairment, it is perceived by fellow non-disabled citizens as somehow 'natural' that lack of mobility should follow. The obvious question seems to be: 'How can anyone expect to get around without being able to walk?'

But if we stop to think about it more carefully we will realize that in modern western societies the amount of walking undertaken by most people is surprisingly limited. Often it amounts to little more that popping out to the corner shop, pushing baby around the park, nipping out to the pub, and an occasional recreational stroll around a beauty spot. Apart from that, in general, our populations take to wheels. What an array of wheels there are: bicycles, scooters, motorbikes, cars, vans, buses, lorries, milk floats, trains. For longer journeys we take to the skies. There is no-one more mobile than astronauts (in terms of distance travelled) and they were not expected to walk to the moon. The important point is that in modern industrial societies the way most distances are covered is by the utilisation of man-made conveyances. The potential that this brings is enormously liberating. The physical inability to walk need no longer place limitations on a person's mobility. We can design and build our way out of that trap. To borrow a phrase from the Women's Liberation Movement, at last we can see that biology is not destiny.

And yet, so deeply is the assumption held that mobility impairment inevitably leads to immobilisation that all too often the means of transportation, and the places to which they transport people, continue to be designed as though mobility impaired people were not part of the travelling public. The entire process then becomes a self-fulfilling prophecy: since mobility impaired people have been designed out of the buses, trains, etc., they are not able to use them and hence become immobilised.

The barriers erected in respect of mobility are not limited to the design of transportation. After all, vehicles are only part of what mobility is all about: they merely carry you to your approximate destination. After that there is the fine tuning, the more delicate process of getting from the bus to the concert hall, from the car into your mum's house. Sometimes people go out for the sheer pleasure of movement, sight-seeing, or just being. At other times there is a more focused purpose, perhaps a visit to the Town Hall to sort out a council tax problem, or going to see the Christmas pantomime at a child's school, or buying a birthday present. In these cases the intention is not just to be *moving* or simply outside, there is also a need to get into a particular building and be able to fulfil the intended purpose there. Many of the barriers that make it difficult for mobility impaired people to achieve these goals have now been well documented and due largely to the efforts of the disabled people's movement, the level of awareness about them in the population as a whole is gradually being raised. Such things as steps without ramps as an alternative, or flights of stairs without lifts as an alternative, are now more likely to be spotted as presenting unacceptable obstacles to mobility than ever before.

The understanding of mobility issues has gone further in some large stores and local authority buildings. Occasionally people with mobility impairments now find themselves welcomed by wide automatic doors. Where these are found, invariably a wheelchair-accessible toilet is not far away. It is such a relief to have this particular need recognised in the bricks and mortar of an establishment! But these developments have often arisen from a formulaic approach which implies that once a ramp has been put in then the barrier has been removed. Such a belief betrays a chasm in understanding between those who are in charge of such things as buildings, transport and the outdoor environment and mobility impaired people who are trying to play their part in the world. The lives of mobility impaired people do not run to a simple formula – like everyone else's they are detailed ordinary day-in day-out affairs made incredibly complex by the mass of barriers erected. Removing the barriers requires a deeper and more subtle understanding than the 'put in a ramp' approach.

One of the ways in which the attempt to create access goes wrong is when, in removing one barrier, another barrier is created. This is a common problem and is frequently encountered with lavatories designed for use by disabled people. Often the lavatories are kept permanently locked. Whether the mobility impaired person is stopping off at a motorway service station, a railway station or a public convenience they will be confronted by the same thing. While non-disabled people can simply walk into a lavatory, or get in for a small price, people with mobility impairments have to send off search parties for someone who has the key, or subscribe (at a cost) to the National Key Scheme operated by the Royal Association for Disability and Rehabilitation (RADAR).

A personal experience: 1

I was unfortunate enough to come across another example of the removal of one barrier creating another when making a business visit to a city centre office building. Here a short flight of stairs separated the entrance from the reception area and the lifts to upper floors. To overcome this barrier one of the tenants had installed a stairlift, but this could be operated only by a member of that organisation, who had to be summoned by someone on reception. Entering the building I was confronted by the stairs, complete with lift, and an expanse of hallway: at some distance was the reception counter where receptionists sat behind protective glass. At the entrance level there was no buzzer or intercom or other way of summoning assistance and the only way I could deal with this situation was to shout. Unfortunately shouting, in English culture, is interpreted as angry, rude behaviour and is frowned upon. Being forced into the position of having to shout to gain access did not do much for my interaction with that organisation. This is a good example of the situation where the attempt to make parts of the environment accessible has been done in such a way as to create frustration, dependency and complication for mobility impaired people.

Another thing that can go wrong is when good or reasonable access is built into the architectural design of a building, but the non-disabled staff and users render this ineffective by the unaware way in which they use it. A disabled toilet full of mops, brooms and a year's supply of toilet rolls is not an uncommon sight and it frequently prevents a wheelchair user getting in. Furniture is often placed so close to doors that the opening width is obstructed and becomes too narrow for wheelchairs to get through; ramped entrances that are not the main entrance to a building are particularly vulnerable to this kind of thing.

A personal experience: 2

Arriving at a women's centre one night for a cultural event, I rang the bell at the top of the only ramped entrance to attract help. After a pause a head popped out of a doorway several yards away, and a voice shouted 'Go round the front!' (to the main, inaccessible, entrance). I was speechless. Someone finally came to let us in, but then we confronted the further indignity that tables and chairs in the room where the event was taking place had been arranged cabaret-style in front of the door that gave access from the ramped entrance and disabled toilet.

In this instance disabled people's needs and rights *had* been remembered in the design or conversion of buildings, but the users had behaved as though we did not exist. In order to access the facilities put there for the use of disabled people I had to make a fuss. Too often disabled people have to hang around while mops and buckets are moved before they can use a toilet provided for their use; while cupboards, tables and chairs are moved away from the entrances to activities in which they wish to take part. Their right to freedom of movement is undermined and they run the risk of being regarded as, and made to feel like, nuisances.

This leads me to the next point. Creating barrier-free environments for people with mobility impairments is something which has a very firm physical dimension and this is generally understood. The wide doors, ramps and lifts are all undeniably physical as are the narrow doors, steps and stairs that went before. But there is a psychological dimension to the changes needed as well. Good inclusive design will send positive messages to disabled people, messages which tell them: 'you are important'; 'we want you to be here'; and 'welcome'. The effect of this on mobility impaired people can be dramatic. The element of struggle so often present in daily life fades, confidence and the ability to function is enhanced and a relaxed and open attitude is more likely to prevail. When making access arrangements this psychological element needs to be considered carefully: if the way that disabled people are expected to get into a building is round the back, past the bins and through the kitchens, what message does that communicate? How will it make a disabled person feel? Will that message and those feelings enhance or undermine their ability to participate?

A personal experience: 3

Some time ago I visited a city centre arts centre to see a vibrant exhibition of carnival costumes. It was imaginatively staged, complete with steel band soundtrack and light show, giving an impression of life and movement. The exhibition was arranged so that dummies wearing the costumes were facing the doorway that led from the stairs to the gallery. People walking up the stairs and coming through those doors had a high-impact experience. It was meant for them. I arrived via the lift. As I entered the gallery all the dummies had their backs to me. I felt as though I was not really meant to be there at all, that I was being let in as a favour and should not expect anyone to take any notice of me, that I should realise that I was second class. I was hurt and angry and my enjoyment of an otherwise excellent exhibition was seriously dented. While the physical access was fine, the psychological access certainly was not.

Related to this notion of psychological access is the role of aesthetics in creating an environment that is accessible to mobility impaired people. The problem of aesthetics barely looms at all when we are thinking about new buildings: architects can incorporate standards that have been developed over the past 20 years harmoniously into their designs. However, many of our towns and cities have a large stock of public buildings that are at least 100 years old, which were built at a time when disabled people were simply not considered either at the design stage or afterwards. To make them accessible adaptations are required. Up to about 10 or 15 years ago there seemed to be a prevailing notion that ramps and other adaptations were inevitably ugly piles of scrap stuck on to otherwise interesting or beautiful old buildings. It was a matter of engineering rather than architectural design. Ken Lumb (1994: 5) writes wittily of this phenomenon in relation to Manchester's Whitworth Art Gallery: 'This structure, or ramp, had the appearance of a load of old scrap metal which had been dumped on the steps and fixed where the pieces lay.'

Not surprisingly, non-disabled people with an interest in preserving our architectural heritage became upset by this tendency, and the shoddiness of adaptations became a reason to resist making any adaptations at all. Preserving the heritage was considered more important than letting in disabled people. The problem was aggravated by the fact that many of the grandest and most architecturally interesting old buildings are also the ones that people most need to get into – town halls and central libraries for example. Many disabled people responded to this situation by sneering at aesthetic concerns. Their freedom of movement was more important, in their view, than arty considerations such as the way things look. To some extent this is understandable, but there was a reason why the Victorians and the Georgians made those buildings so elegant or so grand. It was to do with reflecting and engendering a sense of pride in citizenship, a sense of belonging to something larger than self and family and local community. A sense also of the importance of the activities that take place within those buildings, whether they be municipal functions, learning or cultural pursuits. The grand architecture is a very effective way of communicating those messages. A trip to any older municipal centre always makes me hold my head a little higher and my eyes shine a little brighter. So I wasn't at all happy with the idea that getting my share of what goes on in those buildings should inevitably produce an aesthetic blot on the cityscape. If my participation could only be made possible by some ugly contraption, what did that say about me? What would it do to my sense of pride in citizenship? Would I be able to go into these buildings without first apologising to the conservationists?

Of course, after conservationists and disabled activists had been glaring at each other over committee room table tops for long enough it became clear that the dilemma was a false one. Ramps did not have be made of concrete or stainless steel and grab rails did not have to be made of lengths of steel tubing bolted together with wing nuts. This way of doing things had sprung from the oppressive idea that ramps were not valid architectural features in their own right, but things you had to stick on to buildings to benefit a tiny minority of the population, while spending as little money as possible. Once this mind block had been overcome it was discovered that beautiful ramps could be constructed in the same stone as nineteenth-century buildings and grab rails could be made of brass with elegant Victorian styling. People realised that considerations of style and taste could be applied to adaptations for mobility impaired people as easily as they could to anything else and the result was that buildings which were intended to be entered with pride, *can* now be entered with pride – by mobility impaired people as well as everyone else.

Mobility impaired people want to get everywhere; with the technology and design know-how at the command of twentieth-century western society there is no reason why this desire should not become a reality. But being able to use the environment is about more than being able to 'get about'. At a deeper level it is about a sense of belonging. Until the environment supports mobility impaired people's participation with dignity and pride intact, this sense will continue to evade them.

4
Visual impairment and disability

Colin Barnes

This chapter is written from a personal perspective. The main aim is to discuss my experiences as a man with a congenital visual impairment. In doing so I hope to provide something of an insight into both the practical implications of my condition and my perceptions of the role of medical and/or 'rehabilitative' interventions.

To achieve this I have adopted a biographical approach and divided the ensuing discussion into three separate but interrelated sections. Following the definitions of impairment and disability proposed by the disabled people's movement (Barnes, 1991) the first section focuses on my condition and its effects and the second provides a brief biography outlining my experience of disability; namely, the social consequences of living with impairment. The third section outlines the strategies I have used to overcome the disabling process within the context of school and at work. I conclude by suggesting that medical interventions are appropriate only for minimising and monitoring the negative effects of medical conditions, and that coping with disability can only be learned from people who have experienced it themselves – disabled people. Based on these insights I suggest that there is an urgent need for a thorough reappraisal of rehabilitation-type services.

Impairment

I have a visual impairment caused by a condition known as congenital cataract. This is similar to the progressive cataract associated with ageing and it refers to opacity of the lens of the eye, causing blindness. It is treated by the removal of the affected lens during surgery, and vision is then enhanced with artificial lenses. This can be done in one of three ways (Hillman, undated: 9):

- thick 'cataract' spectacle lenses;
- contact lenses;
- tiny plastic intraocular lenses inserted into the eye during the cataract operation.

Although cataract surgery is now routine and fairly straightforward, in some cases it can damage the eye causing other vision impairing conditions. Two examples include mystagmus and glaucoma. Mystagmus refers to continuous involuntary eye movements; it is non-treatable and can make focusing difficult. Glaucoma is an increase in intraocular pressure which causes the eye to harden; it is controllable with the daily insertion of eye drops and/or surgery to relieve pressure, but if untreated it can result in blindness.

I was born 'blind' because the lenses in both my eyes were opaque. However, as the condition was detected immediately, I had two 'needling' operations on my right eye before I was one year old. This means a hole was made in the centre of the lens enabling me to see. The left eye remained untouched because it was to act as a kind of reserve in the event of anything happening to the sight in my right eye. I understand that although this was fairly common practice in the late 1940s, when I was born, it would not happen today.

As a consequence of the operations, with the aid of spectacles I can see with my right eye but not with my left. This does not mean that I cannot see anything with my left eye, but the images pale into insignificance when compared with those provided by the right eye. The best way I can describe the difference between the two is by comparing them to two television screens placed alongside each other, where one is 'normal' but the other is considerably smaller and extremely dark so the picture is almost incomprehensible. I use the term 'normal' here because what I see with my right eye is normal for me, it is all that I have known. Indeed, my sight has remained constant throughout my life. I cannot remember not being able to see nor can I remember the operations, and I have always worn 'thick' glasses. I have tried contact lenses but I find that the extra magnification spectacles provide is extremely useful, particularly for reading. According to my ophthalmologist my vision with glasses is 6/36 – about one-sixth of that of someone with 'normal sight'.

I also have mystagmus, although this has never caused me any problems. It is only evident when I focus on things which I find difficult to see and on these occasions I have an involuntary tendency to move my head to compensate for the movement in my eyes. Unlike my father (who also has congenital cataract and a similar visual range to mine) I have not developed glaucoma. This is confirmed annually by routine checks at my opticians.

Disability

In practical terms my impairment has caused me few real difficulties – it causes me no pain and, hitherto, has and is likely to remain relatively stable. The problems I have encountered have all been socially created – mainly as a consequence of the experience of segregated special education, and my subsequent perceptions, whether real or imagined, of society's treatment of people with this kind of impairment. However, these difficulties were not unexpected, for I knew that my parents had to deal with similar experiences for most of their lives. Unlike the overwhelming majority of disabled people

I grew up in a household where impairment was not considered a problem nor, indeed, something of which to be ashamed. Both my parents perceived themselves as working class and I was taught from a very early age that society had little to offer people at the bottom of the class structure – especially if they happened to have an impairment.

Both my father and my mother had first-hand experience of the discrimination encountered by disabled people. My father grew up in Montreal, Canada, brought up by my grandfather who abused him both physically and verbally because he could not see very well. He came to England when he was 18 years old and after several attempts to get a job in mainstream employment ended up in a workshop for 'the blind' working for subsistence wages, first as a basket maker and later as a mat maker. My mother came from a solid north of England working-class family; her father was a bricklayer and she had six sisters and one brother. As a result of a cycling accident in her early teens she acquired a slight visual impairment which was corrected with spectacles. In order to supplement the family income she worked extremely hard; while my brother and I were very small this meant her working as a cleaner when our father came home from work and when we grew older she often had two part-time jobs. She also experienced periods of severe emotional distress and was diagnosed as a 'schizophrenic'; as a result, she was frequently admitted to psychiatric hospitals for a variety of 'treatments'.

Although both my parents had impairments they did not consider themselves to be disabled people. They did not mix with other disabled people socially and they associated 'disability' with passivity and dependence – qualities which both of them abhorred vehemently. They were fiercely independent and did their best to ensure that my brother and I 'could look after ourselves'. I was the first of two children and although my brother has no impairments whatsoever and is two years my junior, my parents treated us both exactly alike. Unlike my father's relationship with my grandfather I was never made to feel inadequate because of my impairment. The only difference it made to our upbringing was that my brother was never allowed to help me find things I had lost, and my tendency for blindness-related behaviour (see below) was discouraged.

The reasoning behind not allowing my brother to find things was so that I would learn to put things where I could find them and, therefore, not have to rely on other people to do things for me. Blindness-related behaviour was discouraged because my parents believed that it would stimulate a negative reaction from non-disabled people. For example, like many children with visual impairments I had a tendency to stare at bright lights; they used to tell me not to do this because people would think that I was 'stupid'. This learning process was never conducted in an overtly oppressive manner, though, and my brother received similar condemnation for sucking his thumb. Additionally, both of us were taught from the outset that we must always stick up for ourselves and never succumb to bullies without a fight. I was never made to feel 'different' from anybody else; I only acquired a sense of difference when I went to school.

Although my mother registered me at the local mainstream primary school the local education authority (LEA) decided that I should go to a 'special' school. Hence, I spent the first seven years of my statutory education in segregated special schools: first, in a residential school for 'the blind and the deaf' and later in a non-residential special unit for 'partially sighted' children. In respect of the first one the logic of putting children who have difficulty communicating physically because they cannot see with children whose impairment makes aural communication difficult in a residential setting has never ceased to amaze me. Like many disabled people with similar schooling experiences, I deeply resented this imposition of 'difference'.

Being sent to boarding school at four and a half had a profound effect on both myself and my family; I hated the school and as a result my parents tended to overcompensate for my absence during the holidays and, later, when I was allowed home at weekends. This resulted in unnecessary friction between my brother and myself and caused us to fight a lot. This inevitably resulted in arguments between my parents. I firmly believe that my being sent away to a boarding school, and the ensuing family tensions it created, was one of the key factors which contributed to my mother's depresson and eventual hospitalisation. Although being transferred to the partially sighted unit was infinitely better than the boarding school, because I was living at home the sense of being somehow abnormal was only marginally less oppressive. Our class was much smaller than those in the rest of the school and we, the 'partially sighted kids', did not change classes each year – we remained in the same one. I spent four years in the same class with the same teacher doing the same things. Other children did 'proper' schoolwork while we spent most of our time on handicrafts – such things as raffia work, knitting, basketry – and/or listening to the teacher reading us a story. Dependence was also emphasised by the fact that we were taken to and from school in taxis while the other children made their own way there either on their own or with their parents.

At eleven and a half I went to a mainstream school. This was due mainly to my parents' insistence to the LEA that I would be better off in an 'ordinary' school at a time when educational policy for children with 'special needs' was under review. I relished the experience thoroughly, but my previous schooling meant that I entered the school at the lower end of the academic spectrum. This meant that the boys in my class were the school outcasts and since all I wanted was to be as 'normal' as possible I therefore wanted to be just like them. Being just like them – one of the 'lads' – meant doing as little work as possible, and being able to fight. This approach to school life suited me very well since not working meant that I could conceal more easily the extent of my impairment. Moreover, due to my father's tuition and my experience at boarding school I was well able to look after myself. The level of bullying at boarding school was far greater than that in the other two schools I attended, so with little real effort on my part, and with no extra help other than that provided by my parents, I passed through secondary school without difficulty.

I left at 15, then the school leaving age, without any qualifications and went on to catering college. This was suggested by the school careers officer because he felt that 'my eyesight' would prove less of a problem in the catering trade – an industry characterised at the time by few regulations, low wages, poor working conditions and little job security. Although this was not my choice I went to catering college because my parents were keen that I should get a 'proper trade' in order that I would not end up in a sheltered workshop like my father. I completed the two-year course, left with a hotel and catering diploma, and after working in a couple of hotels went to work in a large industrial canteen as an assistant catering manager.

I remained there until the late 1970s when I decided to do something 'useful' and become a teacher. This decision meant that while holding down a full-time job I went to night school to catch up on my missed education, and then passed on to a teacher training college. Initially I wanted to work with students with special needs but I was appalled at the level of understanding of the problems faced by disabled people at teacher training college; this was the early 1980s when traditional paternalistic approaches to disability had only just begun to be challenged by disabled people. My tutors suggested that in order to study the subject further I should look to sociology. Consequently, from teacher training college I went on to university, studied disability both at the undergraduate and post-graduate levels and received my PhD in 1989.

Throughout my student years I worked with disabled young people in day centres, conducted empirical research on the social construction of dependence (Barnes, 1990), and subsequently went to work in 1989 as researcher for the British Council of Organisations of Disabled People (BCODP) – Britain's national umbrella for organisations controlled and run by disabled people. Since then I have conducted research on a range of disability-related issues including institutional discrimination and disabled people (Barnes, 1991), disabling imagery and the media (Barnes 1992), and national information providers' services to local disability organisations (Barnes, 1995). I am currently a teacher in disability studies, honorary research director for the BCODP, and active in the disabled people's movement.

Living with disability

Experience makes it clear that I have employed at least three main strategies to overcome disability.

1 *Minimisation*: This included various methods of information control in order to minimise people's perceptions of the extent of my impairment so that I could appear as 'normal' as possible.

2 *Overcompensation*: The development of socially valued attributes which deflect attention from subjective limitations (for a discussion of similar strategies used by other disabled people see Goffman, 1968). Until recently I could never pass as 'normal' because of my 'thick glasses'. I now have a pair of contact lenses which make this possible, but I prefer not to use them as my vision is substantially reduced.

3 *Openness*: This involved simply being open about the extent of my impairment and making impairment-related needs known as and when they arise – it is the result of my contact with other disabled people within the context of the disabled people's movement. The disabled writer Tom Shakespeare has likened this process of 'coming out' or coming to terms with a 'disabled' identity as similar to that of lesbians and gay men, who, after years of concealment, declare their sexuality openly following involvement with others of a similar disposition (Shakespeare, 1993).

The first two of the above were picked up, rather than consciously learned, from my parents and, apart from my family and a small circle of very close friends, they dominated social interaction between myself and the rest of the world until the late 1980s.

Probably the best example of minimisation relates to reading. Although reading has never been a problem for me – my parents taught both my brother and me to read before we went to school – like many people with a visual impairment, in order to read 'normal' print I have to place it very close to my face. Like my father I have always found this extremely embarrassing and I avoid reading in public at all costs. When this was not possible I employed several techniques to make it appear as if I was reading normally. At mainstream school, for example, I would conceal an old spectacle lens in my hand and read through it to give the impression that my eyesight was more 'normal' – as I grew older and more confident I simply refused to read in class. I can only remember being asked to read once at special school and that was in front of an adult visitor who commented on the way I followed the line of the text with my head rather than my eyes. At further education college and in the catering industry reading was not a high priority. When I had to read I did it in private; either at home, in the toilet, in the cloakroom, or in an empty office. Even today when teaching I try to memorise the lectures before a class and use a minimum of notes which are hand written in large print – I read in public only when there is no alternative.

With regard to overcompensation, although I had got through secondary education with relatively little effort, upon leaving school I quickly realised that I had to work harder than other people if I wanted to stay in mainstream employment. For instance, languages of any sort were not part of the curriculum in any of my lessons at school. Consequently, at catering college, as well as studying full time during the day, I went to evening classes for several weeks to get a grounding in French since this was a prerequisite of the course I was on. Upon starting work I made a conscious commitment never to be late or absent without a very good reason. At each of my jobs in the catering industry I started work before my official start time and worked right until the very last minute. I took fewer breaks than other workers and never refused to work overtime. When I got the job in catering management I made a point of being at work before the rest of the staff and only left when they had all gone home.

I adopted a similar approach to work when I entered higher education, first at teacher training college and later at university. Although I still have a tendency for overwork, today the motivation behind it is slightly different. In the catering industry I felt I had to work hard simply to stay in employment; now, I enjoy work more. Moreover, my work situation has also been made much easier because I no longer try to conceal the full extent of my impairment. There are a number of reasons for this: first, and most importantly, due to the growing strength of the disabled people's movement impairment, whatever its cause, is no longer discussed solely in terms of individual pathology. Although this might not be the case in society as a whole it is certainly true within some sections of the higher education system; notably, in social science departments. Second, through my involvement in disability politics, and with disabled activists in particular, my self-confidence has grown enormously. Coming to terms with my impairment has meant that when confronted with an impairment-related problem I now ask for help rather than waste time finding ways to overcome it on my own.

To illustrate the point, when I first entered university I spent hours in the libraries finding my way around, taking books down from the shelves and memorising where they were so that I could avoid using the catalogue or asking the library staff for assistance. The catalogue uses normal size print and consequently it is difficult to see unless I hold it close to my face, which is something I tried to avoid. Today, I simply ask library staff for help. Psychologically, this is far less traumatic than my previous experiences in the library, and I have considerably more time to do the things that I am employed to do – teach and do research.

Discussion

I have tried to articulate my experience as a visually impaired man in a society in which any form of impairment remains for most people a passport to exclusion and second-class citizenship. While it may be argued that my biography is not typical of someone with a visual impairment, or that my condition is not particularly severe, I believe it illustrates the type of problems encountered by many disabled people.

I should mention at this point, however, that I do not believe it is possible or useful to make generalisations with reference to the experience of impairment. All human beings are unique; an individual's ability to adapt to a particular condition, regardless of its nature and severity, will vary considerably and be determined by a variety of factors, both subjective and objective, including gender, ethnicity, race, age of onset, social class and so on. This is particularly evident with reference to the experience of visual impairment because many people's visual range alters considerably as they grow older. While some people come to terms with these changes fairly easily others find it extremely difficult. Consequently, the only way to find out about impairment and how to deal with it is to talk to the individual concerned.

However, by focusing upon my education and my working life to date

I have described my experience of *disability*. In contrast to the experience of *impairment* this is an area where I believe generalisations are possible and indeed appropriate. In doing this I have tried to show how my life-style has been influenced both by my impairment and by society's reaction to it. I have described three of the strategies I used to overcome some of the barriers I have encountered, including minimisation, overcompensation and openness, all of which were learned, both consciously and unconsciously, from other disabled people. Although the first two, minimisation and overcompensation, enabled me with varying degrees of success to integrate into the mainstream of community life, with the benefit of hindsight they are not strategies I would advise other disabled people to adopt. With regard to minimisation the constant fear of discovery makes 'normative' social interaction difficult and this inevitably adds to the barriers that all disabled people face: for example, it is likely that my secondary education was seriously inhibited by my attempts to conceal the extent of my impairment. In terms of overcompensation, this has had similarly negative psychological and sometimes physical implications which compounded other problems. Besides having a detrimental effect on life outside work, if nothing else because of the time and effort involved, trying to work harder than everyone else often results in social isolation among working colleagues.

Clearly, being open about impairment is the only way to deal with the experience of disability and this is something that can only be learned from people with similar experiences and in the present context I do not believe this is something that can be achieved easily. Notwithstanding that over the last decade or so our understanding of disability has shifted dramatically, the majority of individuals with visual impairments, as with disabled people generally, are still confronted by a range of social and environmental barriers – only some of which have been touched on here – which restricts to a greater or lesser extent our choice of life-style. At the same time the majority of services for people with visual impairments, as with provision for disabled people generally, is dominated by non-disabled professionals steeped in the traditional individualistic medical approach to disability. While medical interventions may be appropriate for minimising and monitoring the negative effects of impairment they are inappropriate for dealing with disability. Professionals working within this perspective invariably pathologise the experience of impairment and in so doing compound the problems faced by disabled people: directing us into segregated special schools and sheltered workshops are two good examples.

In the short term some of these problems might be overcome by a complete reappraisal of the ideologies underpinning the services currently provided for disabled people. This could easily be achieved through consultation with people with appropriate impairments from organisations controlled and run by disabled people, and by the employment of more disabled workers within the 'rehabilitation' professions. But whichever way you look at it this seems to me to be only part of the solution. There is little doubt in my mind that many of the problems encountered by disabled people can only be eliminated through the creation of a less disabling environment and culture. In the case of visual impairment this would mean the widespread provision of accessible information – large print, Braille and appropriate peer support services – and the introduction of a wide range of policies designed specifically to integrate rather than segregate us from the mainstream of community life. These would include comprehensive anti-discrimination laws similar to those already in place in Australia, America, Canada, New Zealand and other western democracies and the appropriate resourcing of the nationwide network of organisations controlled and run by disabled people to ensure their implementation. Only in such circumstances could the majority of people with visual impairments, and disabled people generally, be completely open about their condition, its effects and their impairment-related needs.

A key feature of any professional's activities, therefore, must be to focus on these particular issues. Any other form of 'rehabilitation' is relatively meaningless. With a few notable exceptions this is something that hitherto they and their organisations, in both the public and the voluntary sectors, have failed to do. It is hoped that this situation will change significantly in the foreseeable future.

5
A hearing difficulty as impairment

Mairian Corker

This chapter explores the experience of people who have difficulty with hearing, considering in particular the constraints which result from different kinds of impairment and the possibilities that exist for rehabilitation interventions. We will focus primarily on the adult population, but it will be necessary to look at the experiences of children in order to develop a greater understanding of the kinds of barriers experienced – and the consequences of that experience – for different individuals. In addition we shall look at the role of personal and professional interventions in determining those consequences. In exploring the responses which people with hearing difficulties make to societal constraints, we will consider differing perceptions of 'impairment' and 'disability' and the origins of those perceptions.

Prevalence and terminology

The Royal National Institute for the Deaf (RNID) estimates that 20 per cent of the general population have 'hearing difficulties'. Of these: 1.4 million adults of working age have a 'clinically significant hearing loss'; 70,000 (5 per cent) 'use hearing aids'; and 24,000 are 'registered disabled' (Honey et al., 1993). Other sources use different terminology such as: 'communication difficulties' (OPCS Survey, 1988); 'sign language users' (British Deaf Association); 'deaf without speech' (IMS Survey, 1993). However, it is not always clear which hearing impaired people are included in which category. Attempts to define hearing impairment accurately in individual terms, especially with respect to the barriers experienced and the outcomes of the experience for life-styles, are difficult, and this difficulty with definition can in itself become a barrier for the hearing impaired person. This is because global group labels can be used indiscriminately as a means of trying to predict the ease with which a hearing impaired person can 'cope with' or 'overcome' the barriers they experience, or the disability they experience, and in some cases is even used to try and predict the quality of rehabilitation interventions.

For example, the commonly used medical classification divides the hearing impaired population into categories described by the type, stage of onset and

HEARING LOSS	DESCRIPTORS			
ORIGIN	Acquired		Congenital	
DEGREE[1]	Mild	Moderate	Severe	Profound
STAGE OF ONSET[2]	Postlingual		Prelingual	
COMMONLY USED LABELS	deafened	hard of hearing		deaf
PREDICTIONS	Least disadvantaged *by impairment*		Most disadvantaged *by impairment*	

[1] Degree of hearing loss is measured primarily by means of a pure tone audiogram which plots the loudness levels (measured in decibels) at which the sound of a range of specified frequencies (measured in Hertz) become audible. In practice, account is always taken of the audiological *profile* e.g. whether there is a greater hearing loss in one part of the frequency spectrum than in another, rather than simply loudness levels
[2] In relation to the development of *spoken* language

Figure 5.1   *The medical classification of hearing impairment*

degree of hearing loss (the *impairment*). This is described in Figure 5.1, which is organised to show how the different systems relate to each other.

The interaction between impairment and disability

The model outlined in Figure 5.1 predicts that hearing impaired people will vary in their linguistic competence or communicative ability in spoken language as a function of the hearing impairment, and that the barriers experienced will be largely communicative, relational or social barriers. However, communication has two primary functions – it is the means by which social relationships are forged and maintained, and it is the means by which information is received from the surrounding environment on a number of different levels defined by Ramsdell (1978) as:

● the *symbolic* level, which includes understanding language;
● the *signal or warning* level, which includes having access to direct signals of events to which the individual makes constant adjustments;
● the *primitive* level, or the 'rumble' of everyday living.

Kyle et al. state that: 'individuals live and work in information environments governed by social and personal norms as well as access features such as speed, intensity and density of information' (1985: 122).

The process of personal and social adjustment to the features of information environments therefore becomes related to the specific level of *control* which the individual determines, in part through negotiation and agreement, in a variety of social circumstances. Hearing impairment, framed in these terms, clearly disturbs the control that an individual can achieve, and the steps taken to adjust to a reduced level of control can be socially intrusive to the extent that a barrier is experienced, as we will see below. In this sense the boundary between the medical model of impairment (which is confined mainly to the information level), and the social model (which describes hearing impaired people's dominant social affiliations and their experience of disability in barrier-laden environments) becomes somewhat blurred. In practical terms, what does this mean for intervention?

'Medical' interventions focus on amplification to boost a diminished capacity to receive information through the provision of hearing aids and remedial language teaching. For example, using the impairment classification above, it is predicted that a deaf person born with a 'profound hearing loss' (whom we will call A) will experience more obstructive barriers and have more difficulty in challenging or overcoming them than a hard of hearing person born with a 'moderate hearing loss' (who is called B). That is to say, *all other factors being equal*, A will manifest a greater experience of disability than B. Further, because B's experience of disability depends on the extent to which environmental characteristics can be controlled to optimise incoming information, interventions focus on increasing the level of control possible or improving the quality of incoming information, and are therefore primarily medical interventions. The level of success people like B have in minimising, or at least rationalising, their experience of disability will depend on how far they can develop the practical skills of lipreading and using hearing aids, and how much time they spend in environments which are not conducive to communication because of the level of background noise, for example parties, busy streets. This is described in a tongue-in-cheek way by Mansfield (1980) in the cartoon shown in Figure 5.2.

Professional assessment procedures that A might experience rely very heavily on the deaf person's ability to understand and use *spoken* language, and because this can be regarded as an alien language, it can be expected often to lead to outcomes which reinforce a negative image of impairment or disability. It could be argued that if a native French-speaker were to be assessed in English, the outcomes would probably be very similar. However, because deafness is stereotyped by professionals in negative terms (as an impairment or a disability) performance on what are, in essence, experientially irrelevant tasks also becomes associated with linguistic impoverishment and underexpectations of linguistic competence. This adds to A's negative self-perception of 'not having the cognitive competence, psychological skills, instrumental resources, and support systems needed to influence his or her environment successfully' (Schlesinger, 1985: 105). Responsibility for social barriers in such circumstances becomes internalised, and shows itself in A's low self-esteem when dealing with difficult or challenging circumstances and social encounters. We will come back to this in a slightly different context below.

The impairment classification in Figure 5.1 indicates that A is seen to require a greater degree of professional intervention and support than a person who

Figure 5.2 *The Adventures of Jill. 'Jill in a Pub' reprinted by permission of Jill Mansfield. Further details of Jill Mansfield's booklets and videos about deafness can be obtained from 35 Taverner Close, Pitwines, Poole, Dorset BH15 1UP.*

acquires a profound hearing loss in adulthood (person C), though the barriers experienced by C will be qualitatively different and centred in the emotional-psychological sphere of communication rather than the linguistic sphere which poses difficulties for A. The experience of disability of people like C is determined by the degree of psychological and emotional adjustment they can make to losing their hearing and the dependency of, or consistency in, existing relationships (Kyle et al., 1987; Cowie and Douglas-Cowie, 1992). It has been demonstrated by these authors that the trauma resulting from the loss of the one function which maintains relationships with others – communication – is likely to be severe in the life-style disruptions that are caused; therefore the experience of disability is more pronounced for C than for either A or B. Both B and C can attempt to minimise disabling factors in the environment, but C may experience greater disability as a result of:

- not having relevant practical skills such as lipreading or signing;
- attitudinal changes in close family and work colleagues as they struggle to come to terms with C's loss and what it means for *them*;
- the effects which C's attempts to adjust have on social relationships.

Some of this is demonstrated by one individual's experience:

> Conversations at parties might elude me, but I seldom fail to pick up on mood. I enjoy watching people talk. When I am too far away to read lips, I try reading postures and imagining conversations. Sometimes, to everyone's horror, I respond to things better left unsaid when I'm trying to find out what's going on around me. I want to see, touch, taste and smell everything within reach; I especially have to curb a tendency to judge things by their smell – not just potato salad but people as well – a habit that seems to some people entirely too barbaric for comfort. (Galloway, 1987: 8)

Interventions in C's case may not be consistent and may move between social interventions such as:

- counselling and hearing therapy (which focus on the provision of human support);
- technological aids (which enable access to information in a familiar language through visual means);
- medical interventions (which aim to 'rehabilitate' C to a semblance of the hearing condition). This can include surgical interventions such as cochlear implants.

Where interventions aim to restore, as far as is possible, the hearing condition, they become associated with the impairment classification. Thus, if the aim of rehabilitation interventions considered appropriate for A is to develop or restore the ability to use spoken language, these interventions are linked to the concept of impairment. However, A might come from a deaf family where sign language is the home language, attend a residential school for deaf children which uses sign language as a means of instruction and eventually become employed in a deaf-sector job teaching sign language, while B may come from a hearing family, attend a mainstream school without specialist support and become underemployed in a hearing-sector organisation. Under those circumstances we must consider the degree of certainty which exists in predictions of the type and extent of barriers which might be experienced on the basis *only* of the disability experienced as a result of the impairment. It is in this arena that the medical classification must

Type and degree of hearing impairment

interacting with

- quality and accessibility of early language environment
- family and community support
- type and quality of professional interventions, including assessment practice and the access to knowledge, skills and understanding which is facilitated by the interventions
- educational achievements
- linguistic competence
- personal characteristics, in particular self-esteem and self-advocacy

determines

- the extent to which communication is blocked or damaged, and information is impeded
- the extent to which disability is experienced
- the control which the individual can exercise in relation to social barriers

Figure 5.3 *Interaction between impairment, potential disabling factors and disability experienced*

be seen for what it is – part of an extremely complex scenario which might be described as shown in Figure 5.3.

The assertion of difference

No discussion on people who experience hearing difficulties is complete without reference to that section of the deaf population who describe themselves as a linguistic and cultural minority and whose lives revolve around the use of British Sign Language (BSL). It is estimated that this group consists of approximately 65,000 individuals, and BSL is cited as the fourth most widely used language in Great Britain (Ladd, 1993), though Gregory (1993) suggests that we should be careful about how we qualify such information. This group are traditionally described as 'Deaf' with an upper-case 'D', to distinguish them from other deaf, deafened and hard of hearing people, though because linguistic and cultural minority status can be acquired and is a measure of chosen social affiliations, the distinction is not always clear. It is therefore in respect of this group that we experience difficulties with the impairment classification, and its implicit definition that Deaf people are imperfect hearing people who are therefore impaired in relation to hearing norms:

> Self-identification with the group and skill in American Sign Language (ASL) should be important diagnostic factors in deciding who is Deaf. But the bounded distinction between the terms *Deaf* and *deaf* represents only part of the dynamic of how Deaf people talk about themselves. Deaf people are both *Deaf* and *deaf*, and their

discussions, even arguments, over issues of identity show that these two categories are often interrelated in complex ways. (Padden and Humphries, 1988: 3, emphasis in original)

This complexity is reflected in the difficulties of viewing Deaf people within the context of impairment, barriers and the experience of disability, for the majority of Deaf people themselves undergo the transition from deaf to Deaf at some point in their lives. This means that they have experience of deafness both as impairment and as disability *before* it becomes enshrined in a cultural difference. Before the transition takes place, they could be said to be acultural, because they have no accessible culture and no opportunity to exercise cultural preferences. This is in part because at least 90 per cent of deaf children will have hearing parents and the majority of these children will attend mainstream schools which deprive them of the primary socialisation possibilities with the adult Deaf community (see Corker, 1989; Gregory, 1993).

This situation arises because in mainstream schools spoken language is dominant, of course, and both the teaching staff and the deaf child's peer group are predominantly hearing. Special school environments are of enormous cultural and linguistic significance for the Deaf community because it is in those environments that a deaf child is more likely to encounter Deaf adults in a variety of roles. The child will also have a deaf peer group, most of whom will use British Sign Language. This is why many people in the Deaf community perceive the closure of special schools as a direct threat to Deaf culture. When Deaf people ask a newcomer to the Deaf community which school they attended the question is one way of asking 'Are you Deaf?' If the name of an unfamiliar mainstream school is given it can lead to rejection because the individual is seen as not Deaf. There is increasing interest in the plight of deaf ex-mainstreamers, who are often unable to find a community to which they feel they belong: they feel rejected in both Deaf and hearing communities. Some Deaf people argue that the Deaf community's apparent rejection of ex-mainstreamers is a transference of Deaf people's childhood experiences, where hearing people demeaned the use of sign language and 'poor speech'. As ex-mainstreamers are often oral communicators they are therefore seen as allying themselves with hearing oppressors (Channel Four television, 1994).

Barriers can be and are experienced by deaf children, young people and even adults whose parents and their experience of the education system denied the existence of what was portrayed as an 'alien' Deaf culture. The life-style constraints imposed can be attributed directly to the difficulty of living with an acquired identity which does not match up to the image of 'normal', and rehabilitation interventions which serve to reinforce this identity:

> The child may deny the deaf self (which is the true self) as he or she feels driven towards acquiring the persona of a hearing person, as objectified in the hearing mother or father. That persona can never be perfect, but it may be sufficient to ward off the 'bad' deaf self to such an extent that it becomes a kind of festering unconscious . . . the 'hearing' persona . . . has a censoring role which, in the presence of reinforcement from the outer world, serves to repress the deaf self . . . a

deaf child who believes their true experience of the world is 'bad' communicates in a vacuum and lives with the pain of knowing that a piece of their self is missing. (Corker, 1989: 5)

The cost of these interventions is clear when we observe the large numbers of deaf adults who remember believing, as children, that they would be hearing when they grew up (Gregory, 1993). We have to ask what happens to the experience of deafness as impairment or disability once the transition from deaf to Deaf is made, for the simple reason that experiential veins run deep.

This relates back to the question of the experience and the techniques of professional assessment mentioned earlier. Deaf people argue that if they were assessed using visuo-spatial parameters and through BSL by Deaf professionals skilled in the use of such testing, the outcomes would be very different, and there is evidence to suggest that this may well be the case (Gregory, 1993; Lane, 1993). As part of the battery of tests currently carried out by educational psychologists, visuo-spatial or non-verbal tests *are* administered, and it is often observed that deaf children produce well above average results on these tests together with below average results on verbal tests. Yet education continues to be focused on medical intervention concepts which aim to correct the 'deficit', at the expense of sign language teaching. Bilingual approaches to education can be observed: Derby School for deaf children uses a bilingual approach and Leeds Education Authority has a policy of bilingual education for deaf children in mainstream schools, but such situations are generally few and far between.

Because the language taught to deaf children does not relate to their experience of the world, it is not an enriching or a stimulating language for them to use in communication. Learning becomes lifeless and frequently focused on what is easy or familiar. Moreover, because interventions tend to place responsibility for action in the hands of the professionals effecting the interventions, as opposed to developing the deaf child's self-advocacy, it has been suggested that deaf children are often the *passive* recipients of this kind of learning (Luterman, 1987; Montgomery and Laidlaw, 1993). This encourages dependency on others for decision making (Redfern, 1991) or perceptions of powerlessness (Schlesinger, 1985). Interventions which are overprotective and carried out over a long period of time in both segregated and integrated environments increase the possibility of the deaf person experiencing an acute shock when, for the first time, they enter mainstream life-styles which carry expectations of self-responsibility. We can see the outcomes of such interventions clearly in the following example:

The personnel director of a large business concern employing deaf persons became greatly alarmed at the number of personal data forms in which the answer 'yes' had been given by the deaf job applicants from this particular school to the question . . . 'Have you ever had fits?' She hurriedly phoned the school principal for explanation, and was promptly reassured. None of the applicants had ever had fits. The problem lay in their reading of the language of the application form. All the young applicants had just completed a course in dressmaking. Great stress had been placed on the need for accuracy in the cut and fit of the garments they had made. What could be more reasonable than to assume the word 'fits' in the question had the same meaning as in dressmaking? So here too, the answer 'yes' seemed entirely suitable. (Levine, 1981: 74)

The question which must be asked about this experience is: if the director had not had the foresight to contact the school principal, would these deaf people have been refused employment? If so, is it the impairment which is the operative factor or is it the quality of the interventions experienced? It is situations such as this where the impairment can be perceived to be a barrier or restriction, which result in the experience of disability.

As a recognition of and response to these negative connotations of the experience of disability, and what is seen to be the displacement of the responsibility for undesirable outcomes of inappropriate medical interventions on to deaf people, Deaf people reject the label 'hearing impaired' because they see being Deaf as a different kind of norm. This norm is determined by a different sensory, predominantly visuo-spatial, experience which finds expression through a gestural-visual-spatial language. The barriers they experience are therefore different in quality, and probably very similar to those experienced by users of other minority languages.

When deaf people affiliate with other Deaf people they do not generally experience blocked or damaged communication because there is a common language and a common culture. In terms of the medical model of disability, it is usual to describe all d/Deaf people as 'communication disabled', but when Deaf people meet with other Deaf people this is clearly not the case. Any disability which is experienced in Deaf–Deaf communication cannot easily be attributed directly to the impairment. It is more likely to be a consequence of two different levels of linguistic competence similar to those we might observe between a university academic who uses jargon to express ideas and a fledgling student who is ignorant of the meaning of the jargon.

When Deaf people have been alienated from the Deaf community by inappropriate educational intervention, for example, they may be socially isolated or have social affiliations which are predominantly hearing; in this situation they may perceive themselves as being 'communication disabled' because they are deaf, rather than as a consequence of having internalised their oppression by hearing people. They believe the situation to be 'their fault'. Deaf people, on the other hand, will commonly attribute their experience of disability directly to that oppresion – that is to say, communicaton difficulties are the fault of hearing society.

For example, assuming the Deaf person's fluency in BSL, the communication barrier is often perceived to be a direct result of others' inability to use sign language, or a sign language interpreter's lack of skills in a particular area, which interferes with access to information:

When they use an interpreter, how do Deaf people know that the interpreter's voice-over[*] of their signing is correct? Have they ever wondered, but could not know for sure, whether poor interpreting voice-over was to blame when communications with a hearing person did not go well? Does it worry these Deaf people that an interpreter may do a poor voice-over at an important meeting, such as a job interview? (Reid, 1994: 19) ([*] *When a Deaf person signs in BSL, they cannot use*

Table 5.1   Summary of the relationships between hearing impairments, the experience of disability and interventions

Impairment	Primary barriers	Experience of disability depends on	Dominant interventions
hard of hearing (medical definition)	communicative (receptive) social attitudinal	practical ability in dealing with barriers extent to which environmental characteristics can be controlled	technological (hearing aids, loop systems)
deafened (medical definition & social definition)	communicative (receptive, possibly expressive) attitudinal social	degree of psychological and emotional adjustment to loss dependency on or consistency in existing relationships	psycho-emotional (e.g., counselling, hearing therapy) technological (hearing aids, palantype, Hi-Linc) surgical (cochlear implants) visual information systems
deaf (medical definition & social definition)	communicative (receptive and expressive) linguistic educational attitudinal	extent to which impairment is accepted or denied quality of educational interventions	remedial language teaching technological (hearing aids, radio aids) visual information systems
Deaf (socio-cultural definition; concept of impairment rejected)	oppression of Deaf identity failure to recognise sign language attitudinal cultural	extent to which can maintain Deaf social affiliations the reliability of support systems cultural awareness and acceptance	sign language interpreters Deaf teachers technological (minicoms, flashing light alarms, door bells) visual information systems

their voice at the same time as BSL and spoken language are conveyed in different modes and have different structures. The Deaf person therefore requires an interpreter to translate what they are signing into spoken language. This is called voice-over.)

The response to the constraints posed is both a professional intervention (improved interpreter monitoring), and an individual response (developing the ability to challenge 'defective' services).

Conclusion

A summary of the relationships between impairment, the experience of disability and interventions in people who have different perceptions of 'hearing difficulty' is given in Table 5.1.

The medical *model* is, by itself, of limited use in describing the processes whereby d/Deaf people interact with society, but medical *classifications* and *terminology* cannot be discounted completely. *Speech* ability, which as we have seen can be an indicator of the d/Deaf person's status within *hearing* society, is linked to the degree and type of hearing loss. In this context, the barriers encountered interact with the impairment to produce the experience of disability. However, because speech is not synonymous with language and many of the interventions we have discussed focus on curing the impairment, the barriers are largely attitudinal and, in the instance where sign language is actively suppressed, can be considered to be 'audist'. Conversely, because communication is the foundation of relationships between people, and is therefore a fundamental part of the functioning of society, no discussion about d/Deaf people's life-styles is relevant without the application of a social model which takes account of the disabling consequences of blocked or damaged communication and determines the attribution of responsibility for communication difficulties. Deaf people clearly place the responsibility on hearing society:

> Disabled people advocate the removal of physical, social or psychological barriers to their access to the dominant culture. The dominant culture should adapt with the aim of assimilating disabled people and thus removing or re-defining disability. Deaf people on the other hand are demanding recognition as a cultural and linguistic minority group. While they root their disadvantage in their treatment by the dominant society, they are demanding for themselves identification as a group with a specific cultural identity. (Gregory, 1993: 5)

The demand for Deaf people's recognition as a cultural and linguistic minority group is one positive and resilient *group* response to the 'cruel legacy' of an oppressive society (Dimmock, 1993) and lack of access to the majority language, but it could equally be said that deaf people's struggles with the forces of oppression are a different kind of response, perhaps more individualised, to the same forces. Likewise, different conceptualisations of impairment hinge on the way in which communication and socialisation are defined, and the ways in which communicative barriers are encountered and managed within society. On one hand, the life-style goal is integration and identification with the Deaf community but on the other the life-style goal is integration, though not necessarily identification, with the wider community from a position of individual strength. This dichotomy has regrettably been submerged in a debate about whether Deaf people are disabled or not within a very narrow definition of the term disability. Other linguistic and cultural minorities are oppressed by the dominant society and some authors are suggesting that there are very similar patterns and trends of underexpectation and inequality within education with respect to children from minority cultures and children who have special needs (Troyna and Siraj-Blatchford, 1993). The real issues are the barriers created by oppression, lack of access and inequality and in this context we should not forget that the wider deaf population is in itself a diverse and pluralistic community the members of which have very different perceptions of and responses to the conditions of impairment or disability. Like the hearing community, this population includes individuals who are black, female, elderly, gay, lesbian, physically or intellectually challenged, and some of them will adopt a different cultural stance to impairment and barriers based on another kind of difference. Perhaps the real subtleties of the relationship between hearing impairment and disability have yet to be understood.

6
Learning difficulties

Sheila Ford

What are learning difficulties?

This chapter begins with a quotation:

> A learning disability is an impairment of intellectual functions, which occurs before adulthood and results in significant disabilities in day to day life. (West Midlands Regional Health Authority, 1993: 60)

The concept of a learning difficulty relates to individuality. In learning, like so many other aspects of human functioning, each person learns things at a different speed depending on many things such as personal interests and aptitudes. The West Midlands Regional Health Authority Report for 1993 states that approximately 2 per cent of the population have a level of learning ability which needs nurturing through specific teaching measures. A learning disability is significant during educational experience and children with a learning disability will often be taught in a special school. As children, people with learning difficulties can be placed in a position that their abilities may develop slowly while other physical and emotional attributes progress according to age-related expectations. Over the last 80 years the health services have provided long-term residential care for people of all ages with a learning disability but with the changes now occurring many people are being moved from hospital into small homes in the community.

The West Midlands Regional Health Authority Report was compiled with the help of the Centre for Research and Information into Mental Disability (CRIMD), which is based at the University of Birmingham; the researchers suggest the following relationships:

- A person with a *mild* learning disability is fully independent in self-care but has only basic reading and writing skills.
- A person with a *moderate* learning disability is likely to have limited language skills, need some help with self-care although fully mobile and able to do simple practical work.
- A person with a *severe* learning disability is able to use some words or gestures for basic needs, will be able to undertake supervised activities but is likely to have some degree of impaired movement.
- A person with a *profound* learning disability will have very limited communication skills and no self-care skills.

The estimated prevalence of mild and moderate learning disabilities is 16.5 to 20.5 per 1000 while those in the severe and profound categories would number 3.5 per 1000. Most interventions in adult life are to the benefit of people whose disabilities are in the severe or profound categories.

The four categories outlined above are only indications used by professionals to ensure that they provide services to meet the needs of individuals. Special Needs Registers (SNR) are being kept in some health districts which give service planners ongoing information on which to base their long-term service needs. These registers include information about individuals who are assessed regularly and their life needs noted. The SNRs are a valuable tool to ensure that everyone gets the services they need when they need them. SNRs have not been compiled in every area yet but it seems they have proved a very effective tool and their use is spreading.

In the West Midlands around 15 per cent of people with a learning disability also have a sensory impairment and 28 per cent have a psychiatric disorder of which 11 per cent are behavioural disorders. According to figures compiled by the National Society for Epilepsy 30 per cent of people with all levels of learning disability and 80 per cent of those with severe learning disabilities are affected. These additional difficulties can cause them concern but they may also gain support from another service area which can be beneficial. In some people there is a lack of coordination and balance is affected as a result of poor body awareness which can lead to an ungainly way of walking. As a result of these additional health difficulties life can be further complicated for people with learning disabilities. Living independently may be out of the question for some and there may also be restrictions on movement around the community. If there are constant restrictions of the freedom of an individual then frustration can be one effect and this can manifest itself through the behaviour patterns that emerge.

The use of long-stay hospitals is being discontinued for all but the most severely learning disabled and in the Birmingham area over 40 per cent of hospital beds have been closed in the past 10 years and only 20 per cent of people with a learning disability are now living in a hospital; 52 per cent live with their family; 26 per cent live in sheltered housing and 20 per cent live independently (West Midlands Regional Health Authority, 1993).

Birth

The birth of a baby changes the ethos of the members of any family. Parents have to develop a new routine, siblings have to learn to accept the new addition to the family and often they may discover feelings of loss which come as a result of parents being so involved with the baby. When the new baby is born with a disability there can be a different sense of loss for the parents as they discover that their expectations for the child have to be modified. Where the child has a learning difficulty it is possible that the diagnosis will not be made for some time; this can be initiated by the parents who begin to realise that development is taking place more slowly than it seems that it should by comparison with other children of similar age. Despite this small degree of possible preparedness, the final diagnosis can come as a shock to parents and how the disability is diagnosed, and how parents are told of it, is a significant aspect of the level of trauma within the family. Some disabilities can be diagnosed almost immediately, for example those with Down's syndrome, although the tests taken at birth will take six weeks to be interpreted. Support for the parents is vital and the need for a positive view of the future can often best be offered by someone who is a parent with experience of the specific disability. When early diagnosis is made contact will frequently be arranged with local associations such as the Royal Society for Mentally Handicapped Children and Adults (Mencap) or the Down's Syndrome Association and their members will be able to take on the task of talking to the parents. Support and information is also available through Values in Action, an organisation which works with and for people with learning difficulties and their families. This sort of support is available to all parents of a child diagnosed as having a learning difficulty, but contact is most often arranged when that diagnosis is made early on. When the diagnosis is made later, which can mean after a few months but sometimes even after years have passed it is somewhat less likely that communication is established between the parent and the local organisation. A new initiative in South East Staffordshire has resulted in a Post-Diagnostic Support Worker being appointed. She is based in the hospital and gives support, information and advice to individuals, and their carers, when a diagnosis of disability is made. It is envisaged that more appointments of this type will be made in other hospitals in the area.

Case study 1

Rebecca was the mother of a child with Down's syndrome but by the time her daughter was nine months old and was growing normally her paediatrician told her that there was nothing more that she could be done so 'there was no point in coming to the clinic again'. Rebecca described this sudden withdrawal of support as 'like being in a boat tossing on a dark sea, with no light to guide me'.

Case study 2

A recent case (see Harris and Rayment, 1994) has highlighted the manner in which parents were informed that their child had Down's syndrome; this caused the father to try to smother the baby which he imagined would 'grow up as a monster'. The QC in this case said that doctors had broken the golden rule that the child should be with the parents when such news is given. The doctors in the case told the parents in the outpatient's department and stated that they 'assumed the parents knew that something was wrong with their baby and did not assume that they would be shocked by the news'. This is an example of the trauma felt by parents on discovering that their new baby is disabled being underestimated by professionals.

A great deal has been written about the way parents should be treated in order to protect them from as much stress as possible when they are informed of the diagnosis; perhaps you can read more about this area.

What is to be considered here is not only the attitude of medical staff but also the attitude of people in general and how their perceptions of a learning difficulty colour their expectations. The expectations new parents will have of a disabled child will depend on their prior experience, which could be negligible. How many contacts have you or your family had with people with learning difficulties?

Parents of a learning disabled child will often feel that they are treated differently from other new parents as people often don't know what to say and this can lead to the family being cut off from much social contact. Rebecca felt that her friends were embarrassed when their children started to develop so much more quickly and this meant that she felt out of place on the trips to the park and other occasions when the mothers and babies got together.

Is it possible to make the situation less stressful?

The most relevant questions here are:

- What can be done to help new parents in the early stages of their child's life?
- Would additional training for doctors help them to give the information to parents in a way which is acceptable?
- Not many people would be comfortable telling parents that their child is disabled and doctors are no exception: how can this situation be managed?
- Parents (such as Rebecca) often feel very isolated in the first few years of their child's life: how may they be advised and helped?
- Self-help groups are often initiated by parents who find themselves in difficult situations: how viable are these as a source of support?

Childhood

Children go to a Child Development Clinic every six months for developmental tests and diagnosis of a learning difficulty is most likely to be made there. The developmental tests are intended to monitor areas of physical, mental and sensory development and should also offer support when a developmental difference is identified. Special nurseries and home support are available to families in order to ensure the development of the child's abilities. One example of home support is the Portage scheme which provides assessment and equipment with which to develop physical skills. Portage is a voluntary organisation which has to find funding in order to provide a service, which is always difficult. There are currently 300 Portage schemes available in this country and everyone involved, at any level, will have wide experience of working with families and children. Developed in rural areas of the United States in the 1970s it helps parents understand the effect they could have on their child's progress. Portage is free and parents can refer themselves or be referred by a local authority or voluntary organisation. A Portage team of home visitors offers a carefully structured but flexible system to help parents become effective teachers of their own children. In the Portage system the child is assessed at an early stage by an organiser who then devises a programme of exercises to be carried out with the child at home. The programme builds on the strengths of the child to develop appropriate skills and ways of behaving and families are taught how to use the programme. Equipment is lent to the family and the exercise programme undertaken by them. Once a week a volunteer will visit them, assess the child's progress and leave the next piece of equipment, after teaching the parents how to use it. For example, a large ball is used to develop reflex actions for balance: the child lies on top of the ball which is then tilted a few degrees so that as the child feels the change of angle his or her reflexes should lift body and arms to compensate. This should be an innate reaction but babies with disabilities have often not developed in a way that permits them to notice the change in their body position. The benefit of this scheme is that it involves the parents throughout, giving them information and activities to undertake with their child rather than passing responsibility over to others. By encouraging parents in this way the scheme strengthens the family by giving them a positive approach.

Special nurseries are available in some areas; these are sometimes attached to special schools and occasionally they are shared between all the local children of nursery age. The integrated nurseries encourage interaction between the two groups of children and the most effective way to do this has proved to be through adults participating in the games, playing a leading or guiding role (Maychell and Bradley, 1991). It is during this time of the child's life that formal assessment will take place in order to make a Statement of Educational Needs under the terms of the 1981 Education Act (HMSO, 1981). This is designed to ensure that the child has additional appropriate support built into the teaching programme. With the changes in legislation over recent times there have been difficulties in getting statements for children. Parents have had to wait a long time for their child's assessment and the additional support needs to be met. One explanation for this could be the level of funding which schools receive to provide extra levels of support for the teaching programme.

This can be another difficult time for parents who may perceive that their child's future is being developed in a different mould from the one they had envisaged and this can also create a further sense of loss. Parents will need to have information such as:

- How many pre-school facilities there are for children with learning difficulties in their area.
- Whether there are adequate numbers of places for the children who need them.
- Whether there is a Portage scheme within reach.
- Whether it is possible to get home support of any kind for the child or parents.

Schooldays

A child who has a statement will have specific requirements which must be built in to the teaching programme whether the child goes to a mainstream school or a special school. Children with learning difficulties are excluded from the local school in favour of special schools which have a larger catchment area, but segregated education involves treating the disabled child very differently from others. Numbers are not available which will indicate how many children with a learning disability are in their local schools as opposed to special schools but there has been debate over a number of years regarding segregation in education as the statement makes it possible for the appropriate support to be offered in either a special or local day school. During childhood friendships are formed as a result of living in the same street or going to the local shops but segregated education often means that children with learning difficulties who do not attend their local school do not develop those friendships. On the other hand, if a child is in an ordinary school but struggling he or she may become the victim of bullying.

Case study 3

Sophie is a girl who is now 15 years old and in a mainstream school where she is often bullied. She is not able to keep up with her work even though she tries very hard and as a result is the butt of jokes and often laughed at which causes her distress. Her older brother went to a special school and her parents do not think it was in his best interest. They feel that the stigma attached to special schools is what has caused him to be unemployed since he left school. The parents have refused to allow their daughter to move to a special school, even though she is bullied, as they want to protect her from the stigma (Goffman, 1968).

The National Curriculum has been modified for special schools; while this is necessary in order to ensure that provision is as appropriate to the abilities of the child as possible it can mean that the academic content of the work is reduced making it very difficult for a child to move back into mainstream schools. Voluntary organisations have been set up which seek to increase the variety of academic work available to children in special schools. Two examples are the North Staffordshire Special Adventure Playground and the Saxon Gymnastics Club. The former is based on a two-acre site with conservation areas, stream, pond and a wide range of indoor and outdoor activities. It is open to children and adults with disabilities and the staff work with nurseries, schools, special units and adult training centres to offer appropriate teaching which includes activities which fit into the National Curriculum, like bird watching and pond dipping. At weekends and through school holidays the centre is open to everyone including families and siblings as well as the young people and adults with disabilities. The Saxon Gymnastics Club in South East Cheshire caters for all children and adults, including those with profound disabilities, those with behaviour problems and those wanting to train as coaches in gymnastics. Although only established in September 1992 one young person with a learning disability has already qualified as a coach. This type of achievement gives credibility to the wishes of other young people with a disability who have aspirations which frequently other people will not take seriously.

Perhaps you know centres like this in your locality? These activities give opportunities for contact with adults and young volunteers who may themselves be disabled.

Even where the academic education is appropriate, social education is limited when children are cut off from interaction with most of their peers. Travelling to school on a special bus or by taxi reduces opportunities for experience of community life, limits the range of communication with other members of the public and even restricts the development of road sense. Many aspects of standards of behaviour are learned from peers but wider role models are restricted in a special school. Restrictions on the breadth of experience of children who attend a school away from the locality where they live extend to holiday periods too. It is not uncommon for the learning disabled children to stay at home, often only with adult company, only accompanying their family on outings, while other children play together in the street, in each other's homes or in the park. This also puts enormous emotional and physical strains on the family members, but the added burdens can be financial too if permanent care for the child must be arranged. Some areas organise summer play schemes which offer some respite to families during the long holiday.

Case study 4

Laura, a lone parent after the break up of her marriage six years ago, has three children and the eldest boy has a learning difficulty and severe behaviour problems. Laura works in a college of further education and her term time commitments fit in quite well with the school term but school holidays can be a nightmare. It is impossible to give her other children time or attention because Malcolm has to be constantly watched, leaving her no time for the others. There is no summer play or holiday scheme available in her area.

Case study 5

Don's experience of residential school was of being bullied by both staff and pupils. He always reported that he was happier during school holidays because he played with the smaller boy who lived next door and was then able to bully him! Don still feels very uncomfortable when walking home from his day centre at a time when the children are coming out of school because his walk is ungainly as his balance is poor; as a result the children call him names which upsets him greatly. The centre arranged for him to go home earlier so he missed the children, but it has now been suggested that reciprocal visits between school and day centre would be extremely beneficial.

A child's first big stepping stone is school and most children will start at a local school. Children with learning difficulties on the other hand will often have to travel many miles to the special school which can be very tiring. As you read this, consider the following:

- Where do most of the children in your area go to school?
- Where is the nearest special school?
- How do the distances compare?
- What are the ways in which schooling for children with learning difficulties can be organised?
- What should be the alternatives?
- What degree of choice is there for statemented children in your local education authority?
- In which ways is society in general segregated?
- How can children with a learning disability be fully accepted by other children?
- What can be done to encourage and ensure this?

Family aspects

Many things affect the smooth running of the family with a child with a learning disability. These can include finance, where apparently simple things can easily affect financial aspects of the family. Often the bus for the special school picks up the children after nine o'clock which means that the hours when mother can take up some form of employment are limited. Yet extra money is needed for many additional costs, including washing and feeding, heating and transport of a child who will be growing bigger and stronger physically but will possibly still need nappies, a push chair and a special diet. These strains do not diminish as the child gets older, and can become sufficiently serious that they cause marital and emotional problems. The availability of support and respite care is greatly valued by families and local needs are again often met by organisations such as Mencap. Social Services have also made this sort of provision. Social Services provided Laura with two hours of respite care each week until recently when the service was discontinued as a result of increased demand. Mencap has a support service for families which provide reliable, trained people who can care for an individual with a learning disability, allowing the parents and carers to have time to themselves. National Mencap records show that this service is offered by 75 out of 435 local organisations, with 1009 people with learning difficulties and their families benefiting in November 1994. This number reflects provision for all age groups, not just children. About half of the local organisations that provide a respite service offer the service to all age groups, the others providing for the over 19 year olds only.

In the teenage years most children move to a new school and this can be a fresh start when any past misdemeanour can be forgotten, their horizons widen and new experiences introduce them to possible careers and hobbies. Special schools are often all-age, however, so it is possible that the children attending them will stay at that school until 16 or 19 years of age, thus experiencing no change of environment or staff. The physical and emotional changes that happen during the teenage years can often create such things as friction between the generations, a degree of rebelliousness and apparent moodiness in all children, and those with learning difficulties are in the same position. Parents can experience problems dealing with this phase of personal development as frequently the degree of the freedom demanded by the teenagers is impossible and this can be exaggerated for the child whose experiences, skills and abilities are limited. This does not mean that the teenagers with a learning disability cannot develop in the same way as others but there must be an awareness that the processes will take longer and care and effort must be put into preparing them. Youth clubs, such as Mencap's Gateway clubs, organised specifically for young people with disabilities, can be a source of assistance but this approach continues to segregate the young people; however, this is often a choice of parents because it offers their child protection from bullying and abusive experiences and this can been regarded as an outcome sufficiently beneficial that it compensates for the exclusion from wider developmental opportunities.

Case study 6

In Tamworth, South East Staffordshire, a group of parents started a group called SPIN – Special People in Need – in 1988. From this original group it was seen that younger children could also benefit and Junior SPIN was started. Through SPIN parents are supported and their children given opportunities to take part in social activities. As the children have grown up a need for long-term support has been identified and the Thaddeus Trust was set up in 1989. Through association with a housing association two houses were opened in June 1994 for eight young people with learning disabilities, as a stepping stone to employment and independent living.

It is not uncommon for parents to provide many opportunities to take part in sporting and similar experiences alongside peers who do not have learning

disabilities. Cathy Hebden was given the opportunity to take part in the Duke
of Edinburgh's Award and went on to win a Gold Medal in 1985, at the age of
23, the first young woman with Down's Syndrome to gain this standard.
    Consider the following:

● Do you know of any voluntary organisations which work with parents of
  children with learning difficulties in your area?
● What services do they offer?
● If you were a parent where would you find information about such support
  groups?
● Are the services well advertised or does it require a high level of tenacity in
  order to find them?
● What facilities are there in the special schools in your area for those over
  16 years?
● How does the school prepare young people for life after school?
● Are the links with outside agencies developed for school leavers?
● Do the special schools in your area have parents' groups?

Post-school opportunities

After school life is over life choices are limited for young people with a
learning disability. The provision made for them by the statutory bodies is
limited and for many of them employment is not an option particularly in the
short term. The provision being made at present is through the social, health
and education services, and that organised by voluntary organisations.
    Social services provision in Adult Training Centres (ATC) is available to
some people aged over 18 who have a learning disability that makes them
unable to sustain regular employment without extensive training or support.
Priority is given to individuals who live at home with their families, as this
provides a respite service as well as providing for the needs of the individual.
As the changes in the legislation take effect the ATC staff are beginning to look
more closely at ways in which they can utilise the resources in the community
which are available to the public as a whole. By utilising the services
appropriate to the needs of individuals in their centre it could mean that
attendance will be for fewer days as they attend other places within the
community, thus relieving some of the pressure on the centre.
    The Staffordshire Social Services Department (1994) conducted a review
of its day services and made recommendations for future service provisions.
Currently there are 1602 people attending the various centres in the county,
the majority of them having a severe learning disability. There are Adult
Training Centres, some with special care facilities; Activity Units; Industrial
Units; Special Placement Schemes (now know as Sheltered Employment
Schemes) and multipurpose day care services. The Health Authority makes
provision for 368 people in residential settings and in day care centres.
Colleges of Further Education have provided full-time courses for young

adults and part-time courses for people attending day centres but the Staffordshire report states 'with the transfer of Colleges of Further Education from control of the local education authority to independent management, the future of some of this provision is unsure'. Concern is expressed that the further education colleges will not have an incentive to cater for people with learning disabilities as the work is not 'cost effective'. Social services also provide support to voluntary groups by employing a staff member to organise the group and estimate that approximately 130 people receive day services through these channels. The SNR suggests that Staffordshire has approximately 2830 people with a learning disability of which 2100 are in some form of day care. It is probable that at least some of these people are living independently of services, having managed to find open employment. In Staffordshire it is estimated that by the year 2000 there will be approximately 650 people looking for a community-based day service as a result of the closure of long-stay hospitals, the number of school leavers and the people in the community who are waiting for space to be available. People are staying in the day centres up to their death and people are living much longer than used to be the case. These facts linked to the Community Care philosophy will affect the way day care provision is organised in the future. The average number of people using these services nationwide is 1.8 per 1000 according to Department of Health statistics. These figures give an overall picture but when looked at geographically it shows that some people have to travel long distances to their day care provision. The main aim of the staff in social services provision is 'to meet each client's individual needs by a planned programme so they can achieve their full potential and become as independent as possible'. Other subsidiary points included the basic personal care provision and the respite for carers as well as the aim to educate the community about people with learning difficulties.

The Community Care Act (HMSO, 1989) has recommended that where possible social services should purchase care from other groups rather than provide it themselves as they have done in the past. Some colleges of further education have provision for young people coming from special schools and adults with learning difficulties who attend social services day centres. Colleges of Further Education are no longer under the control of the local authority but are managed independently by their Board of Governors. Financial concerns have brought about changes because courses which have in many cases in the past been free are no longer so. This has caused difficulties for some other day care services which have to find money to pay for their clients' attendance at college or discontinue their involvement. Skill, the National Bureau for Students with Disabilities, is currently monitoring the situation. Colleges receive much of their funding from the Further Education Funding Council (FEFC). The FEFC has rigid criteria which restrict its funding to courses leading to vocational outcomes. This may be an unrealistic type of course for many people with learning difficulties in the short term. Training and Enterprise Councils (TEC) also provide funding for vocational courses but they concentrate on people in employment who are furthering their knowledge. The FEFC is currently considering the funding requirements for colleges which want to include young people and adults with learning difficulties and other disabilities in their student body. The Tomlinson Committee is responsible for this and has called for evidence from colleges, people with disabilities and any organisation interested in the education of adults with learning difficulties and other disabilities, so perhaps in the future funding can be allocated according to the needs of individuals.

Children with severe learning difficulties were not accepted by the education service until 1971 as a result of the Education (Handicapped Children) Act of 1970. Following that date 16 to 19 year olds, who had until then been placed in junior training centres under the jurisdiction of the social services, were offered places in some colleges. A very high percentage of further education colleges have provision for this age group of students (FEU, 1989; NFER/FEU, 1988; Stowell, 1987) but not every college offers a curriculum for students with more severe disabilities. The FEFC is currently setting up a mapping exercise to discover which colleges provide educational experiences for students with learning disabilities because there is no information available at present which gives an overall picture. Colleges are not always within reach of a would-be student and without the money to pay for bus fares or the mobility to catch a bus to college then the opportunity is of no value.

Some colleges have integrated the courses for young people and adults with learning difficulties into mainstream provision, giving each student an individual timetable including basic skills and vocational areas. The organis-ation of this provision has been done by cross-college Learning Support Departments rather than a separate Special Needs Department. Working in a cross-college role gives tutors access to a wider range of educational experiences for their students than was previously available to them.

Where the college curriculum is planned to meet the educational, vocational and social needs of the individual, and where it continues over a number of years, it has been seen to have given people with learning difficulties time to expand their view of the world, develop social skills through their integration with other students on mainstream courses, learn about employment and have experience of a work placement. This has led to full-time paid employment for many and part-time work for others. Pathway Officers trained by Mencap work throughout the country finding appropriate work for people with learning difficulties and supporting them in the employment until they are able to do the work independently. Success rates have varied but generally it has been a valuable input. The majority of people go to work experience and then part-time working in order that their benefits are not affected but some move on to full-time work.

Case study 7

Graham attended a college for eight years, progressing through courses to vocational training in a mainstream setting. He was very interested in catering as a career but had difficulties with the written word. Nevertheless he was accepted on to the City and Guilds London Institute (CGLI) course and handouts from the teaching staff were recorded on to tape so that he could listen and learn. However, the examination board would not allow an amanuensis for the exam which meant that in spite of knowing the answers to the questions he could not get his qualification. With the initial support of the Pathway Officer Graham obtained a job in the kitchen of a large hotel where he now works full time. The main reason for the successful result was the close liaison between college staff, the ATC staff and the Pathway Officer. Graham's needs were met in a consistent way, each of the services playing their part to ensure that he got the support he needed.

Adult education centres as well as further education colleges offer an enormous amount of support to people with learning difficulties and Jeannie Sutcliffe (1990), a staff member of the National Institute of Adult Continuing Education with funding from the Joseph Rowntree Foundation, undertook a study of the opportunities available in different parts of the country. It makes interesting reading and gives good advice to anyone committed to developing provision for people with a learning disability.

Another source of support for adults with learning difficulties is offered through Adult Training Centres, which are beginning to be known as Social Education Centres. These centres have been the main providers of support to this group of people and they have offered a wide range of techniques for the development of skills for life. They are now being changed as the role of social services changes from provider to purchaser and they use community-based resources. This includes adult education classes, training to encourage appropriate behaviour in places such as libraries, shops and restaurants and training in the areas of travel, safety and road sense using public transport. They carry out mobility training and social training, building up the fund of skills in the individual. The people who use the centres also get the opportunity to take part in assertiveness training and some centres use the *Patterns for Living* course, produced by the Open University for people with learning difficulties (1989). Many people with learning disabilities are not able to predict or assess what is possible for them, but with appropriate and careful organisation of provision a great deal of independence can be achieved, as is shown in Case study 8.

Case study 8

Jenny is a young woman attending an ATC which uses the *Patterns for Living* course. She reported that until she took part in the course she had no idea of the opportunities that were available to her. Until the death of her father six years ago Jenny had lived with him and her brother, their mother having died two years earlier; her father had a number of relatives but they always spoke to her through her father. When her father died, Jenny and her brother decided they would stay together in their own home. Their relatives were not pleased about the decision as they felt that Jenny and her brother needed residential care, because Jenny and her brother both have learning difficulties as well as a visual impairment. Jenny felt that the relatives' objections may have been because they thought a great deal of assistance would be needed, which they were not prepared to provide as they live some distance away. Jenny's mother had a good friend, Anne, who had given assistance to the family over a number of years and when their father died Anne supported Jenny and Colin in their wish to live independently and because of this they were allowed to remain in their home. Anne acts as their advocate whenever necessary and supports them in many other practical ways, particularly shopping. Both Jenny and Colin hold their own benefit books and with Anne's help budget for their daily needs. Jenny also receives a mobility allowance (as a result of her poor sight); this enables Jenny to go out – which she likes – but Anne keeps charge of the allowance so that Colin does not become jealous of the extra money available to Jenny. Jenny uses the services of a befriender, whom she pays, to accompany her to such places as shops, a pub or on a day trip, for she enjoys the activities but without assistance the combination of her poor sight and her learning difficulty would prevent her taking part in them. A mobility officer helps Jenny in the home one day each week and she has marked switches and doors, cupboards and the cooker so that she can manage everyday chores around the house in safety. The mobility officer is also teaching Jenny to use Braille and she has acquired a number of aids such as a speaking clock and an indicator for cups to tell her when they are full.

The mobility officer only works with blind and partially sighted people but voluntary groups have been set up to offer the same mobility services to people with learning difficulties. One group that does travel training is the Paddington Integration Project which is part of a three-year further education course. It is essential to be able to travel independently if employment is the aim and it takes a long time to become confident when travelling alone. The project worker discusses the journey with the individual and his or her parents if appropriate to ensure that everyone involved knows what is being done. Parents are often anxious but the project worker seeks to show the positive effects of independent travel.

Jenny and Colin are very different characters. Jenny is outgoing and enjoys going to the Adult Training Centre and taking part in the activities while Colin is more reserved and prefers to stay at home looking after his animals and his pigeons. Most of the responsibility for everyday living therefore falls upon Jenny as Colin relies on her to make his breakfast and prepare the evening meal for every day. They rely on a number of external sources of support, of which the main one is Anne, and they also have a key worker and a care worker but they are able to manage other things for themselves. A key worker is a person working at the Adult Training Centre who takes responsibility for a number of the clients and acts as their advocate giving hope and advice. By respecting their clients' wishes and enabling them to make their own choices they encourage the clients to develop independence. Life has opened up for Jenny since she discovered that it was possible to have a friend with whom to go to the shops and for a drink in the evenings. This began through the assistance of a Mencap Friendship Project which was operating in the area; Jenny approached them with the help of her key worker and a suitable volunteer was introduced to Jenny. They have been friends now for 18 months and Jenny expresses herself as really happy with the arrangement because they get on so well. She says that her brother is happy with his animals and his pigeons but she always wanted to get out and about more but even without her visual impairment it would not have been easy.

A practical obstacle to development is the reduced social life after the end of the school day. Often the opportunity for young people with learning difficulties to go out is limited to doing so with their parents and this can lead to problems where families are always trying to establish a balance between doing things which interest the parents and doing those which interest the young people. One attempt to address this is the Mencap Friendship Project, which works to link people with learning difficulties, over the age of 16, with volunteers living in their locality. One example of a friendship project is that based in South East Staffordshire. This project offers training to the volunteers so that they will gain an understanding of the needs of the person they will be with and be able to match interests. The project workers always support the friends until they are settled together and they organise shopping trips as well as holidays for all to enjoy. The friends go out together as often as they wish, taking part in activities which they both enjoy. With the support of a project coordinator the friendships can flourish and the life of a young person be expanded to include things that they enjoy but their families do not. A letter from a parent sent to the project leader after her daughter had taken part in a summer scheme organised by the project said 'If you could see her face at the end of her day with you it would make all your efforts worth while'.

Finance can frequently be a source of difficulty. Money is, for many, in short supply and quite often anything that is provided goes into the general family budget. This results in conditions that restrict personal independence and can result in their being treated as a child, such as having few clothes and where the ones they do have are chosen by their mother.

Case study 9

These people are students at a college of further education:

Gareth is 23 and is on a college course but lives with his mother and his sister and has no social life at all. He spends his evenings in his bedroom listening to his music tapes. Over the two years that he has been in college he has worn the same clothes, and although clean he has never had anything different because his mother always gets them for him; he is never able to choose anything for himself. His allowance is considered to be part of the family budget and he is not given any opportunity to budget for his own needs.

Mary is 24 years old and lives with her mother and younger brother. She goes to a youth club with other young people with learning difficulties and occasionally to the cinema with her mother and is always well presented and happy at college. However, when she wished to attend the departmental Christmas party at college her mother was most unhappy and refused to let her attend in spite of transport and staff helpers being made available to her.

These restrictions impede the development of young people and increase their dependence rather than cultivate their independence.

Parents

Parents are often fearful that their children will be bullied or teased when out on their own or in groups. Every parent has a protective instinct towards their young but they have to overcome the tendency to overprotect their children. As we have already discussed, children begin to try to take things into their own hands when they feel ready but children and young people with learning difficulties are rarely given much freedom to try as they are constantly under supervision.

Parents of young people with learning difficulties benefit from the experiences of others. Over the past decade support groups have been organised in many special nurseries and schools, and occasionally in colleges of further education, to enable parents to meet and discuss their concerns.

Case study 10

A parents' group (Clare, 1991) was started for the parents of young people on a full-time course in a Midlands college, and it was discovered that many of the parents who were brought together expressed surprise that there were other families like theirs. One father said that all through the years that his son was in school he had not met the parents of any of his friends and now it felt as if a weight had been lifted from his shoulders as he realised he could talk to others about his son. Parents began to meet each other socially and then encouraged their sons and daughters to do the same. Friendships were encouraged and the young people travelled to each other's homes to stay for the night or a weekend. Parents were invited to make suggestions for the curriculum and to meet the staff from all parts of the college which gave them an insight into the possibilities. Speakers were invited to talk about subjects chosen by the parents. The subjects of benefits and sex education were of interest. The work of Ann Craft (1992) was considered and changes were made to the curriculum so that sex education could be included. This college runs a fully integrated programme for young people with learning difficulties and many of the students graduate on to courses leading to vocational qualifications, such as catering and nursery nursing, and into employment.

It is also necessary to consider the needs of people with learning difficulties who become parents. There is the same variation of fertility as in other members of the public so how can their needs and those of their children be met?

Ask yourself:

● How do you think young people can be supported in their development of independence?
● How would parents be satisfied that the question of safety has been adequately considered?
● How can aspirations be encouraged?
● How can parents be encouraged to develop their child's independence?
● What support do parents need?

Employment

Contrary to what is often thought by those who are uninformed, employment for people with learning difficulties is a real possibility. Training in everyday mobility skills, encouraging social interaction and learning skills in stages can be the key but the attitudes of the others in the workplace will decide whether or not the door will open. In 1978 the Centre for Educational Research and Innovation (CERI) of the Department for Economic Cooperation and Development (OECD) began work on a major Disabled Action Programme. The Further Education Unit was commissioned and one of the publications to come from the work is specifically related to the field of employment possibilities for people with learning difficulties (Griffiths, 1989). The study outlines the issues that are linked to employment and shows how people with disabilities have to take control of their own lives. Parents and professionals need to remember that people with learning difficulties have as much need to be recognised as adults as their peers. To be recognised as an adult we have to take full responsibility for our own life, be financially independent, take an adult role in society and be a non-dependent son or daughter. Employment is a vital element in all these areas so to exclude people with learning difficulties from the job market would maintain them in the role of dependants.

In Kirklees the Metropolitan Council aims 'to ensure that disabled people have full access to all our areas of employment and services' through their 'Into Work' initiative. Guidelines were produced by the council which would help managers target their workforce to reflect the population of the borough (Kirklees Metropolitan Borough Council, 1993).

Using the 1991 OPCS Census data the guidelines suggested that 10.7 per cent of the workforce should be black or from ethnic minorities, 51.6 per cent should be women and 12.9 per cent should have a disability. Each manager sets targets for his or her own department and integrates them into the service business plans and work priorities. This initiative entails all managers considering their workforce and developing strategies which will ensure that barriers to employment for any person are overcome. The council provides funds to meet training costs, gives loans for specialist equipment and access improvement. Kirklees runs Worklink (Kirklees Metropolitan Borough Council, 1993–94), an employment service for people with a disability which is linked to the Sheltered Employment Scheme (SES). The SES is a way of giving disabled people time to get used to employment. Often when starting a new job there is so much to learn that it takes longer to complete a task than it does after practice. Using SES the employer pays the person the wage for the job. The employer assesses the percentage of the job completed by the individual and the SES pays the amount for the additional percentage to the employer. This allows Kirklees to find appropriate employment for individuals either in their own departments or with other employers. In the financial year 1993–94 85 placements were made, bringing the total to 720 since 1986, and 48 people were benefiting from the SES, which is all that funding will allow. There are other initiatives under way which are funded by the Training and Enterprise Council. REAL (Realistic Employment for Adults with Learning Difficulties) is also organised by Kirklees Metropolitan Council (KMC) and looks specifically at employment opportunities for people with learning difficulties. By working with employers and supporting people until they can work alone REAL has helped many people find permanent work. The efforts made by these and other organisations and councils around the country are making a difference to the quality of life for a number of people with learning disabilities and should be encouraged and copied by others. The attitude of employers and other employees is vital in any work situation because without a friendly reception and tolerance a placement will fail.

The Bridle Gate Project is a voluntary organisation based in Leek in the North Staffordshire moorlands which gives training in animal husbandry, organic gardening, nature study and conservation leading to a qualification which gives entry to the Staffordshire Agricultural college. EDIT is a registered charity which facilitates education for disabled people using information technology. The training is provided by Keele University and Newcastle College for people with an interest in employment in the world of commercial office services using computers. Once again, although these opportunities are available to some, they are limited and spread throughout the country so availability depends on where a person lives.

Questions you might ask yourself here are:

- Is it possible in your area to find training for employment for people with learning difficulties?
- What kind of support do you think is required in the employment to ensure that a person will be successful?
- Have you met a person with a learning disability who is employed?

Independent living

As a result of the recent changes in the social services legislation adults with learning difficulties are now assessed by a care manager. The assessment takes into account the daily living needs of individuals and a care plan is drawn up. The care that is required is then purchased for the individual from the services available in the area. According to research undertaken by CRIMD the following items would be included:

- a home of their own;
- social relationships;
- a meaningful occupation;
- leisure and recreation;
- opportunities for education and good healthcare.

The aim of area managers is to purchase a wide range of different services in order to give real choice to people with learning difficulties and their families. Support for daily living is to be provided whenever possible to enable people to live in their own homes. When it is not possible for individuals to live alone a range of other homely accommodation will be available. The support services will include local colleges of further education, occupational schemes, local drop-in centres and integration into ordinary community facilities, befriending services and help in the home. The plan will be to replace day centres with a mixed range of services in a variety of settings. People with learning difficulties need help in learning the skills of daily living and support workers in their home will guide people through a programme built around their needs (FEU, 1992).

Group homes have been set up by local Mencap groups and the young people have done their own shopping and cooking as well as gone out to college or the day centre. One Warwickshire home was opened four years ago and five young people, who had previously lived at home with their parents, moved in together. With support they have settled into a comfortable way of life and with their domestic skills improved they have a new independent life which is working out well.

Consider these relevant aspects:

- Are there any opportunities for people with a learning disability to be supported in their search for employment?
- Do employers in your area include equal opportunities statements in their advertisement of posts?
- What is your local council's policy on employment for people with a learning disability?

Raising awareness

It is important that those who may come into professional contact with people with learning disabilities are educated in the importance of treating people with learning disabilities as people first and addressing the fact that they have that type of disability second. An awareness by the general public would also go a long way towards making life more enjoyable and fulfilling for the individuals concerned.

The new Nursing 2000 training includes placements in special schools which will help nurses develop their understanding of children with learning difficulties and this will hopefully lead to better relationships with the adults they will become. Self-advocacy groups have been started all over the country in colleges and centres, mostly affiliated to People First which is organised and managed by people with learning difficulties. These groups have given them a voice and one group that has been running for seven years expressed how much it had helped them to understand their lives, to express themselves and to open up a little bit more of the world. The group members now go into a local university to explain their experiences and point of view to students on the Social Work course as well as speaking at conferences for social workers. They take up issues in their town and have sent letters to the local council on such matters as access to shops and public buildings for wheelchair users and the location of the post office. The group members also have an input into the organisation and running of the centre which extends to interviewing new staff members but even after seven years of slowly building up the assertion, negotiation and presentation skills some staff members do not agree that the group should continue in this way. Some studies have been done on the effects of self-advocacy and the benefits that have occurred which make interesting reading (Clare, 1990; Sutcliffe and Simons, 1993; Wertheimer, 1989). The Open College in the North West offers a Stage B course for people with disabilities to train as Disability Awareness Trainers who can then tell employers, employees and professional groups how they can develop their awareness of the needs of disabled people. At present there is only one course of this type running and that is at Lancaster and Morecambe College with funding from the European Union.

Conclusion

There are many ways in which the quality of life can be improved for people with learning difficulties but they mostly depend on the willingness of others to change the way they act themselves. Talking over someone's head, using complicated language, staring and name calling all cause distress to people with learning difficulties and could so easily be avoided if society at large took an interest. It would increase feelings of acceptance if people who live in the same street to those with learning disabilities befriend them, allowing them to feel like full members of their community instead of people apart.

The self-advocacy group mentioned above suggested that if possible they would like to get to know the children from the local school and for the children to get to know them through reciprocal visits. The members of the group point out that activities such as these would widen the range of contacts for children and allow them time to get to know the group members as individuals. Can you think of other ways in which members of the community at large can be made more aware of the way their responses affect people with learning difficulties?

When speaking with people with learning difficulties and their parents/ carers the neglect of health matters has been a common experience. One woman with Down's Syndrome, who had a heart problem, went to see the consultant accompanied by her mother. It seems that the problem was bad enough for a transplant to be considered but her mother was told 'it's not worth it, they don't live long anyway!' If this is the response people with learning difficulties get from professionals how can society be anything but disabling.

Every step through life can be improved for people with a learning difficulty with forethought and consideration of their needs by the rest of society. The steps that have been taken in different parts of the country by voluntary agencies show that improvement is possible and that the effects can be excellent. Society in general seems to encourage division. Young men support different football teams and scorn each other's choices, membership of clubs is only open to certain people, everywhere there is conflict between people of different religions and races. What can we do to form links between people? Understanding different viewpoints can be a first step and to do that we need to know more about the individuals concerned. Everyone has a need to be accepted and befriended no matter how they look or speak and we can make a difference by our actions. There is a long way to go before everyone in society gives everyone else the respect that they themselves expect but we can help by breaking down barriers between ourselves and people with learning difficulties.

Useful addresses

Bridal Gate Project, The Mill, Winkhill, Leek, Staffs ST13 7PP. Tel: 01538 308020.

Centre for Research and Information into Mental Disability (CRIMD), University of Birmingham, Queen Elizabeth Psychiatric Hospital, Mindelsohn Way, Birmingham B15 2QZ. Tel: 0121 627 2859.

Centre for Studies on Integration in Education (CSIE), 1 Redland Close, Elm Land, Redland, Bristol BS6 6UE. Tel: 0117 923 8450.

Down's Syndrome Association, National Office, 155 Mitcham Road, London SW17 9PG. Tel: 0181 682 4001.

EDIT, Employment for Disabled People using Information Technology, Unit 10, Burslem Enterprise Centre, Moorland Road, Burslem, Stoke-on-Trent, Staffordshire ST6 1JQ. Tel: 01782 836992.

Further Education Funding Council (FEFC), National Office, Cheylesmore House, Quinton Road, Coventry CV1 2WT. Tel: 01203 863000. The Tomlinson Committee is a committee of the FEFC.

Further Education Unit (FEU), Citadel Place, Tinworth Street, London SE11 5EH. Tel: 0171 962 1280.

Joseph Rowntree Foundation Disability Programme, Norah Fry Research Centre, University of Bristol, 32 Tyndall's Park Road, Bristol BS8 1PY. Tel: 0117 923 8164.

Kirklees Metropolitan Council, Ros Jones, Employment Initiatives Officer, Corporate Resources Strategic Personnel, Pearl Assurance House, John William Street, Huddersfield, West Yorkshire HD1 1BA. Tel: 01484 422133.

Lancaster and Morecambe College, Morecambe Road, Lancaster LA1 2TU. Tel: 01524 66215.

Mencap (Royal Society for Mentally Handicapped Children and Adults), Mencap National Centre, 123 Golden Lane, London EC1Y 0RT. Tel: 0171 454 0454.

Mencap Friendship Project, organised on a local basis. Contact Mencap National Centre or The Coordinator, Mencap Friendship Project, Mid-Staffordshire, 1st Floor, 20 Sandon Road, Stafford ST16 3ES. Tel: 01785 227707.

Mencap Pathway Officers, organised on a local basis. Contact Head of Employment Services at the Mencap National Centre.

Mencap Support Services, organised on a local basis. One contact is: The Coordinator, Voluntary Services Centre, Union Street Car Park, Burton-on-Trent, Staffordshire DE14 1AA. Tel: 01283 567303 or Mencap National Centre.

National Institute of Adult Continuing Education (NIACE), 21 De Montfort Street, Leicester LE1 7GE. Tel: 0116 255 1451.

National Portage Association, National Secretary, Mollie White, 4 Clifton Road, Winchester, Hampshire SO22 5BN. Tel: 01962 60148.

National Society for Epilepsy, Chalfont St. Peter, Gerrards Cross, Bucks SL9 0RJ. Tel: 01494 873991.

North Staffs Special Adventure Playground, Stanier Steet, Newcastle-under-Lyme ST5 2SU. Tel: 01782 717612.

Open College of the North West, Disability Awareness Training Diploma. Storey Institute, Meeting House Lane, Lancaster LA1 1TH. Tel: 01524 845046.

Paddington Integration Project, Beauchamp Lodge, 2 Warwick Crescent, London W2 6NE. Tel: 0171 286 2802.

People First, Instruments House, 207–215 King's Cross Road, London WC1X 9DB. Tel: 0171 713 6400.

Rathbone Society, 1st Floor, Princess House, 105–107 Princess Street, Manchester M1 6DD. Tel: 0161 236 5358.

REAL, Nancy Redhead, Supported Employment Officer, Learning Difficulties Service, Knowle Park House, Staff House 2, Crowlees Road, Mirfield WF14 9PP. Tel: 01924 465151 ext. 5145.

Saxon Gymnastics Club for People with Special Needs, Head Coach, Dave Rozzell. Tel: 01270 665514.

Shaw Trust, Caithness House, Weston Way, Melksham, Wiltshire SN12 4DZ. Tel: 01962 865074.

Sheltered Employment Scheme is operated through the Employment Service.

Skill (National Bureau for Students with Disabilities), 336 Brixton Road, London SW9 7AA. Tel: 0171 274 0565.

Training and Enterprise Councils are locally based. Contact Training, Enterprise and Education Directorate, Department of Employment, Moorfoot, Sheffield S1 4PQ. Tel: 01142 753275.

Values into Action (VIA), Oxford House, Derbyshire Street, London E2 6HG. Tel: 0171 729 5436.

SECTION 3: HOW DOES IT FEEL?

This section is about experience – both of individuals and the general experiences of a section of the population. Sian Vasey begins with a detailed exposition of the way in which she organises her own care support, effectively making the point that anyone who thinks that the provision of care packages is an unnecessary luxury must realise that disabled people cannot rely on friends and volunteers for the help they need – they must be able to pay for it and be in control of their day-to-day lives independently of those around them.

Bernard Leach then follows with a discussion of disabled people and the equal opportunities movement. This gives us a fascinating insight into the way in which a development took place, became a major idea and then seemed to fade away again in certain respects. His chapter makes it clear that there is a requirement for a strong disabled people's movement and there are few signs of the level of theoretical debate that typified activity in the 1970s and 1980s and which have had such a lasting effect.

Sallie Withers delves into the relationship between disabled people and counsellors. She looks at why people seek counsellors and what are the experiences of disabled people. Her comments are illustrated with case histories and she provides a comprehensive structure including considerations of training, co-counselling and peer counselling.

This section concludes with the other side of the coin being provided by Ray Woolfe, whose chapter is about being a counsellor. Ray explains that there is no copyright on the term and anyone can use the description 'counsellor', a situation which makes it even more important that the professionals do it properly. This chapter distinguishes between being and doing, demonstrating that counselling can be conceptualised in two major ways, either as 'something which one person does to another' or as 'a way of being with another'.

7

The Experience of Care

Sian Vasey

I am a wheelchair-using person in need of ongoing facilitation with activities such as getting washed and dressed, going to the loo, cooking and driving. I can function independently when my immediate environment is organised so that things are within reach: for example I am able to feed myself and so on. I do not have personal assistants with me all the time, which I have to say I am glad about. Instead I hire them in for roughly an hour at a time to do what is necessary at appropriate times. To pay for this I receive the sum of £223.50 a week from my local authority. This money is called a care package.

In some ways I do find the arrangement a little minimalistic, although I do have more cover from time to time, on an ad hoc basis. Broadly there are two factors which hinder the development of my arrangement into something more substantial:

- financial constraints;
- my reluctance to have an assistant present at all times.

A constantly present assistant gives me a claustrophobic feeling; I find I prefer to take a few risks and go to places unaccompanied, hoping I find someone to give me a hand on the loo when I get there, rather than take someone with me for the purpose. I am helped in this because for a lot of the time I tend to move in circles where people are attuned to disability, so I find I meet people who are familiar with the issues and who can help me from an informed point of view.

Overall the way my system of care operates is fairly piecemeal, relying on quite a high degree of ingenuity on my part, particularly when I want to do something out of routine. If I had more money I would employ a team of perhaps four people on a full-time basis giving them full employment benefits. This would get me closer to the ideal of total seamless cover, but as it is the system is very much held together with glue and bits of string. The most problematic aspect of my situation, which might seem very obvious, is the fear of being without help at a time of need.

Organising my care

My support network functions quite effectively most of the time. There are twelve people in it and this is enough for them to cover for each other so the system does not really demand too much of my attention. The problems come in two ways. First, during bank holidays, particularly Christmas, it is possible that everyone will disappear – including the people who are on the periphery of the network, but who do come in handy in emergencies. Of course, there are always agencies to fall back on, but these are expensive and most care packages are not designed to accommodate this solution. Second, it is very difficult to make arrangements to stay away from home, either for work reasons or because I wish to take a holiday.

I can find myself in trouble because I have not put my mind to getting organised early enough, so the lesson I have had to learn is to try to plan ahead, regardless of how tedious I may find it. Finding someone to go away with is a particularly difficult business. I find I really have to grit my teeth to get it sorted out and find someone who I actually want to go with, is available and is able. It is quite stressful if I end up in the situation of having a holiday booked and still relatively near the date I have no one to accompany me. For some reason people do seem to be unreliable in this area by saying they can go and then changing their mind. A week, or two weeks away, is a big chunk out of people's lives and because it is only possible to take one person due to cost that one person has to do everything, which can be very tiring and tends to discourage long stays away from home. One possible solution here is to use agency people some of the time while away, although the only time I have done this was recently when I was in York. I hired a driver from the Job Centre in York but I was unable to find someone who could both do the care work and drive. This arrangement became very complicated, expensive and unwieldy because I also had to find someone to drive my van to York, who then travelled back to London on the train. At the end of the week I then had to find someone else to travel to York on the train to drive me back to London. A lot of organising for a week away.

My network of assistants

Earlier in this chapter I referred to my 'network'. It is worth considering who these people actually are and where I acquired them. They amount to twelve people. I found one from a local newspaper advertisement, three from advertisements in sweetshops, two from advertisements in the Job Centre, one started as an agency worker, one was a friend, I found three through friends and I met one through work. Apart from one elderly retired man they all do other things and have a variety of commitments. The knock-on effect of this for me is that I do need to stick with routine, even as a care package recipient; this is a high status to have in the hierarchy of disability and one which implies a considerable level of freedom. However, my reality is that I really do have to get up at the same time every week day, because the person who gets me up has to get to various other jobs, so however much a lie-in might seem deserved, necessary or possible as far as I am concerned, I am very unlikely to be able to have one unless I plan it days in advance. So freedom is not exactly the hallmark of my life. On the positive side this really does assist with personal discipline and I think it has had a major and good effect on my professional life in that I can and do get to places on time even early in the morning, but of course it can be quite tiring.

Being a user of personal assistants certainly creates a variety of mobility difficulties. I have mentioned that it is difficult to have a holiday, but similarly my heart sinks when I imagine moving away from the area in which I currently live. The first thing that would need to be sorted out (which could prove very tricky) is the provision of the money in another borough. A different local authority might take a more rigorous line about the financial assessment of my provision and this could be very problematic. I feel that overall my best bet is to lie low, away from the scrutiny of the authorities – including the one that currently provides me with my package – even though this is not tackling the fact that I am effectively having my fundamental human right of freedom of movement substantially diminished.

The second problem is in the area of recruitment. Although I know it would not really take a long time to find a new team, the business of sloughing off the old one does seem quite daunting. My worries range from the purely selfish to concerns for the workers themselves, who are up to a point financially dependent on me. Although I feel reasonably confident about recruitment, I am not sufficiently confident that I would be able to find someone who is as quick at getting me up in the morning as the person who currently does that job. Many personal assistant users would corroborate the idea that the morning is the crucial time and while a lot of the other jobs can be done by lesser mortals, if you do not have someone who has the morning routine down to a fine art, who understands the niceties of details such as how to do your hair (and who can get through the operation quickly) then life becomes very difficult indeed. The same person has been doing this for me for three or four years now and I suppose while this is obviously a good thing it does increase my feeling of dependence on her. In reality I have found at least two other people within those years, without really looking, who are as speedy, so perhaps that is a worry that is virtually unfounded. I believe that it would, however, be inadvisable to move to a lightly populated area as there just would not be sufficient people there to draw on; similarly an area unpopulated with casual workers would also be difficult to live in.

The basic problem with moving away from my existing set-up is the fact that the assistants I rely on most have become very much a part of my life-style and the business of recruiting new people is genuinely burdensome. I really dislike the process of initiating new people into how to put me on the loo, primarily because it involves an element of some physical danger. It is a procedure that is more about knack than physical strength, but with a new person you can never be absolutely sure that they have understood your instructions or are not going to make a hash of it in some way, resulting in a very uncomfortable accident. I must add that this has never actually happened, but the total experience means that I am seriously put off the idea of moving house to an area where I would not have anybody I know to rely upon. Again the answer lies in advance planning and the problem can be solved, but when I think about moving I almost prefer to live a fantasy in which I am able to just 'manage somehow'. I like to give myself this option mentally as a relief from the daunting constraints of having to be permanently covered, which means knowing incontrovertibly that someone suitable will turn up about four times a day – first thing in the morning, at lunch time when I am at work, at approximately six o'clock and last thing at night – come rain or shine. The issue of moving is one example that reminds me that I am in a position of some power and I should not allow myself to be lulled into a false sense of dependency. It is also a reminder that I have to be tough and potentially able to make a lot of people of whom I am fond redundant.

Employment relationships

Employing people does bring responsibilities and being in an ongoing employer–employee relationship is quite testing. I have to confess that in order to survive I approach it in a fairly cavalier fashion and have been known to treat people quite badly. It is particularly at the beginning of the relationship that problems can occur. I can refer to a recent recruitment exercise when I was looking for someone to make dinner, but at a period in my life when I was working long and erratic hours and finding it difficult to get home at specified times. This is not a good state to be in when trying to establish a routine with a new person. People will only be tolerant once a relationship is established. I found in this case that I did not have the time or energy to sort the new people out properly and everything became quite chaotic for a while. The underlying fact was that I did not have a desperate need for a new person, but was just trying to add to the numbers in my network for greater flexibility.

Management is not my strong point even in a professional capacity. I am the sort of person who relies on liking a person in order to work with him or her. There is a received wisdom in the use of personal assistants which states that they should not be friends with the disabled user. I personally think it is virtually impossible to employ a personal assistant whom the user does not like at some level. However, it is important that the personal assistant clearly understands that the priority is to get the job done and does not expect 10 minutes' chat on arrival. Particularly when a lot of different personal assistants are coming and going regularly, it is quite possible for the user to become swamped in a quagmire of other people and have no time alone at all.

I feel I am quite lazy in that I do not operate a Pay As You Earn (PAYE) system, although it would not suit the workers for the financial arrangements to be too formal. Of course, this in turn is a symptom of the fact that packages are not generous enough to discourage operation from within the black economy, which potentially results in the exploitation of workers. I pay £7.50 for an hour's help with getting up in the morning, £6.00 for visits in the day and £11.00 for assistance to go to bed at about eleven o'clock. I am not sure whether this is reasonable or not, but I certainly have guilty pangs about the fact that these amounts have not increased at all since 1989 when I first started the care package. I could lobby for more money from the council and I could try to sort things out so that the assistants received some benefits such as sickness pay and holiday entitlement. I could do all sorts of things, but I don't because (I suspect like most people) I think that if a system is working reasonably well why should I bother to do anything about it? Also I have a sense that there could be a danger in 'rocking the boat'. Of course the local authority should look after its workers properly, including those employed by contractors, which in a small way is what I am. However, I do not want to engage in this battle and in any case I do feel that if I did so and won it could be a pyrrhic victory as my workers might actually be worse off in a low-paid formal job structure than they are now with the flexibility of cash in hand.

Before getting a care package and relatively flexible assistance I would say my life was a panicky wilderness of stifling dependencies and inappropriate support systems comprising district nurses, Community Service Volunteers, family and friends, and so on, in which survival was my main goal. There is no doubt that this present type of arrangement is liberating and is effective for people with good organising skills. However, once the nuts and bolts are in place and the novelty of the new-found freedom has worn off a bit, the subtle difficulties of being a personal assistant user do become apparent. It is a case of 'after you get what you want you no longer want it'. It inches you nearer towards a mainstream life but does not quite allow you to reach it.

Relationships

The problem for me is centred on relationships and particularly about how you have a sexual relationship when you need help getting to bed, turning over in bed, someone to come into the bedroom in the morning to get you up, and so on. Before one even starts thinking about the problems of intimacy, the issue of more everyday privacy can also be a problem. A lot of partners and potential partners just do not like the constant intrusion of the third party and will therefore drift away. My experience is that it can be awkward and embarrassing having a personal assistant present even in quite innocuous situations. Some partners seem to like doing personal care work and the easiest thing can be to let them get on with it. However, if that happens then inevitably the disabled person's independence is under threat and the relationship will be under some strain, however much the partners might try to resolve the issues. My personal belief is that in order for a disabled person with bed-related care needs to have a long-term relationship, two bedrooms are a necessity unless significant compromises, for example about the time of going to bed, are made on a long-term basis. Being a personal assistant user can be a lot easier when you are on your own than when third parties are involved, so this can encourage the more solitary aspects of one's personality.

Relationships and friendships do become more puzzling when you are a care user. I have occasionally found myself in the position of wondering whether the person I am with would be with me if I weren't paying him or her. This is clearly a result of my personal policy of blurring the boundaries and not treating personal assistants exclusively as staff. On one occasion when I employed a friend we had a long conversation before she started work, which I assumed was just a long conversation, but it transpired later that she expected to be paid for that time. This seemed a little odd to me but I was not assertive enough on that occasion to make any comment.

A trap I have fallen into on one occasion, which with hindsight seems very silly indeed, was to ask a friend to help me on to the loo from time to time when we were working together. I had done this in the belief that my friend genuinely did not mind as help had been offered in this way on many occasions. In the course of time I discovered that my friend was actually quite resentful about being asked and was making comments about it, including suggestions that I must be doing well on the money they perceived I was saving from my care package. Apart from the obvious hurtful implications of this for me I find it is quite a bizarre situation when economics can start to play such an overt part in everyday relationships. I start to think that perhaps I should pay people every time they open a door for me. Clearly I made a big mistake, tempted as I was by the ease of being able to ask someone who just happened to be there, rather then for ever having to arrange a visit and go to the loo at a preordained time. One thing this does illustrate quite effectively, though, to anyone who thinks that the provision of care packages is an unnecessary luxury, is that disabled people cannot rely on friends and volunteers for the help they need – we must be able to pay for it and be in control of our day-to-day lives and independent of those around us.

8
Disabled people and the equal opportunities movement

Bernard Leach

The disabled people's movement began to stir in the United Kingdom in the early 1970s. A letter from Paul Hunt in the *Guardian* on 20 September 1972 started a chain of events which led first to the formation of the Union of Physically Impaired Against Segregation (UPIAS) and eventually to a national coalition of groups and organisations controlled by disabled people.

These were stirring times, as the following quote from the editorial of the first issue of the UPIAS journal, illustrates:

> It is the Union's social definition of disability which has . . . raised the floodgates for a river of discontent to sweep all our oppression before us, and with it to sweep all the flotsam and jetsam of 'expertise', 'professionalism' and 'authority' which have fouled our minds for so long, into the sewers of history. (*Disability Challenge*, No. 1, May 1981)

By the 1990s the 'social model' and policies of the disabled people's movement have seemingly replaced the discredited 'medical model' of disability. A new paradigm appears to be in place. Even the professionals whose control has been challenged (social workers, medical and charity professionals), seem to be at home with the new terminology ('people with disabilities'; 'empowerment') and have become 'disability aware'.

This chapter will look at how disabled people became involved in the political process in order to examine what can be learned from what happened in practice at the level of local equal opportunities initiatives.

Getting to grips with equal opportunities politics

At the same time that groups of activists in the UK were beginning to form a self-conscious 'movement' and raise disability rights as a political issue, equal opportunities initiatives were rising to the top of the political agenda in several Labour-controlled city councils. The predominant aim of the disabled activists was to try and organise their own campaigning groups and organisations. This involved either taking over organisations that were *for* disabled people but not yet controlled *by* them, or setting up their own organisations (such as the Manchester and Derbyshire Coalitions of Disabled People).

This was a productive time for the development of new political and social theories of disability. Until then disabled people had been largely politically invisible. Consideration of the heritage of totally inaccessible nineteenth-century municipal town halls makes it clear how irrelevant disabled people were to the local political process. They were socially visible only as patients, clients or welfare/charity cases – under the control of medical and other disability-related professionals.

When disabled people began to assert their rights they often used as their model the theories and tactics of other groups (for example, women, black people, the gay community) that were fighting for political influence. In addition, by demanding the right to control both their own lives and their own organisations disabled people were also challenging the power of the disability-related professions. For the theoretical or political debate about disabled people's rights to have any practical effect disabled people themselves had to become involved in the political process. At a local level this often meant becoming involved with local authorities who are major providers of services (through day care centres, residential homes, meals-on-wheels, and so on) and employment opportunities to disabled people. Councils were a potential source of power at the political level and they could also provide access to grants.

One shining possibility for funding and influence were the burgeoning equal opportunities initiatives being launched by local authorities. Disabled activists found themselves being whisked into town halls on the coat-tails of the black people's, women's and gay movements, but initially disability was not high on the agenda of the leftish Labour councils with equal opportunities initiatives. In Manchester, for example, while there were gay, feminist and black politicians who were councillors or influential in the local Labour Party, there were no corresponding disabled activists. Disability was seen as a separate, almost non-political, issue. Where there were 'Disability Units' they were often managed by non-disabled people and based on a social services 'client' model with no notion of accountability to disabled people.

In Manchester and Derbyshire UPIAS activists had very different experiences of local authority initiatives. In Derbyshire the County Council provided funds for the Derbyshire Coalition of Disabled People, which became a model for such coalitions across the country. In Manchester UPIAS effectively controlled the City Council's Disabled People's Subcommittee (which had been established in 1985) and they could see their impact slowly spreading across the council.

Certainly there was an (equal) opportunity cost involved: many activists moved from voluntary activism to paid employment in the new posts that were on offer in local authorities. Disabled people have found (and still find) it a struggle to maintain their own organisations; in the meantime equal opportunities initiatives have come and (largely) gone.

Disability groups such as UPIAS became involved in local authority equal opportunities initiatives because for the first time there was a perception of a chance of access to power and resources on terms of their own making. Local authorities could either involve the disabled people's movement on its own terms (that is, representation from disabled-controlled organisations *only*) or risk a boycott. In several cases disabled activists began to steer equal opportunities policies in the direction of their choosing (Davis, 1986). In Manchester, for example, an equal opportunities subcommittee consisting of representatives of disabled-controlled groups only was established in 1985.

We must consider what disabled people have gained from their involvement in equal opportunities, asking what changes they managed to effect in terms of improved physical access, employment opportunities, service improvements and changed attitudes.

The first problem was to have disability accepted as an equal opportunities issue by both elected members and council officers. Councils of all political persuasions were proud of their record of building segregated residential institutions for disabled people. Vested interests in the caring professions within town halls were also extremely effective at defending their power rather than being willing to share it with disabled people. Typically, social services departments were more at ease with regarding disabled people as clients rather than as colleagues.

The second problem was that once disability was put on to the equal opportunities agenda, it became difficult actually to effect change in a complex and often hostile town hall environment. It soon became apparent that while it was possible to carry out the democratic function of passing motions and establishing policies, nothing seemed to change. Disabled people still appeared to be outside the political process; few of them were councillors or officers and they were unaware of the complex routes that comprise decision making before implementation is possible.

Disabled people also had to face up to the fact that by aligning themselves with equal opportunities initiatives, they were faced with the consequences of being labelled as part of the 'loony left'. After giving a talk to a group of trade unionists about disabled people's involvement in Manchester's equal opportunities initiative the author was approached by a senior trade unionist who came up to me first to praise what disabled people were doing, but also to warn against being associated with such other pressure groups as the gay and lesbian community; this response was by no means uncommon. However, disabled people generally found no problem in aligning themselves with other oppressed groups even (or especially) if it meant losing 'sympathy'.

In the 1990s, after a series of budgetary reductions, nearly all local authorities have abandoned high-profile equal opportunities initiatives. Equal Opportunities Units and departments were disbanded and while the policies may remain in place, the drive to implement them has largely given way to other political priorities. This leaves us with the questions:

- What has been left for disabled people now the Units have closed?
- Is there a legacy of anything more than the rhetoric entombed in long-forgotten policy documents?
- Was it all a waste of time?

From my own experience the answer is that it was worth while where local authorities accepted the principle that the authentic voice of disabled people were organisations controlled *by* disabled people. In Manchester, for example, disabled people were consulted as never before over everything from access improvements to setting equality targets for council employment. Millions of pounds were spent on access improvements which have turned buildings like Manchester's Gothic town hall 'from access nightmare to access showpiece' (Manchester City Council, 1990). However, just as important have been the lessons that disabled people have learned about the political process. There are now disabled councillors (meaning councillors who are both disabled and see disability as a political issue – not necessarily the same thing); there are more disabled officers, many of whom have been disabled activists; and there is also a realisation that some changes takes a long time. Ironically, some of the main benefits of the equal opportunities initiatives may be felt long after they have fallen down the political agenda.

A good example of this is Manchester's Disabled People's Equality Targets. These were part of a policy adopted by the City Council in 1989 which outlined an eight-year programme to change the composition of the workforce to reflect the city's population as specified by ethnic origin, gender and disability (Manchester City Council, 1989). The steps that needed to be taken to make this a reality show the complexity of turning policies into practices. First, because there were no adequate figures on numbers of disabled people in the city, a survey was carried out on the advice of the disabled people's subcommittee and based on self-definitions of disability (Manchester City Council, 1987). This concluded that 9.2 per cent of Manchester's population of working age were disabled people. The Council then adopted a policy which aimed to have 9.2 per cent disabled employees by 1997, the baseline being the 2.74 per cent that were actually employed in January 1989. However, as the Council had had a policy of employing 5 per cent registered disabled people since 1948, it was clear that a policy by itself was not going to be enough.

The next stage was to implement a monitoring procedure which would enable details of the composition of the workforce to be accessed. This was no easy task in that there were technical problems and some resistance to the collection of the data: by 1991 it was clear that while the equality targets policy was working reasonably well for black people (the percentage employed rising from 2.88 per cent in January 1989 to 5.44 per cent in January 1991), few inroads were being made on the employment of disabled people which had only moved from 2.74 per cent in 1989 to 3 per cent in 1991. By now new recruitment and selection procedures were in place which aimed to remove barriers to the employment of the target groups.

At this point a think-tank meeting was held of representatives of disabled people's organisations to work out a positive action programme. This led to a 'Disabled People's Jobs Open Day' in March 1992, which while successful in terms of the fact that 31 disabled people were directly recruited from it,

Table 8.1 *Recruitment monitoring (disability), January–July 1993*

TRS Departments	Housing and social services	Rest of authority
Total number of posts advertised	49.0	22.0
Percentage of disabled applicants	9.0	2.1
Percentage of disabled people in all shortlisted	10.7	1.1
Percentage of disabled people in all appointed	11.3	0

Source: Manchester City Council (1993).

was only a one-off event. More importantly a long-term strategy was agreed upon – the Disabled People's Targeted Recruitment Scheme (TRS).

The TRS was piloted for six months in the housing department in 1991. All single vacancies were advertised as open to all, but the selection panel shortlisted and interviewed only the disabled applicants (Manchester City Council, 1992). Only if no suitable candidate was found did they then shortlist the able-bodied candidates. The overall results were encouraging – one in five of the applicants was disabled and 20 out of the 54 appointed were disabled (37 per cent). It was therefore agreed that the TRS be extended to the chief executive's department and the education department with the aim that all departments would be operating the scheme by summer 1994. As the figures in Table 8.1 show, the TRS does seem to have had an effect.

The current aim is for the 9.2 per cent target to be achieved by the year 2000. Progress is slow – by January 1993 the percentage of disabled people in the workforce was still only 3.55 per cent.

The method of implementing the TRS scheme in Manchester was very different from that of Lambeth Council, which in 1986 adopted a policy of recruiting only disabled people until they met their statutory 3 per cent requirements. This led to political uproar and bad publicity from the popular press which reported the latest in 'loony left' policies. The result of this was that the policy was abandoned within a few months of its implementation. The flaw in the Lambeth approach was that the policy was imposed from the top and applied across the board; few disabled people played any part in the development of this policy. Lambeth's new 'disabled-people only' rules meant that able-bodied people were not allowed to apply if a suitable disabled applicant could not be found, which led to resentment and hostility to the initiative from some parts of the workforce and the claim that services were suffering because of unfilled staff vacancies ('Disabled policy: services suffer', *social services insight*, august 9–16, 198, p. 4).

By contrast Manchester's policy had been worked out carefully and implemented in stages. At each stage departments were 'won over' to the policy which meant they were committed to adopting it. For example, all the people involved in recruitment attended training sessions given by consultants from the Greater Manchester Coalition of Disabled People. The TRS is being implemented at a time when Manchester City Council is dismantling much of the equal opportunities structure that enabled such policies to be implemented. The Equal Opportunities committee has been abolished, as has the disabled people's subcommittee. The Equality Group (previously the Equal Opportunities Unit) is being considerably weakened. It is ironic that the political will to support equal opportunities initiatives has faded away at the same time as the results of the early struggles were beginning to bear fruit.

Implementing a radical Targeted Recruitment Scheme was based on long-term planning and monitoring and the development of effective recruitment and selection procedures. Despite all this, progress has been very slow and the 9.2 per cent target is still a long way off.

The TRS works, but it seemed to work better in the housing department than the social services. It is hard to draw any firm conclusions as yet, though, as there are so many other factors that could come into play. For example, the housing department benefited directly from having the Jobs Open Day just prior to the launch of TRS and the number of new jobs available dried up as central government budget cuts began to bite. More jobs need to go through this process so that the TRS can be analysed properly and lessons learned. The slow progress made also indicates the general problem of implementing good equal opportunities practice in a context of discrimination in the wider society which leaves disabled people less educated, more likely to be unemployed and therefore less likely to be able to meet job specifications. As Dalgleish (1994: 192) states: 'the percentage of the population of economically active people with disabilities who are unemployed is around twice that of the population as a whole. People with disabilities are also likely to have less skilled jobs.' Manchester provides an example of an attempt to link disabled people's issues into an equal opportunities initiative. Disabled people took full advantage of the political leverage gained by others, specifically women and gay men, who had become part of an equal opportunities movement within the local Labour Party.

In the 1990s political interest in equal opportunities seems to have waned; nevertheless there have been substantial achievements. Manchester may not yet qualify as 'Access City', as it aimed to become in the 1980s, but improvements in access to buildings and in the built environment are there to stay. On the employment front, the TRS may yet deliver its target of 9.2 per cent of the workforce being disabled people, even if it takes a bit longer than first hoped for.

This chapter has focused on initiatives where groups of disabled people (in particular UPIAS members) have been involved in equal opportunity initiatives on their own terms. In the short term they were successful in Manchester and Derbyshire, but much less so in London. In the longer term, however, pressure on local authority finance has meant that even 'successes' were short-lived, with grants withdrawn and units closed.

Elsewhere in the country there was little evidence of disabled people being involved in equal opportunities initiatives. Nevertheless there has been widespread acceptance in local authorities that 'disability jobs' (access officers, disability officers) should go to disabled people and that the views of organisations controlled by disabled people should be taken seriously. For example, in Kirklees (Yorkshire) the local authority has actively encouraged involvement from disabled people in designing its disability services. While there were initially no strong disabled people's organisations to consult the local authority set out to create such a voice: 'In 1991 the Disability Services section of Social Services has . . . held a public election involving over 300 people to create a steering group of fifteen people with disabilities to guide and support the setting up of the Disability Access Points' (Kirklees Metropolitan Borough Council, 1992: 49).

This 'top down' approach has not been without its problems, in that once having helped to set up a disabled people's organisation local authorities have sometimes found it difficult to accept that such an organisation might have views different from the authority's and might want to have its own control over resources. For example, Kirklees Council and Level Best (the disabled people's organisation), together with Manchester-based activists, established a disabled people's Electronic Village Hall (EVH) at Dewsbury Day Centre. This EVH provides access to the latest computer and communications technologies for disabled people; it was opened in April 1993 and was supported by the local authority with the commitment to hand over control to a local group of disabled people. In fact it was not until December 1994 that the disabled people were able to gain control of the EVH for themselves.

Conclusion

What conclusions can be drawn from these examples? First, it is easy to criticise the lack of disabled people's involvement in many equal opportunities initiatives, but where they have become involved real changes have occurred. Second, there is no one right model and disabled people have to grab opportunities when they arise and make use of able-bodied allies and groups with similar goals.

However, there is a danger that the professions who make a living out of disability have now learned the new language of the social model of disability. The rhetoric is all there about 'people with disabilities' and 'empowering' but in reality there is little evidence that attitudes and practices have significantly changed unless they are tied into practical policies. While the rhetoric of community care, for example, is about disabled people negotiating their own care packages, decisions concerning who will be entitled to what resources are still firmly in the control of social services departments.

Disabled people's groups need political allies if they are to succeed in promoting radical policies to improve disabled people's opportunities. The demise of equal opportunities initiatives makes such alliances harder to make. Disabled people remain as vulnerable as ever to downturns in the economy and changes in government policies. Recently, local authorities have started to move increasingly to 'outsourcing' the provision of disabled people's services, often in the independent sector: 'In the future the Local Authority may be less and less of a provider as the independent sector takes over much of the direct provision' (Liam Hughes, Chief Officer Kirklees Social Services, in Kirklees Metropolitan Borough Council, 1993). Such outsourcing of service provision is both a threat and an opportunity to disabled people's groups. It is a threat because it means a move away from grants to voluntary organisations towards a system of competitive tendering for the provision of services which could also include private sector organisations. For example, Manchester City Council has accepted a recommendation 'that members agree to an open tender process whereby bids are invited and received from voluntary organisations, not-for-profit and appropriate professional business/agencies' (Manchester City Council, 1994a).

On the other hand, if disability groups can organise themselves effectively, there is an opportunity for disabled people to be collectively in control of services they receive for the first time. An example of this is the Service Specification agreement between Manchester Disability Forum (MDF) and Manchester Social Services Department. This provides for the MDF to 'provide day care services providing personal care and social/emotional care, including the management of the whole premises . . . [of the Frank Taylor Centre]' (Manchester City Council, 1994b).

Such a shift requires disabled people to be well organised and efficient. Having learned to live with the local authority equal opportunities initiatives in the 1980s disabled people's groups are now having to adapt to a changing political and funding climate. To do this effectively requires a strong disabled people's movement and while there are many encouraging local initiatives there are few signs of the level of theoretical debate that typified the activities of such political groups as UPIAS in the 1970s and 1980s and which have had such a lasting effect.

9

The experience of counselling

Sallie Withers

'I can talk to you and make these decisions because you have no axe to grind.'

'This is useful because you aren't trying to change me. I will do the changing – if I want to.'

'I can cry and be angry here. Out there I can't; I feel I would be letting the side down. I am so tired.'

'Would I choose to be made "normal"? I've thought about that. No, I'd choose to be the same as I am now. When I was younger I might have wanted to be the same as everyone else.'

'I'm so angry because they don't understand. You understand because you've gone through it yourself.'

'Why was I not offered the chance to talk about how I feel before? Right after the accident it would have saved me so much bewilderment.'

'I'm not sure who I am anymore. I'm the same person I was but I get treated differently. It's like I'd died.'

These remarks, all made to a disabled counsellor by disabled clients, represent some of the reasons people with disabilities seek out a safe place and a trusted person with whom they feel able to explore feelings and make important decisions. These clients chose a disabled counsellor; others choose non-disabled counsellors. For most this choice does not exist – professionally trained, experienced disabled counsellors with independent supervision are as yet not numerous.

Why seek counselling?

Disabled clients seek counselling for the same reasons as anyone might: for example there may be physical symptoms, there may be anxiety or sadness. The client's purpose is often to relieve some burden or find a way out of feeling stuck and frustrated. Often what emerges is a struggle over identity. The questions, 'who am I?' and 'do I matter?' are particularly faced by people around the times of adolescence and major change. People born with impairments may never have had their identities affirmed by being recognised as whole people. Those with acquired impairments (through accident, illness and age) may struggle to reconcile their new selves with their former non-disabled identities. The disabled client may have faced discrimination at work or be anguished about whether or not to start a family; others come after an adverse diagnosis. The existential questions mentioned above are seldom the overt reasons for seeking counselling but they are often implicit. What all clients want is to be contained safely while they struggle to effect change for themselves.

Disabled clients' experiences of counselling

Counselling is expensive unless it is obtained through the National Health Service, and this is relevant because disabled people often do not have paid work. Indeed, not having a job may be part or all of the problem. Even those in work may be using much of their available energy doing the job, so for many expense is a real problem. A man with, for example, spina bifida who is unable to drive because of seizures which have no detectable organic cause, finds his chances of getting work lessened and his self-esteem affected. To make any improvements he knows he needs help but cannot afford it. His experience of counselling is non-existent. Even organisations offering counselling to disabled people, such as Sexual and Personal Relationships Problems of the Disabled (SPOD) and the Association for Spina Bifida and Hydrocephalus (ASBAH), charge commercial rates. Some potential clients know they cannot afford not to have counselling.

Case study 1

A man in his 40s and divorced lost his job because of discrimination and was then disabled by anger for which he could not find a channel. His need for work overcame his feeling of helplessness and he found a non-disabled counsellor and negotiated a manageable fee. A year later he understands how to manage anger so that it does not spoil his life; he has found work and made a success of a training course but he still needs his counsellor. There remains the problem of discrimination but this time he has more chance of understanding how some people are used as scapegoats and so is less likely to be one again.

Case study 2

A woman with cerebral palsy who has spent 30 years in residential care is now living in the community. She says she is bored and wonders about what life means for her. She sought a disabled counsellor because she thought he would understand how it feels to live with disadvantage. She has difficulty speaking and sees this counsellor as being more inclined to persevere with communication. Because she is used to being manipulated by carers (who refer to *her* as 'manipulative'!) she is testing her counsellor's boundaries to make sure they are strong enough to contain the sheer weight of bewilderment and panic she often feels under the heading 'bored'. She is beginning to see that her parents were not strong enough to hold on to her, and put her in residential care and she cannot yet believe that her counsellor values her and will not send her away empty. She needs to practise on her counsellor how to manage her carers without being afraid of reprisals. Much of her struggle is about whether she has a right to exist as a separate person. She is now enjoying a real relationship for the first time since the age of nine.

Case study 3

Pat was born minus a hip and with a short leg. Brought up by accepting parents to be 'normal' she failed to see her difference as important until a crisis triggered by the suicide attempt of a family member. At university at the time, she went to the counsellor who scored a hit by recognising that her weak leg did not belong to her. She cautiously became a client and continued to work on retrieving disowned bits of herself for 18 months. She was asked whether she would like to have legs the same length and 'be like everyone else' and said that she preferred her different body although for years she had fought and denied it. Her counsellor was not disabled; for her it was important that he was male and not seducible.

Newly disabled clients

The National Health Service has started to employ psychologists in rehabilitation hospitals, although there is a point of view that suggests that counsellors would do better and disabled counsellors better still. The medical mind seems to need labels like 'clinical' and 'psychologist' to merit trust, but even so at last people with spinal and other major permanent injuries will have a person to listen alongside the physical help they need.

Case study 4

When in rehabilitation a few years ago Denise desperately wanted a listener. She is still angry with staff who tried to force her to 'think positive' when all she wanted to do was to cry. She feels strongly that she has held on to her non-disabled identity and can face the future with more confidence than those born with impairments and many would agree. She also feels she was left alone to cope with feeling dreadful and split off from her body which was being made to do ordinary things. She is still angry and puzzled at lack of care of her as a whole person. There is wide scope for individual and group work with people with similar impairments in a hospital as well as with mixed groups at home. Arrangements to co-counsel could be made from such groups and potential leaders would emerge who could go off and lead more groups. The spin-off of such a scheme might be that newly disabled people could come to trust each other and learn about the existing disabled community without having to go through the demeaning and mistaken phase of feeling that disabled people are dependent on non-disabled experts.

Older people who become disabled often do not wish to consider a new identity, nor are they likely to be offered counselling. There is the problem of finance and a perceived lack of interest among counsellors in older clients, a perception which is unfortunately often accurate. Frequently spouses and other carers are the ones who seek counselling and also battle with identity aspects. Phrases like 'she isn't the person I knew' are often heard from the spouses of people with communication difficulties or conditions such as Alzheimer's disease. A period of adjustment is clearly needed as well as respite from the unsought task of caring. There is a movement towards working with elderly people by helping them speak or write their life stories; such a procedure needs to be thorough and properly set up but if it entails good listening then it may help.

Case study 5

Ellen is a telephone client of my own. She knows I am disabled and uses me to make her feel better. 'At least I'm better off than you are' she says triumphantly but the more times she repeats it, the more hollow it sounds. It is necessary for her that I do not retaliate in the way I would if we met socially. I am whatever she wants me to be in imagination. She can be angry and offensive, lonely and funny and she needs to know that I will listen and understand the unsaid things that can't quite make it into words. If I died I think it would be very difficult for her yet at the same time it would prove that she was 'better off' than me. Often counsellors need simply to survive!

Case study 6

Harry is newly disabled through a road accident. He is in his 50s and can now move one finger only. In hospital a friend suggested counselling because Harry was unable to decide where and with whom he wanted to live when discharged. The counsellor happened to be disabled. Harry did not wish to make a contract at first, asking 'How can you be any good? You're disabled too.' Soon, however, he started to use the counsellor while still denigrating her value. He found her useful because she did not have any agenda other than his. In three months of weekly interviews he got himself unstuck and moving towards a chosen destiny but not before going through an extremely rough patch when he was unsure whether to go on living. Because counselling is paid for by the client and the contract is negotiated by both client and counsellor, the client's purpose provides the objective of the work. The quality of that work reflects the quality of the client/counsellor relationship and involves the commitment of both including the work the client is prepared to put in and the reliable, consistent containment provided by the counsellor.

Case study 7

A woman in her 50s with paralysis and life threatening strokes sought a counsellor who had the same impairments. Locally this was not available but when a wheelchair-using counsellor was found and work started, it seemed that the client felt she could only be understood by someone with identical experience. She had a secret which she felt could be imparted only to someone who she felt might identify with her.

Training in counselling

Whether disabled clients are better off with disabled counsellors will be decided by individuals, but there is already a need for disabled counsellors to be trained and for that they first and foremost need to have been clients – this is the most important pre-condition for any counsellor on to which they build practice skills and learn theory. There is a good deal of counselling training but very few disabled students are going through it and where they do many experience difficulties with trainers who often seem to be overcome with pity, anger, embarrassment and other disabling conditions. Some get enmeshed with the student and neglect their boundaries. Some neglect the student and fail to adapt the courses beyond simple, modifications such as the use of accessible buildings and the supply of (some) books on tape. Disabled students of counselling have to overcome barriers which others do not even see. What is the student to do when the trainer tries to write the student's notes? What is to be done about the trainer who says, 'You won't be able to do this exercise'? Of course there is disability equality training for trainers and providers but often it only seems to stir the conscious mind as far as ramps and tapes. Frequent 'forgetting' of the disabled student's needs serves to prove that unwelcome difficult information is indeed repressed into the unconscious!

Some adverse experiences

Some disabled clients report that they spend too much of their expensive time educating their counsellor in the art of living in a hostile environment. Some report that hard-won access to buildings is lost when the counsellor moves offices and 'forgets' that the client will not be able to gain access or that counsellors write a letter about private matters to a visually impaired client – a letter which will have to read aloud by a third party. Such examples are caused by counsellor ignorance and need to be addressed outside the time for which the client is paying.

Confidentiality is an important issue and one that is stressed by the ethical code of the British Association of Counselling. The presence of third parties to interpret or enable has not been adequately addressed: perhaps many counsellors think this is acceptable as long as the client thinks it is. We have to ask ourselves if this is good enough: an alternative approach would be for the counsellor to learn the client's mode of communication but that would take a long time. We must also ask:

- Do clients who bring enablers really trust or value the process?
- Do they even understand it?
- Are the enablers covert clients?

Displacement can be a real problem: just as a spouse may push a marriage 'problem' on to the partner and dispatch him or her to counselling to save the marriage, so enablers and managers refer disabled people to counsellors because they have projected their own problems and in the process have labelled the (now) recipient of counselling 'disturbed'. Because the disabled person has different communication, the enabler comes along too. The 'client' of course agrees to the enabler's presence – he or she has no clue as to what's going on. Badly trained and poorly selected care staff often fall into the category of 'compulsive carers': people who have not been well cared for as children and who become possessively involved with people who need assistance and live vicariously through them. This is extremely dangerous for disabled people because they may become attached and confused about where they stop and the other person starts. For instance, many disabled people have a problem with body boundaries which may be broken for necessary medical reasons. They need help in owning their bodies and establishing lives separate from the lives of helpers. It is not uncommon for counsellors to see disabled people who are bewildered by the behaviour of carers who veer wildly between doing far too much or far too little. Compulsive carers will need much help themselves and should not be employed in this work unless they have it.

Co-counselling and peer counselling

Co-counselling is a low-cost option in which two people take it in turns to be counsellor and client. A short period of training is necessary in the person-centred approach (a 40-hour weekend training is available, for example). The advantage is that both people get to be a client frequently and for some it opens the door to longer training and further work on personal growth. The snag is that people can get 'hung up' on catharsis – feeling they can only be getting better by feeling worse and then handing that on to others. People attracted to this technique should ensure that they take part in enough training to start, learn to make a good contract with their partner in counselling by establishing ground rules, and pick up enough theoretical background to enable them to know that they need to know more! At its best it works well and costs little except time, commitment and energy. Doing it without any training is not advisable as there is a danger that the apparent democracy can tilt dangerously to one or other partner; there can be little to distinguish it, when done badly, from a chat with a friend. Specific training for disabled people would not come amiss in this field.

Peer counselling

I would prefer to call this peer advice or consultation. There is a lot of confusion about what counselling is: one thing it is *not* is advice and information giving. In counselling the emphasis is on the client becoming his or her own adviser. Requests for advice are standard fare to counsellors who do not supply answers but turn round the request for guidance with, 'What do YOU think you should do?' Peer consultation within the disabled community is common and enormously valuable because there is no other place available to disabled people for good, reliable information about what is available or what is going on in their community. Non-disabled people are automatically disqualified. Those providing the knowledge and guidance are known to be available in the informal networks, often by phone. People looking for information, befriending, support and advice seek it from others they know have faced dilemmas they now face. These seekers are not plagued by ambivalence or confused about who they might be and whether they are valuable; they want hard news and views. I believe appropriate training exists for peer councellors in some areas.

Case study 8

A disabled traveller, new to wheelchair use, was asked to run a course in Florence at short notice. He booked a flight with a travel agent and made sure the wheelchair was entered in to the computer. While packing he began to wonder if the travel agent would *really* cater for him at Gatwick and if so, just how would he be transferred to the plane? And where does his chair go? So he spoke to a friend whom he knew travelled by air with chairs and armed with that information returned to the travel agent for more detailed planning.

Case study 9

A pregnant disabled woman was offered an abortion when what she wanted was a child. She knew what she wanted and also knew that she may have a fight on her hands; however, she knew of others who had become parents. She contacted them both for affirmation and for confirmation that the course she had chosen, while it may be difficult, was possible. She was reassured that others had done it – and experienced continuing support until she felt able to cope alone. After she had her child she became a peer consultant herself.

Case study 10

A young recently disabled woman, having done some work on her new identity incorporating her disability, completed an application for Living Allowance. She remembered a friend's sound guidance that these procedures need to be carried out together with a not-too-close acquaintance who can monitor one's assessment of performance in domestic life. Pen in hand she telephoned a branch of Disability Information and Advice Line (DIAL) where she knew there were disabled employees or volunteers who had been through this process. After a lengthy interview she felt that so many negative aspects had undermined her stable ego-functioning. Even if she does not require professional attention, she can contact someone in her network to ventilate anger: it is better that she finds a way of getting affirmation of her identity as a whole person rather than kicking the dog, crashing the car or fighting her partner.

Peer support is cheaper than counselling, although telephone bills mount up, and it is effective. Perhaps the litmus test for when peer *support* is not enough is when the disabled person nearly decides on a course of action, contacts peers to confirm details and get more good information . . . and discovers that he or she is neither listening to nor using what is coming to him or her. Instead, a feeling of inadequacy, panic or loneliness may be the result. It is hard to listen to another person coping so well when you know you are not ready for whatever the action may be. Then a counsellor may be of more use as 'emotional blotting paper' or a 'mirror to see yourself in'.

Loss theory and disability

Many counsellors believe that any loss, whether through death of a person, loss of a faculty or loss of a body function, needs to be mourned; that grieving is a process with stages involving:

- denial
- anger
- adjustment
- reinvestment.

Newly disabled people in particular are assumed to be 'in denial' if they do not in some manner progress through the model. As Oliver (1990) points out, if we deny that this is how it feels to us, we cannot win. There seems to be a debate between disabled people and non-disabled people and between bereavement counsellors and those subscribing to behaviour and social construct theory.

Hypothesis

This hypothesis is based on personal and professional experience. Those born with impairments often have invasive and frequent medical interventions which attempt to keep them as 'normal' as possible, but they often do not work fully. As babies we have acted out on us the hopes of parents and doctors and we come not only to know about disappointment, but we come to expect it. Naturally, we defend ourselves against too much of it. As soon as a small loss occurs, we go into action but we do not usually remember the earliest episodes. We do not, I believe, deny the loss: we do not see ourselves from that angle. We know something happened and we know that we need to activate our own mending. When 'Pat' (in case study 3 above) badly injured her knee aged 11, she lay in bed fending off pain easily enough and facing with equanimity the prospect of no more gym and tennis and riding bikes and running. She knew she could handle that because she had already handled worse before. What made her distraught that night was the prospect of an anaesthetic next day. A counsellor might have spotted that 'Pat' needed urgent help over a chronic anxiety about forced loss of consciousness which felt like death. What worried parents and medical people was the impossibility of restoring her functioning. She knew something would happen which would make life fulfilling again in a different way – she took up the clarinet and poured herself into the struggle to play well. She survived intact.

The same mechanism works in people (disabled or not) who greatly fear a mental breakdown and take this fear to counsellors. Good counsellors can spot those whose fear is about an apparently future event which has already happened in the past and sense the strength the client already possesses but has 'forgotten' because the earlier breakdown was too painful to remember.

By the time disabled children grow up, they are so expert at the art of self-mending that they confuse the professionals who have only the perspective of 'normality'. Loss theory is fine for those experiencing loss consciously. Clients who say they do not feel it need to be believed. I think non-disabled loss counsellors project the feelings they imagine they would have in the disabled client's position.

This is necessarily a simplistic hypothesis. There is little, if any, research by disabled professionals on disabled infants and without it support for this hypothesis cannot be found. But, through having been a client in analysis, I know who I am and I know I matter. Discovering this same knowing in disabled clients is my joy. Prospective counsellors must, however, be alive to the pain involved in being with clients in their pain.

10
Being a counsellor

Ray Woolfe

In recent times counselling has become a much overused word. People describe themselves as 'debt counsellors' and 'double glazing counsellors' and are able to do so because there is no copyright on the term. Anyone can use the description 'counsellor' because there are no legal restrictions. The common understanding of counselling, as reflected in dictionary definitions, is that it is a form of advice-giving and from this perception it is hardly surprising to find it being used in contexts like business and finance.

At its most basic counselling is a form of helping and perhaps it can be best described as a 'helping activity'. One of the common characteristics of such activity is that it often happens spontaneously; most people have had the experience of a friend, relative, neighbour or colleague suddenly coming out with a personal problem, stressful event or area of life concern. This may be accompanied by unexpected displays of emotions such as crying or anger. A standard response is of the 'let's sit down, have a nice cup of tea and talk about it' variety. The person seeking help talks and perhaps there are further displays of strong feelings.

The listener may feel helpless in this kind of situation but somehow the act of being listened to, with no other participation, seems to help. It is as though listening is itself of therapeutic value. Whether the listener realises it or not the person has been helped and without necessarily being consciously aware of the fact the listener has in the process employed some of the basic skills of counselling. These include active attending, listening to the feelings of the other person; focusing on the other person's feelings rather than one's own immediate concerns and generally being accepting and uncritical even if one disagrees with what is being said.

Counselling and counselling skills

A major characteristic of this type of helping event is that it often happens spontaneously. The person asking for help is not a client or a patient and the person offering help is not necessarily labelled a counsellor. Identifying this fact allows for an important distinction to be made. This is between

- the practice of counselling skills, and
- the practice of counselling within a more formal framework.

In the second case a specific contract exists between two parties.

Counselling skills are used by nurses, doctors, psychologists, social workers, youth workers, teachers, managers and many other helping professionals in the course of their work. Yet these people are not counsellors and would not identify themselves as such. They may use counselling skills, but their primary professional identity is not that of counsellor. Similarly, counselling skills are also used by a vast variety of volunteer workers operating in self-help or advocacy settings. Once again, these people are not counsellors, yet are employing counselling skills in the process of giving advice, coaching, teaching, guidance or whatever helping activity in which they are engaged. Counselling skills are communication and interpersonal skills and these are frequently employed in helping. Yet counselling is something more than the practice of these skills. The crucial difference relates to the contract in which the relationship between the two people is framed.

The distinction between counselling and counselling skills is articulated by the British Association for Counselling (BAC), the umbrella body for counselling individuals and organisations in Great Britain. In the following definition, the distinction between a planned and a spontaneous event is spelled out:

> People become engaged in counselling when a person occupying regularly or temporarily the role of counsellor, offers or agrees explicitly to offer time, attention and respect to another person or persons temporarily in the role of client. (British Association for Counselling, 1985: 1)

Key ideas within this definition are first the notion of 'offers or agrees' and second the word 'explicitly'. It is the presence of these which defines the boundary between the ad hoc use of counselling skills and the specific practice of counselling. The boundary between the two activities is the major safeguard for the rights of the consumer and is vitally important. Many helping relationships offer great potential for role confusion and conflict. For example, a social work manager may have the task of counselling a worker for whom s/he has line management responsibility or a tutor may have counselling responsibilities for a student whom s/he also teaches. It is this sort of potential confusion which the use of the terms 'offers', 'agrees' and 'explicitly' attempts to clarify or as the BAC definition further explains:

> clarification of the opportunity offered, in a way that the client can understand, differentiates the counselling task from other mutual responsibilities in the perception of both client and counsellor. (British Association for Counselling, 1985: 2)

Being and doing

Counselling is sometimes conceived of as something which one person does to someone else. In this sense it becomes rather like the performance of a set of technical skills. However, there is an alternative way of looking at counselling and this is to see it as a way of being with another person.

In the first sense it is rather like the performance of a set of technical skills. However, in the second sense it is the quality of the relationship between counsellor and client that is the crucial therapeutic factor. The difference between these two approaches can be described as between a *skills-centred approach* on the one hand and a *person-centred approach* on the other. Understanding this difference is the key to understanding what is involved in the modern practice of counselling. However, it is necessary to lead into the discussion by first saying a few brief words about the oldest counselling tradition of all: psychoanalysis and its contemporary cousin, psychodynamic counselling.

The psychodynamic paradigm

Modern counselling has roots which go back into the nineteenth century and the pioneering work of Freud. This psychoanalytical tradition is still important in counselling practice and many of its ideas have become assimilated into contemporary practice. In particular, the idea that past, unresolved developmental issues are being unconsciously played out in the present is widely acknowledged. So too is one of the corollaries of this: that feelings from past relationships are transferred by the client on to the therapist in the present. There is not the space in this chapter to enter into a more detailed account of contemporary psychodynamic theory and practice. Interested readers might look at the work of Michael Jacobs (for example, Jacobs, 1988) who offers an accessible introduction to these ideas.

Despite its continuing influence, the psychoanalytical approach came under heavy criticism, particularly in postwar America, not least for the pessimistic view of human nature which it incorporated. Its perception of human beings as dominated by powerful, somewhat unconscious urges was at odds with the American image of people as free individuals, basically good and optimistic and in charge of their own destinies. In addition, the belief (whether true or not) of analysis or therapy taking many years and costing huge sums of money was at odds with more egalitarian beliefs about accessibility. Moreover, the medical model of illness and disease with therapists 'curing' patients seemed at odds with the ethos of a more open society in which self-help was seen as a virtue.

The person-centred paradigm: the authentic self

Out of these criticisms emerged what has come to be known as 'humanistic psychology'; its key belief is the inherent potential of human beings given the right conditions. One of the key figures associated with this movement is Abraham Maslow, whose reference to 'self actualisation' (Maslow, 1962) as the goal of personal development has become a common term. However, the significant person in terms of the development of counselling was Carl Rogers, who is widely regarded as the founding father of counselling in its present form.

Through his work as a psychologist, therapist and researcher, Rogers developed what has come to be known as 'person-centred' counselling, though there are also references in the literature to 'client-centred' (Rogers 1951) and 'non-directive' practice. The basic truth as Rogers saw it was that clients know best what is right for themselves; it followed from this that the counsellor's task was not to advise or guide clients, or tell them what to do. Rather, the role of the counsellor was to assist clients to get in touch with their own inner resource. In this process the quality of the relationship between counsellor and client was of crucial importance.

Rogers saw human beings as essentially good, born with a potentially positive self-concept, an authentic self. However, the experience of being rejected and disapproved of by significant others (of whom the most important are parents) may lead to the individual developing a poor sense of self-worth. Self-esteem may become dependent upon the receipt of approval from others. Gradually they may become divorced from what the person-centred literature refers to as the 'real' or 'authentic' or 'organismic self'.

Left to itself, the organismic self knows what is best and what it needs. However, if the need for approval from others is too great, it comes into conflict with the organismic self and the individual gradually becomes more and more estranged from this organismic self. The result may be a loss of self-confidence and trust in self, feelings of anxiety and insecurity and a general feeling of lack of worth. This may be accompanied by a fear of new experiences and an adherence to rigid patterns of behaviour. Speech may be peppered with the use of conditional terms like 'should', 'ought' and 'must'. By contrast psychologically healthy people are in touch with their organismic self, do not feel threatened by experiences, act spontaneously and have the capacity to become what Rogers called a 'fully functioning person' (Rogers, 1961).

As an example, it is not too difficult to imagine how this process might work particularly heavily in the case of a physically disabled child who has to face the enormous pressures of a disabling world which is less than fully accepting and which presents constant messages of not being wanted; of being embarrassing; of needing always to try harder than others or conversely of little being expected from him or her. Oliver (1978) argues that the meaning that disability has for individuals is created and negotiated through interaction with significant others. He warns against the danger of always directing the disabled person's attention inwards as if the disability was itself the source of, for instance, mobility or access problems caused by lack of suitable transport and poorly designed buildings.

The person-centred paradigm: the core conditions

The person-centred counsellor believes in the inherent goodness and worth of human beings and believes that each individual has the ability to realise this potential. What is required is for the right conditions to be set up in which individuals can tune into their own inner resources and get back in touch with the authentic self. Central to the work of the counsellor is that there must be no repetition of the process whereby the person comes to rely on a significant other for advice about how to be or what to do. This would simply perpetuate the old pattern of dependency on others. Counsellors, therefore, regard themselves as facilitators and not as experts. Their role is to provide the conditions in which the clients can get in touch with their own potential. One might say that their objective is to empower the other person.

Mearns and Thorne (1988) refer to the conditions for growth, in a clear introduction to the paradigm, as 'the growth producing climate'. As Rogers saw them, these conditions are threefold. They are

- empathy;
- unconditional positive regard;
- genuineness.

These three are now consistently referred to as the 'core conditions'. It is helpful to think of them as personal dispositions which the counsellor must demonstrate. Virtually all schools of counselling accept that these conditions are important, if not fundamental, to the formation of a good working alliance between counsellor and client (see Lambert et al., 1986).

Empathy

Empathy is the ability to see the world from the point of view of another person, through their frame of reference, through their conceptual and emotional spectacles, so to speak. It is not to *be* that person, for that is impossible, but to be 'as if' one was that person and to imagine how it feels to be them. The 'as if' quality should be emphasised. Without this quality, empathy becomes sympathy. Sympathy involves collusion with the other person, taking sides and becoming judgemental. In contrast, empathy involves being detached and dispassionate and remaining non-judgemental and non-evaluative.

Empathy is expressed or communicated by a number of skills; a key skill is reflecting back the emotional content of the message from clients in one's own words. This enables the clients to feel that their message has been understood. In this and similar ways, a working relationship based on trust is gradually built up between counsellor and client.

Unconditional positive regard

This is sometimes referred to as 'warmth' or 'acceptance' and involves a non-judgemental acceptance of clients for what they are, 'warts and all'. People often seek help because they feel bad or unworthy and the very act of asking for help may be seen as an admittance of weakness or failure. If the counsellor is able to convey a sense of warmth and acceptance (to prize the other person) it becomes easier for them to re-evaluate their own worth and to love and prize themselves. This offers the prospect for change. Perhaps the key skill here is to differentiate between the *person* and the *behaviour*. Only by feeling accepted will clients feel safe enough to explore the emotional issues which brought them to a counsellor in the first place. The issue of acceptance illustrates that a prerequisite to effective counselling lies in counsellors working continuously to understand their own feelings. If counsellors have not worked through difficult emotional issues and do not feel a sense of self-esteem, it is difficult to see how an unconditional acceptance of others is possible.

Genuineness

Sometimes known as congruence or authenticity, this condition refers to counsellors being honest with themselves about their own feelings and being open in communicating these feelings to clients. The counsellor who is able to be genuine or congruent provides a model for the client and thus facilitates both the development of the relationship and the latter's willingness to take risks in exposing painful or hidden parts of self.

This does not mean knee-jerk responses to one's own feelings or that counsellors must always overtly express all feelings which are present in a situation. For example, counsellors sometimes feel irritated or even angry with clients. The latter sometimes expect counsellors to offer instant solutions without making much effort themselves. It doesn't help for the counsellor to shout or thump the arms of the chair, though this may be the impulse. Genuineness involves noting the feeling and then finding ways to express it in a measured and clear fashion which the client can understand and will not find threatening. An example of incongruence is the person who says, through clenched teeth and white knuckles, 'I am not angry.'

Genuineness means that people are communicating openly without 'front' or 'façade' and that people are presenting themselves as they really are. Once again, this condition demands a life-long commitment on the part of counsellors to find ways of monitoring their own feelings.

Necessary and sufficient conditions

In the person-centred approach, the key variable in helping the client is the quality of relationship between counsellor and client. While this is an attractive and still influential position, it has a rather dated feel about it. Notions like self-actualisation do not fit comfortably in the harsher and more mechanistic world of the 1990s, characterised as they are by high unemployment, significant levels of homelessness and an emphasis on auditing, efficiency and throughput.

It is now widely argued, therefore, that these core conditions (which are essentially personal dispositions) are necessary but not sufficient conditions for effective counselling and that they are most likely to be effective when embedded in the practice of specific skills.

The skills-centred paradigm

The notion of a skills-based or task-based approach is now common in social work and it has also achieved prominence in counselling. The most influential figure in the field is Gerard Egan, whose book *The Skilled Helper* first appeared in 1975 and in 1993 appeared in its fifth edition (Egan, 1993) having influenced a generation of trainers and students.

Egan adopts a problem-solving approach which is typical of skills-based models and incorporates the idea of stages as a key theme. In fact, he envisages three stages, which he describes as:

1 The present scenario.
2 The preferred scenario.
3 Getting there.

Stage 1: The present scenario

This is an exploratory stage and involves helping the client to tell the story and to identify and challenge blind spots. It also involves the search for what Egan calls 'leverage', which involves helping clients to 'identify and work on problems, issues, concerns, or opportunities that will make a difference' to their lives.

Stage 2: Developing a preferred scenario

This is a focusing stage and involves helping clients to examine what a better future might look like. Having done this, the client needs help in translating preferred scenarios into a concrete agenda. In other words, objectives or goals have to be set which when translated into action will turn the preferred future into reality. For example, a person who says that he or she wants to have better communication with a partner may be asked what this would actually mean in practice. Finally, this stage involves the identification of incentives which will help clients to commit themselves. By the end of this stage, clients should know what they want to accomplish even if they do not yet know how to achieve the desired goal.

Stage 3: Strategy – getting there

Having identified goals, the issue now is how to achieve them. Egan sees this process as involving brainstorming a range of possible strategies and selecting a strategy that best fits a client's personal needs and emotional and social resources. Finally it involves turning the chosen strategy into a step-by-step procedure for achieving the selected objective(s).

Integration

The difference in emphasis between Egan and Rogers is at first sight quite marked. For Egan, a key word is 'action'; the whole point of the exercise is to get there and to do this involves directly encouraging acting as well as talking. In other words, the emphasis is on doing rather than being. However, to be fair to Egan, it should also be said that he consistently refers to the importance of a good working relationship between counsellor and client and many of the key first-stage skills, which help to build this alliance, such as those concerned with exploration, bear a marked resemblance to the Rogerian skills of active listening, reflecting, asking open-ended questions, encouraging concreteness, and so on. Nevertheless, in the final resort counselling appears to be a problem-solving, skills-based activity; something one *does*. In contrast, for Rogers counselling clearly involves *being* rather than *doing*.

Perhaps both are necessary. Without the personal characteristics emphasised by Rogers, it would be difficult to build up a trusting and safe working relationship in which skills can be deployed. Conversely, without the skills there may be a danger that a relationship will lose purpose and direction. Putting this another way, it may be tempting for the counsellor who focuses on the relationship never to get beyond the exploration stage. But equally dangerously, it may be all too easy for counsellors who emphasise problem solving to rush to the action stage, thereby perhaps meeting their own need to demonstrate to themselves that progress is being made, without rooting this in the necessary preliminary process of developing a relationship and thoroughly exploring where the client is at.

At the time of writing, a buzz-word in counselling is *integration* and a useful book which brings together the elements of both person-centred and skills-focused paradigms in a straightforward model is that written by Culley (1991). She employs a three-stage model consisting of beginnings, middles and endings and looks in detail at aims, strategies and skills within each stage.

Conclusion

It would be good if the competencies of counselling could be reduced to a simple recipe but unfortunately it is not an activity which lends itself to such niceties. There are a variety of approaches to counselling and this chapter has in no way exhausted the list. However, in the final resort all of them would agree that a key component in being a counsellor, without which change is unlikely, is that most elusive of all human activities, namely the quality of the relationship between two people.

SECTION 4: MAKING IT WORK

This is a diverse section, introducing the reader to a range of aspects surrounding the difficulties of turning ideas – however good – into practicalities. Sally French begins this with a detailed consideration of the use of simulation exercises. These are a not uncommon feature of training aimed at developing 'disability awareness', but French takes a careful look at what they actually achieve in the light of the fact that many disabled people and their organisations are convinced, not only that the practice does not work, but that it is positively harmful. She explains that there is little evidence that such exercises bring about positive attitude change, and indeed states that it would appear that rather than helping to produce more positive attitudes towards disabled people and to gain a clearer understanding of the meaning of disability, simulation activities do just the reverse.

Ken Davis then supplies a consideration of the use of legislation in the context of rights. This finely-structured analysis leads us to understand that 'it is ironic that the Queen has been placed in the position of being able to give the Royal Assent to laws which protect disabled people from discrimination in the farthest corners of the Commonwealth while being unable to offer the same protection to us here on her own doorstep.' He feels that 'quite clearly, those in power feel they can brush our interests aside with impunity'.

This is followed by the examination of the purposes and pitfalls of legislation in a specific context. Deborah Cooper examines the legislative framework as it applies to education. This makes it clear that legislation can *require* certain things to be done, *enable* the provision of services or *prevent* certain things being done. This chapter has a very useful listing of legislation as it applies to educational provision.

Brenda Smith writes about the choices that have to be made in the field of work. This is not just limited to the more obvious questions of what type of work and how to obtain training, but addresses more complex issues such as 'should I work at all?' She makes it clear that in spite of the social pressures on us to work, the decision about whether or not to seek paid work may not be as easy as many would have us believe.

This section is brought to an end by another chapter by Sally French: this time a discussion and review of the literature relating to the attitudes of health professionals towards disabled people. She considers the three components – cognitive, affective and behavioural – and concludes that although research evidence shows some conflict, there is room for improvement in the attitudes of health professionals towards disabled people.

11

Simulation exercises in disability awareness training: a critique

Sally French

Simulating physical and sensory disabilities where, for example, people are blindfolded or obliged to use wheelchairs, is an activity which is frequently used in disability awareness training. It is believed that the personal experience of 'disability' is vitally important in giving both children and adults an insight into the problems, difficulties and frustrations disabled people face, and that such activities have the potential to bring about positive attitudinal changes towards disabled people. Chaffin and Peipher (1979) simulated a moderate hearing loss of 60 decibels in a training programme for care workers working with hearing impaired children. The care workers accomplished a variety of tasks, such as shopping, working and going to restaurants, while experiencing the simulated hearing loss. When discussing their experiences they spoke of feelings of isolation and self-consciousness and how they had gained only a superficial understanding of what was going on. They found the restaurant experience the most difficult to handle as they felt inferior and viewed themselves as attracting unwanted attention. Communication was extremely tiring and night-time activities were described as producing 'genuine fear . . . approaching terror' due to the limitation of both auditory and visual cues. The care workers believed that their attitudes had become more positive towards hearing impaired people as a result of these experiences and that they had gained a greater awareness of the psychological difficulties hearing impaired people face.

Morris (1976) used simulation of visual impairment as a training device for those working with visually impaired people. They were required to wear sight-reducing goggles to carry out activities in various settings including a classroom and a kitchen, in order to develop their awareness of the limitations, problems and frustrations faced by visually impaired people. The participants found pouring transparent liquid the most difficult task, and in the kitchen, where they were required to make a jam sandwich, most chose to spread grape jam rather than apple jam on the white bread because it provided a greater visual contrast. When asked to take a seat on the far side of the table most were slow to move and many had an initial reaction of 'I can't do it'. Marte (1988) reports a disability awareness exercise among nurses where they wore ear-plugs, sight-reducing glasses, and slings or splints to gain insight into the situation of elderly people, and in the article 'Children experience dilemma of disabled' (*Therapy Weekly*, 1991) children are described as either having their arms tied behind their backs, sitting in wheelchairs, using crutches or standing on one leg to simulate various impairments. The people who devised the training were of the opinion that the children were experiencing for a few hours 'the endless dilemma of their disabled contemporaries'. A video was made of the children undergoing these simulation exercises to be used in schools to promote discussion and was regarded, by those who made it, as 'graphically illustrating the continuous daily problems faced by disabled children' (*Therapy Weekly*, 1991: 3).

Wood (1990) had eight- and nine-year-old primary school children simulate various physical impairments by using wheelchairs, putting their limbs in splints and slings and painting pictures using their mouths. Following these activities many of the children said they would feel unhappy if they were disabled and that they would not want to be treated differently or to be left out. They believed they would feel sad and lonely if they were disabled, and upset if they could not join in games with other children. One child commented: 'I would feel stiff and lonely and would be sad looking at the people having a good time on their bikes and I am stuck in a wheelchair.' Others spoke of the practical difficulties they experienced, for example getting the wheelchair near enough to the desk, opening drawers and managing in the toilet.

The Understanding Disabilities Educational Trust has produced training packs to be used in primary schools to help children understand visual, hearing and physical impairments and learning difficulties. The organisation also provides training for teachers who want to use the packs in their classrooms. The aim of the training is to educate non-disabled children about disability and to change their attitudes towards disabled people in a positive direction.

In this scheme the children are first taught how the relevant part of the body works, and are then 'temporarily disabled' to 'help them "feel" what certain disabilities may be like'. Other aspects of the training include video, the chance to talk with disabled guests, and the opportunity to try out various pieces of equipment which help disabled people to function independently (Understanding Disabilities Educational Trust, promotional literature).

Reynolds (1991) reports on a simulation exercise organised by Buckinghamshire County Council undertaken by 15 architects, designers and building officers where they were obliged to get around in wheelchairs. They were positive about the training, saying they had discovered the problems of unramped kerbs, steps, unadapted toilets and restrictive fire regulations.

What is wrong with simulation exercises?

At first glance simulating disabilities may appear to be a good idea, yet many disabled people and their organisations are convinced, not only that the practice does not work, but that it is positively harmful. On closer inspection it is not difficult to understand why.

There appears to be very little evidence that simulation exercises have a positive effect on the attitudes of those who undertake them. Wilson and Alcorn (1969) report some success, but only if the participants have a realistic impression of disability and the chance to experience the reactions of strangers. Clore and Jeffrey (1972) found that under these conditions attitude change was maintained four months later. Semple et al. (1980), on the other hand, found no attitudinal change in a cohort of physical therapy students after they had simulated various physical impairments, and Pockney (1989), of the Understanding Disabilities Educational Trust, states that she knows of no research into the value of exercises which simulate disability, although such exercises are increasingly being used. She goes on to explain that young children will not tolerate being lectured to for very long and that part of the reason for using simulation activities in their disability awareness training is to actively involve them, 'to give the girls and boys something to do' – an argument which, to say the least, is weak and inadequate. She also emphasises that the exercises are 'in no sense a simulation of disability – merely of some of the *effects* of being temporarily disabled' (Pockney, 1991, emphasis added). Such insights are welcomed, but one is left wondering why this is not made more explicit in the promotional literature or why, indeed, the exercises are used at all if they do not simulate the real experience of disability. The Royal National Institute for the Blind uses simulation exercises in *Finding Out About Blindness* (RNIB, 1991) a pack for schools, although RNIB does admit that this only gives an idea of what visual impairment might be like.

It would appear that rather than helping to produce more positive attitudes towards disabled people and to gain a clearer understanding of the meaning of disability, simulation activities do just the reverse. As noted earlier, the children in Wood's study (1990) came to the conclusion that being disabled would be a very negative experience – something almost guaranteed to cause misery and loneliness – yet these are the very ideas which disabled people and their organisations have worked so strenuously to dispel. The training was perceived by those who devised it as a great success, even though there is no evidence to suggest that disabled people are any more inclined to be sad, miserable and lonely than anyone else and who may, indeed, find the experience of disability enriching.

It is ironic that at the same time as these programmes are being introduced into schools, many disabled children are still being educated in segregated establishments. Their integration with non-disabled children would not guarantee positive attitudinal changes, but personal contact, especially when the partners are of equal status, is one important ingredient in bringing about such change (McConkey and McCormack, 1983). Disabled professionals, including teachers, would also provide children and adults with positive role models, yet many accounts and studies show the enormous discrimination they face (Kettle, 1986; Morris, 1987; French, 1988; Ladd, 1988).

Richardson (1990) describes a simulation exercise for student nurses where they spent a day in a wheelchair. Although he admits that the exercise could do no more than 'make a single scratch on the surface of the experience of real people who have a permanent handicap' (1990: 68), the participants were confident that they had been given a true insight into the experience of disability. They spoke about lack of self-esteem and feeling sexually unattractive while sitting in a wheelchair as well as being embarrassed about asking for help with their personal needs. Although some disabled people may feel this way, to imagine that such feelings characterise disabled people is a gross overgeneralisation which reflects the negative perceptions of disability which non-disabled people have, rather than the real experience of being disabled.

Simulation exercises give a totally false impression of what it is like to be disabled. I have a visual impairment and have many visually impaired acquaintances and friends yet, with regard to Morris's (1976) study, I know of no visually impaired person who finds the task of pouring water overwhelmingly difficult, or would think twice about moving to the other side of a table. Likewise, I doubt very much if hearing impaired people would experience fear, let alone terror, when performing activities at night due to the lack of visual cues. Yet Chaffin and Peipher (1979), when discussing the experiences of the care workers who underwent simulated deafness, state that 'It is unlikely that the youngsters with whom the child care worker is normally assigned would feel any differently.'

Simulation exercises have the aim of informing non-disabled people of the situation of disabled people, but they clearly provide false information. At best these exercises only simulate the onset of disability, but even that is not achieved because the people concerned know very well that at the end of the day, or at any time they choose, they can stop being 'disabled' and return to their non-disabled status. It is quite obvious that if a person is suddenly deprived of his or her hearing, sight, or ability to walk or use his or her hands, difficulties will be experienced and fear and frustration may be felt, but this is not the situation disabled people are in because they have had time to develop coping strategies or unusual dexterity or strength in other areas of their bodies, and are therefore likely to be far more calm and able than the non-disabled person's experience would suggest, which is not to minimise the difficulties they do experience.

The focus on difficulties, problems and the disabled person's supposed inabilities and inadequacies is both inaccurate and depressing and gives rise to some very damaging stereotypes and misconceptions. I am reminded of a story, which may well be apocryphal, of the headmistress of a school for blind children, who blindfolded herself, attempted to eat a boiled egg elegantly, failed miserably, and as a consequence banned boiled eggs from the breakfast menu!

The belief that disabled people are in the same situation as non-disabled people engaged in simulation exercises, also has the effect of making disabled people appear superhuman and heroic and non-disabled people, in contrast, helpless and ridiculous. A friend of mine who works with visually impaired people, has spoken of the obvious delight experienced by the disability awareness trainer when the 'silly sighted people' could not even manage to walk across the room with their blindfolds on. These images of heroism, courage and fortitude, on the part of disabled people, which are encouraged by simulation exercises, are ones which disabled people and their organisations have vigorously discarded as false, misleading and damaging. On the other hand, the many social and psychological difficulties disabled people may experience, and which tend to build up over a lifetime, cannot be addressed by simulation exercises and can never be comprehended through them. These difficulties include the effects of poverty, a hostile physical environment, unemployment, the inability to gain access to a good education and the obstructive reactions of others. They are largely the result of social, environmental and attitudinal barriers rather than the product of impairments themselves. Finkelstein (1991b), referring to the article by Wood (1990), believes that simulation exercises are insulting to disabled people because they trivialise disability; he states that:

> disability has nothing to do with standing on one leg, using a wheel-chair, or bumping around in the dark with one's eyes closed . . . Disability is not a dilemma, it is about lifestyle, about discrimination and about ignorant able-bodied service-providers who inculcate narrow medical and paramedical stereotypes into the minds of the future generation. (Finkelstein, 1991b: 5)

The experience of disability is all pervading and to attempt to simulate it as a way of understanding it is as fruitless as a man disguising himself as a woman in order to gain insights into her experiences. In the article 'Children experience the dilemma of disabled' (*Therapy Weekly*, 1991) the non-disabled children are encouraged to 'get under the skin' of disability, but Finkelstein (1991b) believes that this is as stupid as painting white children black in order for them to 'get under the skin of racism'.

John Hull, a man who went blind in adulthood (Hull, 1991), believes that total blindness is superficially the easiest impairment to simulate, for all we have to do is close our eyes, but that simulation gives totally false information because the sighted person 'doesn't have a blind man's brain'. Talking of his own experience he explains that 'one begins to take up residence in another world' and how he is gradually 'moving deeper into blindness'. It should also be remembered that impairment is just one facet of the disabled person's entirety, thus the ways in which any individual perceives and manages his or her impairment will be the product of many interacting attributes and characteristics.

It is also the case with simulation exercises, that no account is taken of the fact that the sighted person who blindfolds herself or the hearing person who stuffs cotton wool in his ears, has the benefit of a lifetime of visual and auditory experience on which to draw, which the visually impaired and hearing impaired person may lack because it has never existed or because it has faded. Lewis (1987) makes the point that young sighted children, when blindfolded, tend to perform better on a range of tactile and auditory tasks than blind children because sight helps to integrate information from all of our senses and helps us to make sense of our other experiences.

In addition to all these limitations, the accurate simulation of an impairment is impossible to achieve; the physically able person who sits in a wheelchair knows nothing of the real experience of paralysis, lack of balance, sensory loss and bladder dysfunction which the paraplegic person experiences. Duckworth (1991), of the organisation Disability Matters, is scornful of the way in which rubber gloves have been used to simulate sensory impairment and believes that simulation exercises are only favoured by non-disabled people. Morris (1976) freely admits that the sight-reducing goggles worn by his participants were inaccurate; for example the people using goggles simulating a loss of central vision, had far more sight around the edges of their visual field than a person with a true loss of central vision would have.

A further concern, particularly with regard to the simulation exercise undertaken by the architects and designers (Reynolds, 1991), is that they only attempted to 'understand' one type of impairment when presumably they should be planning for all disabled people simultaneously, including those with visual and hearing impairments, poor dexterity and learning difficulties. Unless a broad view is taken of disability it is highly likely that any adaptations architects make will further disable people with dissimilar impairments. The lack of knowledge and poor attitudes which some of the participants admitted to having is also alarming, and would suggest that a full and detailed disability equality programme is needed. One person, who said he knew quite a lot about designing for disabled people, admitted that before the simulation exercise his main thought about disabled people was that they only constituted 1 or 2 per cent of the population – and therefore, presumably, were hardly worth worrying about.

Simulation exercises very often degenerate into a situation of boisterous hilarity, indicating that the people undertaking the training are not experiencing anything like the real onset of disability. The Understanding Disabilities Educational Trust, for example, refer to the training they provide as 'great fun', and McConkey and McCormack (1983: 105) speak of 'The embarrassment, mickey-taking, giggling etc. at the thought of facing up to this new, and for some, threatening subject', though they view the behaviour as a relatively harmless emotional release which can easily be dispensed with. This type of behaviour can, however, be very offensive to disabled people. People undergoing simulation exercises do not appear to perceive themselves as disabled, but rather as the participants of a funny game, like 'blind man's buff'. Given the unrealistic situation they are in, and the novelty value of the tasks they must perform, their behaviour is, in my view, entirely natural; I can remember the exuberant giggling and horseplay when, as young physiotherapy students, we attempted to manoeuvre ourselves in wheelchairs or tried unsuccessfully to get up and down stairs on our crutches, though we were not simulating disability but merely learning practical techniques to assist injured and disabled people. But disability is not intrinsically amusing and for non-disabled people to treat it as such, especially in the context of disability awareness training, is in bad taste. Cassell (1985: 155) states that, 'Disabled humour appears to debase and degrade. Disabled humour clouds reality with an air of non-seriousness or unreality.' This is not to deny that disability can be extremely funny; indeed Cassell believes that if it is not a legitimate object of humour it may be stigmatised as having 'unusual, hushed, non-human qualities which are not included among the more normal humour themes' (1985: 154). Disabled people may, on occasions, choose to have a good laugh about their experiences (indeed this is a common pastime of people with visual impairments), but it is offensive for non-disabled people to initiate disabled humour, especially in the absence of disabled people.

Simulation exercises individualise disability

Disabled people, such as Oliver (1990) and Finkelstein (1991a), as well as organisations of disabled people, have for many years fought strenuously to redefine disability in terms of social oppression, where disability is viewed, not as the property of people with impairments, but rather as a product of an oppressive physical environment and social system, where the needs and rights of people with impairments, for example accessible transport and housing, are not taken into account. Although some mention may be made of social and environmental restrictions in disability awareness training which includes simulation exercises, the overwhelming emphasis of simu- lation activities is on impairments rather than disabilities, with discussion focusing on the participants' feelings about their 'impairments' rather than on how society could be altered to reduce or eliminate disability. Thus the Understanding Disabilities Educational Trust start their training by explaining 'how the relevant part of the body *does work* and why sometimes it *does not*' (my emphasis). The children then go on to examine and experiment with all the *special* equipment used by disabled people. To be fair, they also consider environmental barriers and how to remove them, but it seems to me that the training is strongly oriented towards impairment rather than disability. Barnes (1991: 51) believes that:

> The information provided by this organisation adheres rigidly to the traditional individualistic view of disability . . . It is profoundly divisive since it assumes that its audience, both teachers and pupils, will be ablebodied. It presents impairment as the primary cause of disability and ignores social factors such as prejudice, the built environment, and gender and cultural differences between disabled individuals and groups. In short, the pack foments and perpetuates the ignorance and discrimination which it is designed to undermine.

Similarly in the training devised by Wood (1990), disability was discussed in the overall context of 'movement' and the children experimented with *special* equipment, such as wheelchairs and the Chailey Chariot, although they did also consider environmental restrictions and how to remove them.

The London Boroughs Disability Resource Team (LBDRT) (1991: 21) believe that simulation exercises form:

> part of the medical model approach to disability and serves to reinforce the negative view that disability is only some terrible personal tragedy and cannot encompass the view of disability as part of a fulfilling or unfulfilling life experience.

Disability equality training

The LBDRT (now simply known as the Disability Resource Team or DRT) advocate two-day workshops run by highly trained disabled people where participants learn about disability through facilitated discovery rather than through lectures or straight information giving. This includes small group discussion, case studies, and examining the portrayal of disability and disabled people in the media. Role play exercises are also used but the participants are never asked to simulate impairment. It is discrimination that is tackled rather than attempting to make people aware of 'what it is like to be disabled'. The disabled trainers act as powerful models as they run the training in a self-assured and positive way.

Disability awareness training was developed after race and gender awareness training, so disability awareness trainers have had the advantage of learning from this. Two of the major problems found in race and gender awareness training were that the participants were often left with unresolved feelings of guilt and blame for the oppression of these groups, and that they frequently went away feeling enlightened but frustrated as no guidance was given on how to put the ideas into practice. The LBDRT (1991: 10) states that:

> Some people find the discovery process painful, which is an experience common to all forms of equality training. This is to be expected when exposing societal oppression and the part an individual participant would have unconsciously played in it. It is, therefore, necessary to have a consecutive second day to channel and to deal sensitively with the new awareness.

The LBDRT believes that the environment in which the training takes place must be emotionally safe and that everybody's self-esteem must be kept intact. They also point out that the trainers are exposed to a great deal of negativity regarding disability and that they need to be part of a supportive peer group where counselling can be provided.

The underlying idea behind Disability Awareness Training is that negative attitudes underpin discrimination against disabled people. Disability Equality Training, on the other hand, has its roots in the struggles of disabled people to gain equal opportunities and social justice. Disability Equality Training is primarily about changing the meaning of disability from individual tragedy to social oppression; it emphasises the politics of disability, the social and physical barriers disabled people face, and the links with other oppressed groups. Swain and Lawrence (1994: 92) state that disability equality training:

- Is about disability rather than about impairment.
- Is about challenging understanding of disability, and changing practices, rather than about improving general attitudes towards disabled people.
- Promotes a social rather than an individual tragedy model of disability.
- Is seen as part of the wider struggle for equal opportunities in both policies and practices (for women, black and minority ethnic people, and lesbians and gays).
- Uses discussion-based methods for teaching and learning rather than simulation.
- Is devised and delivered by disabled people themselves.

Disability equality training provided by DRT encourages participants to concentrate on their responsibilities towards disabled people rather than their attitudes. Issues of gender and race are woven into the training and at the end of each course the participants are asked to complete an action plan. Rather than loading guilt and blame on to the participants it is assumed that they are doing their best within the context of social, economic, and political structures which are uninformed and unenlightened about disability.

Although disability awareness training may be helpful in removing prejudice and discrimination, Chinnery (1991) warns that if nothing else is done to combat it, the training may be little more than a tokenistic gesture which serves as a convenient veneer to hide the real causes of disability. Making people aware of their own prejudices is certainly not enough. What is needed is training in how discrimination against disabled people can be prevented or dismantled by employers, organisations and unions and how disabled people are affected by discriminatory practices. This sort of training places discrimination and prejudice in a social context and gets away from treating disabled people as individual victims and non-disabled people as individual oppressors.

Conclusion

Disabled people, who run disability equality training courses or devise disability equality training packs, such as Finkelstein (1990, 1991c) and the DRT (London Boroughs Disability Resource Team, 1991), never use simulation exercises. In training such as this participants explore how disability is defined, their own feelings and behaviour towards disabled people, the identity of disabled people, the oppression disabled people encounter and how to remove it through equal opportunity policies and empowerment. The voice of disabled people themselves is central at all times. It is strongly recommended that recognised disabled trainers should be approached if disability training is required, for as Finkelstein (1991b) states:

> professionals should listen to the voice of organisations of disabled people and follow the example of awareness/equal opportunities training courses run by

recognised disabled trainers who never trivialise disability by providing so-called simulation exercises. (1991b: 5)

Note

A version of this chapter was originally published in *Disability, Handicap & Society* (1992), 7(3): 257–66. Carfax Publishing Company, PO Box 25, Abingdon, OXON OX14 3UE.

12

Disability and legislation: rights and equality

Ken Davis

For over four centuries in Britain, where disabled people have been among those singled out for legal treatment, we have been dealt with as a problem in need of special treatment and not as equal citizens with a right to full participation in the social mainstream. Countless millions of pounds have been and are spent on research into why we are the way we are, on attempts to cure us, or rehabilitate us, or conductively educate us, or in some other way make us approximate to able-bodiedness, or make us fit into a society designed to serve and perpetuate able-bodied interests. However, when (despite all this effort) we don't quite fit, or can't quite function, or we can't find jobs, millions more pounds are spent on social security, or welfare services, or heart-warming charitable endeavours designed to compensate us in some way for the personal tragedy that has befallen us.

Over time, disabled people have moved from acquiescence to uncertainty, discontent and, in recent years, to outright anger with this situation. We have been saying through our own organisations that our disability is caused not by the state of our bodies, but by the state of our society. We have said that we do not want legislation which treats us as people with special needs, but which instead outlaws and requires removal of the environmental and social barriers which prevent us from participating on equal terms in the ordinary activities of daily life. We have pointed out that we need legislation which enables us to take control of our lives, live independently and make a contribution to society. We have warned that until this kind of legislation has been enacted countless millions more pounds will be wasted just keeping us in a state of dependency and second-class citizenship.

In order to get this message across campaigns have been launched, initiatives taken and efforts of many other kinds made to try to bring to a halt this continued waste of public funds. Despite this, the vast majority of disabled people seeking work remain unemployed; millions exist on a state benefit system which is under attack; and we still find ourselves segregated, excluded and discriminated against in almost every aspect of social life. The disabled people's movement, through its national representative voice, the British Council of Organisations of Disabled People (BCODP), has been driven, as a result, to demand that the government takes action to bring an end to discrimination and secure for disabled people a proper legal foundation of equal citizenship. The remainder of this article considers some of the background events and issues, and reviews aspects of recent legislative activity which have moved disabled people into this position of political struggle.

Early paternalistic state provision

At first it can seem hard to understand how it can be that, in the face of all the improvements brought about in our lives by the Welfare State compared with the days of the Poor Law, disabled people are still unable to share equally in the society of which we are part. Yet it is our experience that most of the things the Welfare State provides have never been requested by disabled people; they segregate us in a way which is a disgrace in any civilised society; they make us dependent and unproductive; and often they make us feel as though we should be eternally grateful for the beneficence of a caring state. It is plain enough that 'Poor Law paternalism' has simply been replaced by a new era of 'Welfare paternalism', as commentators like Oliver (1994: 12) have pointed out:

> social policies, state provision and professional practice has failed disabled people ever since the welfare state began . . . I suspect I won't be giving disabled people news that they didn't already know and won't have experienced for however long they have been disabled . . . the Welfare State has been based on paternalism at least since 1945 and if you don't think so, read the Beveridge Report, read the preamble to any of the legislation, the National Assistance Act and any of that stuff – it is paternalism.

On reflection, it seems that the Welfare State was far from revolutionary in its approach to dealing with the basic risks, requirements and contingencies of life. As with some of the earlier social welfare measures brought in at the time of Balfour and Lloyd George around the turn of the century, Baron Beveridge's grand plan sought to spike the guns of socialism. This version of welfare based itself, not on a scheme of free allowances from the state on the principle of 'from each according to his means, to each according to his needs', but by paying benefits as of right by virtue of contributions paid on the insurance principle first established in the 1911 National Insurance Act. The new scheme very much emerged out of the incrementalist and paternalistic mould in which the character of British social policy development was set.

The National Assistance Act of 1948 (referred to by Oliver, 1994) starts with the somewhat over-optimistic preamble that 'the existing Poor Law shall cease to have effect and shall be replaced' (Fraser, 1984: 229). However, it perpetuated the means test, continued the 'dumping' of disabled people in institutions and in line with the 43rd Act of Elizabeth in 1602 (the Old Poor Law) required inmates to be charged with the cost of being isolated and segregated from the social mainstream (Fisher and Jurica, 1977). It also fostered the use of segregated services like workshops and hostels run by charitable voluntary organisations for disabled people which, since the middle of the nineteenth century, have become a powerful vested interest in disability services.

All this is not to suggest that the idea of welfare is wrong, nor to indicate that it does not bring undoubted benefits for its beneficiaries. We should, however, be keenly critical of the form it takes in our own lives and our present-day demand for welfare which supports our independence, social integration and equal citizenship is an expression of that duty. We can understand that in the feudal Britain of the fourteenth century, say, when the earliest seeds of future disability legislation were being sown in the precursive legislation to the Old Poor Law, it would have been a very different matter. Early poor relief, like later welfare measures, came out of a fear of social unrest by the ruling class and was a product of its own time, although successive generations of poor law officials, welfare administrators and caring professionals have turned it to their own advantage. Now we must ensure that the State maintains the collective commitment to fund welfare provision, but that it is used to secure our full participation and equality.

In this sense, we can see that early disabled people's groups like the British Deaf Association (1890) and the National League of the Blind (1899), which adopted an approach to welfare which was to last at least until the 1970s, were responding appropriately to the harsh circumstances facing their members around the turn of the century (Pagel, 1988). In the context of a growing labour movement and emerging social welfare arrangements, they were taking up a progressive position. The League campaigned hard (NLB, 1988) for the 1920 and 1938 Blind Persons Acts, which brought some advances for visually impaired people. But these groups, as with the Disablement Income Group (DIG) some 40 years later, were less interested in the underlying reasons as to why welfare was needed than in improving the immediate circumstances of their lives, and gaining for themselves some equivalence with non-disabled contemporaries.

Later legislation – denial of our rights

In order to bring about the kind of legislation needed to break the mould of paternalistic state provision, disabled people first had to break the mould in which our own expectations were set. We needed to overturn the power of the medical model and what Oliver (1990) has described as *the personal tragedy theory of disability* which underpinned welfare benefits and services. Among the ways this change came about were our own struggles to change institutional regimes (Hunt, 1992: 30) or escape them (K. Davis, 1993); developments in integrated and independent living abroad; the unfulfilled promises of the Chronically Sick and Disabled Persons Act (CSDPA) of 1973; and the failure of DIG's campaign for a national disability income.

Once the Union of the Physically Impaired against Segregation, set up in 1974 to spearhead a collective struggle for change, had defined disability as being socially caused, the way had been paved for a civil rights campaign to outlaw discrimination. It has been suggested that this

> signalled the end of the welfare oriented 'begging bowl' period, and with it the idea that the 'experts' could administer away disabled people's problems for them. This made the early Seventies the pivotal period in the development of the movement. From this point on, the emphasis was to be less on appeals to able-bodied people's better nature, polite petitions or orderly marches on Parliament Square, but more on the mobilisation of a democratically organised, politically aware movement. (K. Davis, 1993: 288)

In the face of a more critical approach to disability issues which followed the formation of the Union, the CSDPA, presented as being the start of a new era for disabled people, was shown to amount to little more than a repetition of the well-worn parliamentary device to stifle the growing demands for more substantial social change. It had been weakened when the bill was in committee stage, a process noticeably applied in sections which might enable disabled people to participate in the social mainstream: housing, public buildings and facilities and so on. As a result, its main focus is not on socially caused disability, but on individuals and their presumed welfare needs. The state of mind of the drafters of this legislation can be judged from the kind of welfare needs that can be met under Section 2 of the Act, which includes things like telephones, wireless and television, educational and library facilities, lectures, games, holidays and outings.

Even the 1990 National Health Service and Community Care Act, accompanied as it has been by political rhetoric about independence, choice and control and backed by the belief in the power of market forces to produce it, has failed to break the chains which bind us into unnecessary dependence. It gives disabled people no rights, and indeed has supplanted what limited rights to representation and assessment for services could have been available to us, had the government chosen to implement the relevant sections of the 1986 Disabled Persons (Services, Consultation and Representation) Act.

An important adjunct to community care in the shape of an Independent Living Fund, which placed payments directly in the hands of disabled people in order to purchase, under their own control, personal assistance for independent living, has been supplanted in 1993 with a new fund which restores the binding link to and dependence on professionally provided social services. To underpin and secure this preservation of professional power and control the government has consistently refused to introduce legislation which would make it legal for local authorities themselves to make direct payments which would put some purchasing power, choice and control back into disabled people's own hands. The Derbyshire Coalition of Disabled People (DCDP), commenting on the implementation of community care in the editorial column of its newsletter said:

> Instead of giving us rights, the Community Care Act puts us in the Limboland of uncertainty between a mixed market place of providers on the one hand, and professional controllers of services on the other. Never has there been such a need for a completely new approach to welfare: the kind of welfare which is based on

individual, enforceable rights and entitlements. The right wing view of the market place as the source of meeting our needs is as hopeless and redundant as the hope that they will somehow be met through the state controlled system of democratic accountability – which in practice is accountable not to us, but the infinitely more powerful interest groups which feed on our artificially created dependence. (DCDP, 1993)

This call for a new approach to the idea and practice of welfare echoes many of the arguments which were being developed 20 years earlier by the Union of the Physically Impaired. In those days, UPIAS held firmly to the view that the proper way forward for disabled people was through a 'serious struggle for the right to paid, integrated employment and full participation in the mainstream of life' (UPIAS, 1976). This view has gradually come to be adopted more widely as the disabled people's movement has grown and now finds expression through the campaign led by BCODP for anti-discrimination legislation (ADL), referred to in the opening paragraphs of this chapter (Barnes, 1991).

The fight for anti-discrimination legislation

The first steps towards putting ADL on any parliamentary agenda, however, were taken not by UPIAS but by the Committee on Restrictions against Disabled People (CORAD) under the chairmanship of Sir Peter Large. Set up in the final days of the Labour administration in January 1979 as a way of furthering the work of the Silver Jubilee Access Committee (SJAC), CORAD was charged with the task of considering 'the architectural and social barriers which may result in discrimination against disabled people and prevent them making full use of facilities available to the general public; and to make recommendations' (Large, 1982: 1). The first of the Report's 42 recommendations was that 'there should be legislation to make discrimination on the grounds of disability illegal' and that it should cover such instances wherever they might occur, although particularly in the areas of employment, education, transport and the provision of goods, facilities and services (Large, 1982). When CORAD began its work, there was a good deal of optimism that its findings would find their way on to the statute book since the committee had been set up by MP Alf Morris. However, the elections of May 1979 and the arrival of a Conservative government completely altered the climate of political support.

By the time the CORAD report had been produced in 1982, despite the arousal of a heightened sense of public awareness which was generated by the designation of 1981 as an International Year of Disabled People, the chances of any anti-discrimination bill finding a majority in Parliament had almost completely disappeared. Several attempts to introduce such legislation in one form or another failed repeatedly throughout the 1980s. Barnes (1991) notes nine such tries between 6 July 1982, when Lord Ashley (then Jack Ashley MP) introduced the Disablement (Prohibition of Unjustifiable

Discrimination) Bill and 6 February 1991 which saw the presentation of John Hughes's Disability Discrimination Bill.

Elsewhere in the world, however, the situation has been more hopeful and positive.

Canada

The Canadian government took steps to give some constitutional protection to disabled citizens in 1983.

United States

In 1990, and after long campaigning by disabled people and their supporters in the United States, the much more comprehensive Americans with Disabilities Act (ADA) came into being. Justin Dart, one of the disabled campaigners who worked on the ADA, echoed the same economic basis of argument which was the basis of the UPIAS case for change in Britain during the 1970s, as part of the pressure which was brought to bear on the Bush administration of the time. Just before the ADA Bill was passed by Congress, Dart said that the economic cost of segregating millions of disabled people from the productive mainstream of American life was running at $300 billion per year and failure to enact ADA:

> would lead directly to more unemployment and increasing dependency on massive, paternalistic welfare systems. It would guarantee higher taxes, higher government, business and family budgets, and higher public deficits. An effective ADA will free millions of people with disabilities from the bondage of dependency, enabling them to become employees, taxpayers and customers. It will save billions for government and directly profit every business and every citizen. (Dart, 1990: 1–2)

Congress finally passed the bill into law on 26 July 1990, acknowledging in the preamble that some 43 million disabled Americans had historically suffered and continued to suffer isolation, segregation and discrimination in critical areas such as employment, housing, public buildings, education, transportation, communication, recreation, health services, voting and access to public services. They accepted the depth of institutional and various other forms of discrimination, as was contained within with the BCODP case for ADL here in Britain:

> including outright intentional exclusion, the discriminatory effects of architectural, transportation, and communication barriers, overprotective rules and policies, failure to make modifications to existing facilities and practices, exclusionary qualification standards and criteria, segregation, and relegation to lesser services, programs, activities, benefits, jobs, or other opportunities. (ADA, 1990: s.2(a)(5)).

Congress concluded that the cost to the United States involved billions of dollars in unnecessary expenses resulting from dependency and non-productivity. The continued existence of unfair and unnecessary discrimination and prejudice was thus intolerable, and they agreed that the nation's proper goals would be to assure equality of opportunity, full participation, independent living and economic self-sufficiency for disabled people in American society.

Australia

In Australia the Disability Discrimination Act 1992 (DDA) received the Royal Assent on 5 November 1992; its object was:

(a) to eliminate, as far as possible, discrimination against persons on the ground of disability in the areas of
   (i) work, accommodation, education, access to premises, clubs and sport; and
   (ii) the provision of goods, facilities, services and land; and
   (iii) existing laws; and
   (iv) the administration of Commonwealth laws and programs; and
(b) to ensure, as far as possible, that persons with disabilities have the same rights to equality before the law as the rest of the community; and
(c) to promote recognition and acceptance within the community of the principle that persons with disabilities have the same fundamental rights as the rest of the community. (DDA, 1992: Part 1.3(a) et seq.)

New Zealand

In New Zealand, the Human Rights Act 1994, which is designed to consolidate and amend earlier race relations and human rights legislation and give better protection for minority rights in New Zealand in line with United Nations declarations extensively includes disabled people among its provisions. This Act seeks to make discrimination against disabled people unlawful in relation to access to public places, vehicles and facilities, in the provision of goods and services and in a variety of other circumstances and situations. In each of these anti-discrimination enactments, unlawful discrimination in employment matters takes a prominent place, indicating that the adverse economic aspect of socially caused disability (discrimination) is a feature, the undesirability of which has finally dawned in the consciousness of the governments concerned.

The extent to which this was understood in the United States is indicated by Dick Thornburgh (1990), then US Attorney General, in a speech to the Eighth Annual Government Conference on the Employment of Persons with Disabilities. Referring to widespread job discrimination in the private sector which had left 58 per cent of disabled men and 80 per cent of disabled women jobless, he picked up on the question of comparative cost, that is, the cost of passing or not passing the ADA. He said that, for example, widening a door to permit wheelchair access could cost as much as $300 to $600 per door, but it was also known that the widening must be done, not only because it is right:

but because it is in truth, the only cost effective solution to a dependency that costs our society well over $100 billion a year. Only through empowering this first generation and all coming generations as productive citizens can we overcome this defeating equation. Dependency equals a $45,000 annual cost to maintain each unemployed person with a disability or $2 million over an unwillingly dependent and idle lifetime. (Thornburgh, 1990: 2)

Nevertheless, the effect of pressure and lobbying by groups with a vested interest in stopping or neutralising the effect of ADL can be seen in the variety of conditions, exceptions and delaying devices built into the US as well as the Australian and New Zealand legislation, echoing the resistance to earlier civil rights measures. Dart (1990) noted in the United States that powerful vested interests were pushing for 'separate but equal' facilities and other discriminatory barriers which would perpetuate the unemployment, impoverishment and welfare dependency of disabled people, but went on to argue on the eve of the passage of the Americans with Disabilities Act that:

> this landmark legislation – a world first – provides citizens with disabilities the same 'clear mandate for the elimination of discrimination' which other minorities attained more than two decades ago . . . (yet) . . . professional lobbyists are flooding Congressional offices and the public media with student claims that ADA would force backbreaking costs and lawsuits on business. These claims are groundless. They reflect the same obsolete attitudes, unfounded fears and erroneous doomsday predictions that have greeted all previous extensions of basic civil rights protections. (Dart, 1990: 1)

The extent to which deployment of the economic argument and the link with other civil rights legislation has influenced current moves by the British Government to legislate is hard to judge. Conservative opponents of civil rights have argued that, unlike women and black people, disabled people are not a homogeneous group and people with different kinds of disability experience different kinds of discrimination and thus (almost as though they were unaware of ADL elsewhere in the world) it would be too complicated to legislate.

After the failure of John Hughes's Disability Discrimination Bill in 1991 and the 'talking out' of Alf Morris's Civil Rights (Disabled Persons) Bill early in 1992 the 1992 Bill was re-introduced in February 1993. Morris then deployed the economic case by referring to the gains in terms of national economic wealth to be made by the integration of disabled people into mainstream social life:

> enacting civil rights legislation . . . adds to wealth by reducing their dependence on benefits and increasing the contribution they can make. This is no academic point. When the Americans with Disabilities Act was passed through Congress, the realisation of that effect secured the support of more and more of its former critics. They began to talk more not only of its possible cost, but also of its undoubted economic and social value. (Hansard, 1993: 1142)

However, to date, no amount of polite argument has been able to change the government's position on comprehensive civil rights legislation. The chosen course has been well articulated in a broader context of managing public pressure and protecting the government's policy of cutting public expenditure and requiring individuals to provide for themselves. Until the Parliamentary events of the summer of 1994 referred to below, the management of pressure from the disability lobby was achieved by way of pointing out the success of their 'education and persuasion' and 'sector by sector' approach. This approach was reinforced by casting doubts on the effectiveness of overarching ADL where 'the costs are unquantifiable and . . . likely to lead to excessive bureaucracy and a beanfeast for the legal profession' and where it 'would imply considerable costs for employers, suppliers and the Government' (Hansard, 1993: 1178, 1185).

Conclusion

When this article was first prepared for publication in the opening weeks of 1994, I concluded by comparing the civil rights campaign led by the disabled people's movement in Britain, with the many attempts that had been made in the past to abolish slavery and extend the franchise to women. At that time, the government had rejected some 11 attempts to outlaw discrimination against disabled people. This has now risen to more than 15.

However, noting the relentless build up of pressure, I suggested that disabled people could expect the government 'to try and hold its established policy line with a pre-emptive legislative strike designed to avoid more radical measures' (Davis, 1994: 247). By the end of 1994 that had happened, although few would have predicted the dramatic way in which it came about. The development was triggered when the then Minister for the Disabled, Nicholas Scott, inadvertently delivered a high-profile publicity gift to disabled people in the information he gave to Parliament about his office's role in the defeat of the Civil Rights Bill in the summer of 1994. An opportunity to embarrass the government was successfully seized by the opposition and Nicholas Scott was replaced shortly afterwards in a ministerial reshuffle.

His successor, William Hague, quickly embarked on the Disability Discrimination Bill. Organisations of disabled people, led by the British Council of Disabled People, branded the bill as being weak and toothless. They reaffirmed their commitment to the more comprehensive and enforceable Civil Rights bill, which had been introduced by Harry Barnes. So far, the BCDP have carried with them a much wider coalition of supporting charities and organisations for disabled people under the banner of the Rights Now Campaign.

At the time of revising this conclusion, that is, in the summer of 1995, the Disability Discrimination Bill is proceeding through the House of Lords prior to its enactment. Most attempts to strengthen it by way of amendments have been defeated, and Harry Barnes's Civil Rights Bill has also suffered from the government procedural machine. Yet another reshuffle has produced yet another Minister for the Disabled – Alistair Burt – who will no doubt steer his government's bill between the covers of the Statute Book later in the year.

Previously in this chapter, I referred to the pressures on those with an interest in the field of disability to divide into two camps: one overtly in support of our movement and its demands for full and enforceable civil rights, and the other covertly against. Certainly, as the prospect of the lesser legislation looms ever nearer, these pressures will intensify, and are bound to put the Rights Now coalition under considerable strain. It is important that this pressure does not lead to the disparate organisations in the Campaign breaking ranks. As always, however, the ultimate outcome will depend on disabled people ourselves.

Note

A version of this chapter was originally published in S. French (ed.) (1994), *On Equal Terms: Working with Disabled People*. Oxford: Butterworth-Heinemann Ltd.

13

Legislation: a practical example – young people and education

Deborah Cooper

To many people new legislation simply represents more bureaucracy and a set of complicated words that might at best offer some promise of something they want. But if you get a little closer, untangle the red tape and turn the formal language into accessible and practical explanations, you can see how legislation is a most powerful way of affecting people's lives in practice, because it can open the door to services and close the door to undesirable activity. This chapter attempts to explain some of that power and some of the underlying issues.

Some key issues

New legislation is being introduced all the time. Almost all of it will have some impact on everyone, whether disabled or not, simply because we live in this country. However, some legislation has a particular impact on people with disabilities, either

- because it is specifically about services for disabled people, or
- because it is about issues that particularly affect disabled people.

Legislation can have a range of effects. It can:

- *require* people or organisations to provide certain kinds of services or do specific things and/or therefore give individuals rights;
- *enable* organisations or individuals to provide services or do certain things;
- *prevent* people or organisations from doing certain things.

Each piece of legislation is linked to others, and may make previous Acts obsolete. However, sometimes the links leave gaps, even if they are designed to be smooth. For example, the same person may receive services as a result of one Act, but not receive another service which is provided by another Act, even though both are needed equally.

Individuals' access to services often depends on exact interpretations that are generally, but not always, included in the legislation. This includes definitions:

- a definition of those people designed to benefit (for example, young people with disabilities);
- a definition of which services are affected (for example, transport, housing);
- a definition of who has responsibility (for example, local education authority).

Finally, it is not just the Act that affects what happens in practice, but also the regulations, circulars and other papers that are produced to explain in detail what should take place. The scope of these depends considerably on how 'wide' the legislation is and how much it leaves to government ministers to interpret and decide about detail.

It would take a major work to explain how all these issues affect all the services that disabled people need or use. This chapter concentrates therefore on one particular aspect: key education and training services that young people most need when they leave school. For simplicity it only refers to the situation in England. Other parts of the United Kingdom have parallel arrangements, decided in the same Parliament, but implemented separately for the most part. The chapter picks out three key aspects of major legislation:

1 The basic services offered.
2 How the guidance supplements the legislation.
3 The definition of the people entitled to benefit.

Education legislation

The Further and Higher Education Act 1992 was implemented on 1 April 1993 and reorganised the responsibility for ensuring provision of further education. The Act divides responsibility for funding further education between a Further Education Funding Council and local education authorities. Each of these bodies has specific responsibilities to ensure provision of education to young people and adults (outlined in Sections 2, 3 and 11). In addition, they are required by the Act to: 'have regard to the requirements of persons with learning difficulties' (Section 4).

School-based provision is basically governed by the Education Act 1993. The legislation is important for further education as it provides for a Code of Practice that makes arrangements for transition plans for pupils with special education needs. These are designed to help smooth the way to opportunities after the age of 16.

Guidance on implementation

The Department for Education (DFE) Circular 1/93 (Further and Higher Education Act 1992), provided guidance to local education authorities on their responsibilities to all students, including those with learning difficulties and disabilities, under the Act. This includes assessment of needs, provision for statemented pupils, discretionary awards, transport to further education provision, and a responsibility for ensuring adequate provision of certain kinds of further education.

Further Education Funding Council circulars (of which there were 37 in 1993 and 31 in 1994) cover the whole range of responsibilities of colleges. These include frequent explicit and implicit references to students with learning difficulties and disabilities. Four circulars so far have been exclusively about students with learning difficulties and disabilities: Circular 92/06, Circular 93/05, Circular 94/03 and Circular 95/07.

Definition

The definition of learning difficulty in relation to further education comes from the 1992 Further and Higher Education Act (s.4) and mirrors that in other education legislation. Disability is included as part of learning difficulty, as follows:

> a person has a 'learning difficulty' if
> (a) he has a significantly greater difficulty in learning than the majority of persons of his age, or
> (b) he has a disability which either prevents or hinders him from making use of facilities of a kind generally provided by institutions within the further education sector for persons of his age.

Various guides (for example, Department for Education Circular 93/01; Skill's guide to the Further and Higher Education Act 1992, updated annually) provide further details.

Social services legislation

From 1 April 1993, as a result of the National Health Service and Community Care Act 1990, every local authority, through its social services department, took on full responsibility for assessing their local people's needs and arranging appropriate care, whether in their own homes or in a residential or nursing home. April 1993 also saw the start of the transfer of funds from the Department of Social Security to local authorities. Each department also has to have a published complaints procedure. In practice this most frequently means that adults in receipt of 'community care services' from the local authority will have a care plan giving details of their assessed needs and each local authority will have an annually updated community care strategy.

Services available are based on those listed in the Chronically Sick and Disabled Persons Act 1970, Section 2.

> 2.–(1) Where a local authority having functions under section 29 of the National Assistance Act 1948 are satisfied in the case of any person to whom that section applies who is ordinarily resident in their area that it is necessary in order to meet the needs of that person for that authority to make arrangements for all or any of the following matters, namely
> (a) the provision of practical assistance for that person in his home;

(b) the provision for that person of, or assistance to that person in obtaining, wireless, television, library or similar recreational facilities;
(c) the provision for that person of lectures, games, outings or other recreational facilities outside his home or assistance to that person in taking advantage of educational facilities available to him;
(d) the provision for that person of facilities for, or assistance in, travelling to and from his home for the purpose of participating in any services provided under arrangements made by the authority under the said section 29, or with the approval of the authority in any services provided otherwise than as aforesaid which are similar to services which could be provided under such arrangements;
(e) the provision of assistance for that person in arranging for the carrying out of any works of adaptation in his home or the provision of any additional facilities designed to secure his greater safety, comfort or convenience;
(f) facilitating the taking of holidays by that person, whether at holiday homes or otherwise and whether provided under arrangements made by the authority or otherwise;
(g) the provision of meals for that person whether in his home or elsewhere;
(h) the provision for that person of, or assistance to that person in obtaining, a telephone and any special equipment necessary to enable him to use a telephone;
then, notwithstanding anything in any scheme made by the authority under the said section 29, but subject to the provisions of section 35(2) of the Act (which requires local authorities to exercise their functions under Part III of that Act under the general guidance of the Secretary of State and in accordance with the provisions of any regulations made for the purpose), it shall be the duty of that authority to make those arrangements in exercise of their functions under the said section 29.

This section makes it clear that social services departments can fund educational provision as well as transport and other facilities to enable education to take place. Indeed recent circulars have encouraged social services departments to think about such provision. However the kind of provision social services departments will fund may be restricted to the element covering 'care' or that element that would be considered 'day care' or 'social care'.

Guidance on implementation

Department of Health Circular LAC(92)15 *Social Care for Adults with Learning Disabilities (Mental Handicap)* includes 'enabling the use of everyday education, leisure and other facilities in the community' and 'helping develop occupational skills, finding employment and helping to support the individual in work' as part of its definition of social care (paragraph 15). The annex to the circular refers specifically to further and adult education and the importance of joint discussions (paragraph 16).

Department of Health Circular HC(84)9/LAC(84)8 enabled joint care funding (funding providing for joint health/social services funding) to be paid to local education authorities to benefit disabled people.

Definitions

The definition of disabled people used by social services departments (and the Department of Health) is contained in the National Assistance Act 1948, s.29. All social services and health legislation using the term disability (or similar) refers back to this. The definition is:

> persons who are blind, deaf or dumb, or who suffer from mental disorder of any description, and other persons who are substantially and permanently handicapped by illness, injury, or congenital deformity or such other disabilities as may be prescribed by the Minister.

Since the 1992 Circular referred to above [LAC (92) 15] the Department of Health and Social Services Departments have ceased referring to 'mental handicap' and now refer to 'people with learning disabilities'.

The Children Act 1989 was designed to replace many other pieces of legislation with one unified Act. It includes provision for children with 'special needs' who are defined in the following way (s.17):

> For the purposes of this Part a child shall be taken to be in need if –
> (a) he is unlikely to achieve or maintain, or have the opportunity of achieving or maintaining, a reasonable standard of health or development without the provision for him of services by a local authority . . .
> (b) his health or development is likely to be significantly impaired, or further impaired without the provision for him of such services; or
> (c) he is disabled.
> For the purposes of this Part, a child is disabled if . . . blind, deaf or dumb or suffering from mental disorder of any kind or is substantially and permanently handicapped by illness, injury or congenital deformity. 'Development' means physical, intellectual, emotional, social or behavioural development; and 'health' means physical or mental health.

This is not quite the same as the education definition of special needs for school age children. While many, if not all, young people with disabilities and learning difficulties are likely also to fall within the Children Act definition of 'in need' (if not through disability, then through their need for services), the two definitions are serving different purposes and have different implications. Many children may be entitled to services as children 'in need' under the Children Act, even though they might not be defined as having learning difficulties under the Further and Higher Education Act 1992. However, the services to which they are entitled are not the same.

Links between education and social services

Sections 5 and 6 of the Disabled Persons (Services, Consultation and Representation) Act 1986 were designed to make a smooth transition from full-time education to adult life. It gives local education authorities, and the Further Education Funding Council (following amendments contained in the Further and Higher Education Act 1992), specific responsibilities to make sure students with statements of special educational needs, who fit the above 1948 description of disabled, are known to social services departments.

Guidance on implementation

Department of Health and Social Services Circular LAC(88)2, which is also Department of Education and Science Circular 2(88), gives details, some of which are outdated by the Further and Higher Education Act 1992. Department for Education Circular 1/93 gives more up-to-date, but less detailed, information. Department of Health Circular LAC(93)12 provides further updated details to social services departments.

Definitions

The key definitions involved are those within education and social services (see preceding two sections).

Training

The Employment and Training Act 1973 was a wide-ranging Act that enabled the Secretary of State to provide a range of training and employment services. This has allowed the government to set up YOP (Youth Opportunity Programme), YTS (Youth Training Scheme) and YT (Youth Training) as well as TVEI (Technical and Vocational Education Initiative) and many other programmes without further legislation.

Guidance on implementation

Government policy has been adjusted regularly in relation to training for people with disabilities and learning difficulties. However, currently this is encompassed in the Training and Enterprise Council Operating Agreement which is annually amended and enables Training and Enterprise Councils (TECs) to fund actual provision and any support necessary for trainees to gain access to training including transport.

Definitions

The Employment and Training Act 1973 contains no definition of disability or similar. The term 'special training needs' is often used, but has no basis in legislation. When a definition is required the one used is that of the Disabled Persons' (Employment) Act 1944 (which is likely, however, to be superseded in 1996 by the Disability Discrimination Act).

Careers guidance

The Employment and Training Act 1973 also provided the framework for the Careers Service and the Employment Service guidance services for many years. The careers service provision, previously provided by local education authorities (LEAs), is now the subject of the Trade Union and Employment Rights Act 1993 which provides for alternative forms of management, including partnerships between LEAs and TECs. This requires the Secretary of State for Employment to 'have regard to the requirements of people with disabilities' when discharging his or her duties.

Guidance on implementation

There is a code of practice for careers services which gives detailed guidance and specific reference to people with disabilities and learning difficulties.

Definitions

There is no definition of disability in the legislation but a list of those included is in the code of practice.

Physical access

The Chronically Sick and Disabled Persons Act 1970 makes clear the overall responsibilities of colleges in relation to physical access to buildings, in section 8:

8.–(1) Any person undertaking the provision of a building intended for purposes mentioned in subsection (2) below shall, in the means of access both to and within the building, and in the parking facilities and sanitary conveniences to be available (if any), make provision, in so far as it is in the circumstances both practicable and reasonable, for the needs of persons using the building who are disabled.
(2) The purposes referred to in subsection (1) above are the purposes of any of the following:
(a) universities, university colleges and colleges, schools and halls of universities;
(b) schools within the meaning of the Education Act 1944, teacher training colleges maintained by local education authorities in England or Wales and other institutions providing further education pursuant to a scheme under section 42 of the Act;
(c) educational establishments within the meaning of the Education (Scotland) Act 1962.

More detailed guidance on access is contained in Part M Building Regulations.

Conclusion

The legislation described here is also summarised in the three appendices at the end of the chapter. The legislation is complex and changes regularly but from the current range, several points emerge. First, some of the legislation is specifically designed around people with disabilities (Chronically Sick and Disabled Persons Act) but more legislation is designed for everyone but specifically mentions disabled people (for example, Further and Higher Education Act 1992).

Second, some of the legislation is 'enabling'. For example, the Employment and Training Act 1973 gives the Secretary of State wide powers to create training opportunities. Little legislation related to service provision (unlike criminal legislation) is designed to prevent actions. Much of the legislation on the contrary, requires public bodies to provide services (for example, the Further Education Funding Council (FEFC) to ensure education is available). However, although this almost amounts to an individual right (to education) the legislation does not say this. In practice, this can lead to problems because the FEFC and LEAs are only required to secure either 'adequate' or 'sufficient' provision and there is no definition of these terms. Furthermore, even though the FEFC and LEAs must 'have regard to' students with learning difficulties and disabilities, there is no legal definition of what this entails. In practice it can mean students are refused an educational opportunity they want and need.

Third, although some legislation (for example, the Disabled Persons Act 1986) is designed to co-ordinate legislation, most is not. The gaps between legislation are sometimes wide, particularly when expensive services are included, or when authorities are given discretionary powers. For example, the LEAs have responsibility for deciding about providing transport to education, and social services departments also have powers, but further education is often funded by FEFC. Students are sometimes mid-course when their transport ceases to exist.

Fourth, definitions of the people intended to benefit from legislation vary considerably, from medical descriptions designed in the 1940s to more recent descriptions. This can also lead to anomalies. For example, someone with moderate learning difficulties would come within the education definition, but may fall outside the help offered to disabled people by social services departments.

This variability can be, and often is, softened by helpful guidance in codes of practice, circulars and regulations. These are not, however, legally binding in the way Acts are and change more frequently. They cannot reverse major problems between different Acts. For this reasons there has been growing interest from disability groups in passing anti-discrimination legislation to ensure that disabled people do not have to appear separately (if they do) in different legislation, but have a general right to services on an equitable basis. The United States, Australia and New Zealand have taken this step. Legislation is likely to be passed in the United Kingdom during 1995, but is unlikely to be comprehensive.

Legislation about services for disabled people is fascinating and ever changing. It is also confusing to people removed from its operation. However, this examination of one small aspect of the legislation demonstrates the power it has over people's lives.

Appendix 13.1   Provision, legislation and funding

Provision	*Key legislation*	*Possible funding – responsible bodies*
Education and training provision itself	Further and Higher Education Act 1992	LEA or FEFC
	Employment and Training Act 1973	TECs/Employment Service
	Chronically Sick and Disabled Persons Act 1970 National Health Service and Community Care Act 1990.	Social services departments of local authorities
	HASSASSA 1983	Health authority funding for education and training
Transport to education	Further and Higher Education Act 1992	LEA
	Chronically Sick and Disabled Persons Act 1970	Social services departments
Assessment of needs/Careers guidance	Education Act 1981	LEAs for assessments linked to statements of special educational needs
	Further and Higher Education Act 1992	LEA/FEFC responsibilities not in legislation but linked requirements outlined by Secretary of State
	Chronically Sick and Disabled Persons Act 1970	Social services departments
	Disabled Persons (Services, Consultation and Representation) Act 1986	LEA/college governors and social services departments
	Employment and Training Act 1993	Department of Education and Employment
	National Health Service and Community Care Act 1990	Social services departments
	Trade Union and Employment Rights Act 1993	Department of Education and Employment
	Children Act 1989	Social services departments

Appendix 13.2   Legislation, definitions and services provided

Legislation	*Definition used*	*Legislation governs*
Education Act 1993	Special educational need/ learning difficulty: includes learning difficulty and physical, sensory and other disabilities	Educational provision in schools
Further and Higher Education Act 1992	Learning difficulty – essentially same as Education Act 1993	Further education of all sorts, i.e. all education other than in schools, + services linked, e.g. transport, discretionary awards (grants)
Disabled Persons (Employment) Act 1944	'disabled person'	Support into and in employment
Chronically Sick and Disabled Persons Act 1970	Based on National Assistance Act 1948 definition of 'disabled'	Welfare services including education and/or transport to education
Disabled Persons (Services, Consultation and Representation) Act 1986, Sections 5 and 6	As above	Assessment of disability and link between education and welfare service at end of education
NHS and Community Care Act 1990	As above	Welfare services for disabled people
Employment and Training Act 1973	None – broad legislation for all adults	Range of training and employment services
Trade Union Reform and Employment Rights Act 1993	None – refers to people with disabilities. Code of practice gives comprehensive list	In this context, careers services to all, including specifically people with disabilities

Appendix 13.3   Notes on English legislation and related documents

The Disabled Persons (Employment) Act (1944), set up provision for sheltered employment and other support for disabled people.

The National Assistance Act (1948) laid the groundwork for postwar services and gave the definition of disabilities still generally used by social services departments.

The Chronically Sick and Disabled Persons Act (1970) brought many new services, and 'enabled' departments to fund transport, educational activities and other services linked to education. It also required 'reasonable' access to be made available to public buildings including educational sites.

Community Care: Agenda for Action (The Griffiths Report), HMSO (1988) was the report which led to the White Paper *Caring for People*.

Caring for People, HMSO (1989) was the White Paper on Care in the Community, which followed the Griffiths Report.

The NHS and Community Care Act (1990) gave the legal framework for Care in Community policies that resulted from the Griffiths Report and the *Caring for People* White Paper.

The Children Act (1989) outlined a new framework for legislation related to children, including those with special needs and their transition to adult services.

The Disabled Persons (Services, Consultation and Representation) Act 1986. Designed to fill several gaps, including that between education and social services as young people leave school – Sections 5 and 6.

The Education Act 1981 is the legislation that formed the basis for special education within schools until the Education Act 1993 was passed. A few sections of the Act are still in force.

The Education Act 1993 is the legislation affecting school-based provision and introduced transition plans for pupils with special educational needs.

Education and Training for the 21st Century. This was the White Paper that initiated the Further and Higher Education Act 1992 and also foreshadowed the Careers Service reorganisation as well as the extension of Training Credits, Compacts and the National Vocational Qualification (NVQ) system.

Education and Training – Working Together (1986) contained proposals for TVEI national extension and setting up the National Council for Vocational Qualifications and framework of NVQs.

The Employment and Training Act (1973) was legislation dealing with the Employment and Careers Services and various training opportunities.

Employment for the 1990s, Employment Department (1988) was the White Paper that initiated TECs (LECs in Scotland).

The Further and Higher Education Act (1992) restructured the provision and funding of further and higher education.

The Health Circular HC(84)9/LAC(84)8, Department of Health (1984) enabled joint care funding to be paid to local education authorities to benefit disabled people.

New Training Initiative 1981. A programme for action which contained proposals for Youth Training and other skill development initiatives.

The Trade Union Reform and Employment Rights Act (1993) changed the management and funding arrangements for the Careers Service.

Training Credits for Young People: A Prospectus, Training Agency (1990) invited TECs to run pilot schemes.

14
Working choices

Brenda Smith

Most people in Western society expect to work. The question often asked of young people 'What do you want to be?' is not seeking to know what kind of person they want to be but what kind of work they want to do. The concept of work does not just mean external paid employment but also incorporates other forms of meaningful activity including housework, child care and voluntary work; however, our social and individual expectation is that work for most people will include paid employment or self-employment. Indeed the stigma attached to unemployment serves to strengthen the links between job and social status, job and sense of self-worth. We expect and are expected to make a contribution to society through the work we do.

> Work is a central part of western life and society. The vast majority of people will always have to provide for themselves, either directly (as did our ancestors) or indirectly through contributions to society which are rewarded by support and income. Furthermore our occupational life is organised in many ways to satisfy our requirements for companionship, achievement and gain: people are aware of positive benefits of working which extend well beyond a grudging acceptance of its necessity. Most people would continue working even if they could afford not to. (Warr and Wall, 1975: 10)

Although we share expectations and aspirations about work, the extent to which these are met for any individual will be influenced by a variety of factors, including their work preferences, their skills, qualifications and experience, the employment opportunities in their locality, their willingness and ability to be mobile, their access to information about available options, their expectations of reward (both monetary and in terms of satisfaction), and their knowledge and confidence to make appropriate choices. Their success in achieving their employment aspirations will also be influenced by an elusive 'perceived employability factor', which refers both to the extent to which an employer thinks they can meet the needs of the job, and the extent to which their face 'fits'. Intrinsic and extrinsic organisational factors (for example, actual as opposed to advertised job demands and the reality of the organisation's internal culture compared with its public image) will also have a part to play.

The work expectations and aspirations of disabled people and the extent to which these are met for any individual are subject to these same influences. However, the range of choices available to them and their opportunities to make choices are often constrained by additional factors which will be discussed in this chapter.

Should I work?

In spite of the social pressures on us to work, the decision about whether or not to seek paid work may not be as easy as political policy makers would have us believe. Although the unemployment rate for disabled people is around twice that for the population as a whole, survey findings tell us that there are large numbers of disabled people within the work force (Martin et al., 1989; Prescott-Clarke, 1990). However, for many disabled people the financial and psychological risks associated with employment may seem to outweigh the advantages of being in work.

There is therefore a balance to be sought between the system of work and the system of support of those not in work. Although various attempts have been made during the last 25 years to address the shortcomings of the benefits system as it affects disabled people (Bolderson, 1991) some of its effects still include:

- Putting pressure on people to work, regardless of whether this is truly helpful to them.
- Financially penalising people who are working, but for low pay or short periods of time.
- Marginalising people in a part of the labour market which commands low wages.

In addition, the abilities and potential for work of disabled people are commonly, and inappropriately, assessed by medical rather than vocational criteria. For example, the assessment of 'work capacity' in deciding eligibility for Incapacity Benefit measures the length of time someone can sit or stand, rather than their aptitude for the job. As a result the focus is directed towards disability rather than ability. This has a combined and compounding negative effect. It forces disabled people to become even more aware of their limitations rather than their strengths, and possibly reinforces an existing low level of confidence. It raises questions about their potential value as employees, including for example their productivity and attendance at work which may be wrongly assumed to be lower than average. Most importantly, it obscures limiting factors imposed by the working environment, with the result that the disabled person rather than the workplace is more likely to be labelled as 'inadequate'.

Work is often assumed to be good for us, and many research studies have identified aspects of work which are regarded as therapeutic, especially in relation to mental health and in comparison with unemployment (Warr, 1987; Vostanis, 1990). However, personal accounts suggest that work experiences for most people include both good and bad aspects (Keay et al., 1994). The work experiences of some disabled people have been so consistently negative that an association has developed for them between work and failure: they expect to fail at work. A self-fulfilling prophecy may be in operation whereby the fear and expectation of failure contribute to further negative work experiences. The choice then becomes one between work as failure, or non-work as failure. The decision of whether or not to work has become a 'no win' situation.

Competitive or sheltered work?

In theory, and as established under the 1944 Disabled Persons (Employment) Act – on which employment policies and services for disabled people in the UK are still based – there is a choice to be made between open competitive employment or self-employment for the majority, and sheltered employment where open employment is thought to be inappropriate.

In reality, very little choice exists. The decision about whether competitive or sheltered employment is more appropriate is based not on personal preference but on the productivity level a disabled person is thought able to achieve in comparison with a non-disabled 'norm'. The validity of this is questionable: the survey carried out by Prescott-Clarke (1990) suggests that many disabled people who would be assessed as suitable only for sheltered employment are in fact working in open employment. In fact, more disabled job seekers are thought to find work through general channels than through specialist disability services.

When sheltered work is undertaken, the type of work performed is more likely to be decided by what is available in the locality than by the person's interests and aptitude. Most sheltered employment has traditionally consisted of light manual work undertaken in workshops run by local authorities or voluntary organisations, or in Remploy factories. The lack of training and promotion opportunities (Smith et al., 1991) and the low wage levels, have in the past been compensated for some people by the security offered, although the number of sheltered employment places available has been inadequate to provide for all those eligible, and the viability of many workshops is increasingly threatened by the demands on them to compete with private sector organisations for contract work.

The introduction of the Sheltered Placement Scheme was seen as an innovative attempt to bridge the gap between sheltered and open employ-ment, providing opportunities for disabled people assessed as being between 30 per cent and 80 per cent productive to work in open employment organisations, with the employer paying the relevant proportion of a full salary and the Employment Department making up the difference. The scheme proved to be too successful, with the result that numbers of places available were frozen, in spite of the Department's statement that:

> Wherever possible sheltered placements should be the preferred form of provision
> . . . employment in sheltered factories should be confined to those who cannot be

supported properly under sheltered placement arrangements. (Employment Department, 1990: 12)

Various other initiatives have developed to provide alternatives to sheltered and competitive employment, including social firms and other forms of supported employment, and cooperatives. Most of these are small, local projects which often have a far more equitable involvement of disabled people at all levels than exists in sheltered employment (McAnaney, 1994), but which rely on inadequate short-term funding and have to struggle for commercial viability. Most of these newer initiatives have been developed for specific groups of disabled people, particularly for those who have had mental health problems, so they are not usually available to everyone as an option.

Equality at work?

In spite of the fact that many organisations proclaim themselves to be 'equal opportunity employers', the reality is that disabled people are more likely to face inequality both in terms of getting work and developing careers. One reason is that in the United Kingdom we have not had anti-discrimination legislation requiring equality for disabled people, as we do have in relation to discrimination on the grounds of race and gender. Draft legislation in the form of the Disability Discrimination Bill is currently before parliament to address this anomaly, but 20 years after the Sex Discrimination Act (1975) and the Race Relations Act (1976), it is still legal in this country to refuse someone a job, or promotion, because they are disabled.

A second major reason for inequality in employment is the widespread ignorance of the barriers which lead to the under-representation of disabled people at work, both in terms of unemployment and underemployment. People in organisations, particularly those in decision-making roles, may or may not be aware that barriers exist. They frequently fail to recognise their own role in erecting and maintaining such barriers, and hence their ability to reduce and remove them.

The employment barriers experienced by disabled people take three main forms: physical, procedural and attitudinal (Smith and Povall, 1994). Physical barriers are usually associated with lack of access. This arises from the design of buildings and workplaces and the lack of appropriate equipment to do the job, but it includes other access issues, for example the dissemination of information and the provision of training in formats which do not meet a range of communication needs. Procedural barriers may be experienced more indirectly and often without the knowledge of those affected by them. They include recruitment, assessment and promotion procedures which discriminate by applying criteria irrelevant to the job, or which allow decisions to be made based on assumption rather than fact. Attitudinal barriers, which are often based on fear, ignorance or misconception, may be the most pervasive, influencing behaviour directly but also underpinning other types of employment barrier.

Several years ago I was asked to carry out research for a major company which wanted to know how it rated as an employer of disabled people. Interviews were carried out with disabled members of staff, and with their colleagues, supervisors and managers, as well as senior decision-makers in the organisation. The following case study highlights a range of employment barriers experienced by one person.

One disabled member of staff was a member of a typing pool who sometimes found herself alone in the large open plan office, usually because she arrived early or left late in order to earn some overtime. She told me that the first time this happened she was a little anxious, because as a deaf person she was unable to hear the fire alarm located in the corridor outside. She later asked her supervisor whether it would be possible to have a visual alarm installed inside the office, facing her desk.

The supervisor raised the issue with the line manager, who directed the enquiry to the company's health and safety officer. Having reviewed the situation, this officer reported back to the line manager that although the suggestion seemed sensible, approval for the necessary expenditure could only be given if the Company Doctor made a case on medical grounds. After consultation, the doctor reported that this was not an issue requiring a medical decision. The necessary expenditure for a visual alarm was not approved.

One outcome for the deaf member of staff was a suggestion from her line manager that it might be better if she stopped working any overtime and made sure there was always someone else in the office when she was there. Her comment to me was 'I expect they want someone to go to the coffee machine with me as well!' A second outcome was that she was turned down for promotion to an administrative post on the grounds that she would be unable to meet the demands of the job. It was assumed that she would be unable to use the telephone or be flexible about where she was located.

The employment barriers experienced by this member of staff were evident to an outside researcher, as were ways to overcome the most obvious of the physical barriers (a vibrating personal alarm carried in the pocket and a Minicom system installed in selected locations). Less easy to deal with were the procedural and attitudinal barriers. Failure to designate responsibility and a reluctance to recognise the disabled person as the expert are common disability management problems in organisations (Smith et al., 1991), as is the tendency to equate disability with illness, leading to assumptions of inability:

> We are seen as 'abnormal' because we are different . . . but the truth is, like everyone else, we have a range of things we can and cannot do, a range of abilities both mental and physical that are unique to us as individuals. The only difference between us and other people is that we are viewed through spectacles that only focus on our inabilities, and which suffer an automatic blindness – a sort of medicalised social reflex – regarding our abilities. (Brisenden, 1986: 175)

The paradox in the situation described was that the member of staff involved was teaching hearing people at evening classes and holding executive positions in two voluntary organisations, one of which was heavily dependent on her administrative skills. As she said: 'I would like a more demanding daytime job. I do the boring things at work during the day, and the interesting things – the things which stimulate me and use my abilities – in the evenings and at weekends.' She had not chosen typing work. This had been recommended by a school careers officer on the grounds that 'you don't have to be able to hear in order to type'. She would not have chosen to work in a typing pool but had applied for an administrative post. The recruiter instead offered her a job in the typing pool, with the expectation that she would be able to take over the less popular copy-typing jobs, leaving audio-work and administrative tasks for the hearing typists. Her working choices had been made for her by other people, and were based on assumptions and misconceptions, with very little reference to the individual herself. This is the reality of work for many disabled people.

15

The attitudes of health professionals towards disabled people

Sally French

Attitudes are enduring mental representations of various features of the social or physical world. They are acquired through experience and exert a directive influence on subsequent behaviour. (Baron and Byrne, 1991: 138)

This chapter explains the nature and function of attitudes and reviews the literature on the attitudes of health professionals towards disabled people. It concludes by considering various strategies for attitude change.

The nature of attitudes

Most definitions of attitude comprise three components:

- cognitive;
- affective;
- behavioural.

The cognitive component refers to our beliefs about the object or person to whom the attitude is directed. We may believe, for example, that blind people have a 'sixth sense', or that the number of patients referred for therapy has increased; our beliefs may or may not be correct.

The affective component refers to our evaluation of the object or person to whom the attitude is directed. We may think, for example, that the 'sixth sense' of blind people makes them superior beings, or that the rise in patient numbers is placing an unfair burden on therapists. These evaluations are based on the underlying values we hold which represent ethical codes and social and cultural norms; whereas beliefs represent what we know, values represent what we feel. Gross (1987) points out that in order to convert a belief into an attitude a value ingredient is needed. The more important or central our beliefs and values, the more difficult they are for ourselves or for others to change. This is because they tend to underpin our other attitudes and may influence the way we behave.

Our beliefs and values may, in turn, affect our behaviour. We may, for example, fail to assist the blind person when he or she needs it, or display resentment towards the clients queuing up for our services. These ideas are

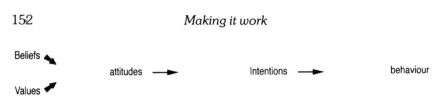

Figure 15.1   *Attitude components*

summarised in Figure 15.1; our beliefs and values constitute our attitudes which may, in turn, influence our intentions and behaviour (Fishbein and Ajken, 1975). It can be seen that behaviour is sometimes viewed as a component of an attitude and sometimes as a separate entity.

Prejudice

Prejudice literally means to pre-judge or to form a strong attitude without sufficient information (Reber, 1985). Although, in its pure form, a prejudice can be either positive or negative, it usually refers to an extreme negative attitude. Reber defines prejudice as: 'A negative attitude towards a particular group of persons based on negative traits assumed to be uniformly displayed by all members of that group.'

Prejudices, like attitudes, have cognitive, affective and behavioural components. The cognitive component is a stereotype (an overgeneralisation) which is, in itself, neutral. The affective component is a feeling of liking or hostility, and the behavioural component may manifest itself as aggression, avoidance, discrimination, or preferential treatment. Holmes and Karst (1990) believe that professionals learn to rely on culturally acceptable stereotypes of disabled people as a way of handling their clients and surviving the organisations where they work. They state:

> it may take less time to use a myth as a basis of action than it does to learn something firsthand from a client . . . stereotyping allows humans to infer characteristics at the cost of distorting and restricting awareness of people and individuals. (Holmes and Karst, 1990: 21).

Stereotypes of disabled people may strengthen negative attitudes towards them. Disabled people may be expected to behave in various ways, as passive recipients of care for example, yet when they comply their behaviour may validate and reinforce prevailing attitudes that they are inferior or incapable of self-determination. A particular set of behaviours, often referred to as the disabled role, may be expected of disabled people so strongly that those who do not conform are viewed in negative terms (French, 1994a). Funk (1986) believes that self-advocacy is not generally considered part of the behavioural repertoire of disabled people and Holmes and Karst (1990) maintain that disabled people who take control of their lives may be viewed as aggressive, while passive clients may be viewed as cooperative. As choice of rehabilitation facilities is usually non-existent, disabled people are frequently forced to conform to the stereotyped role prescribed for them.

Disabled people are, of course, members of society and the prejudices which are held against them may become part of their own self-identity and view of the world leading to a 'self-fulfilling prophecy'. These processes are rarely at a conscious level so health professionals do not necessarily guard against them or even think about them. This situation is exacerbated by the big, impersonal organisations where most health professionals work. Although professional ethics may demand the self-determination of patients and clients, bureaucratic organisations and professional self-interest may insist that professionals remain in control (Holmes and Karst, 1990). According to Brown (1986) two factors are particularly important in breaking down prejudice: non-competitive contact of an equal status, and the pursuit of common goals which are obtainable through cooperation.

The relationship between attitudes and behaviour

Our attitudes and behaviour tend to be poorly correlated; Wicker (1969) estimates that only 10 per cent of the variance in our behaviour can be explained by our attitudes. This is because factors other than attitudes, such as habits, social norms, and group pressure, influence our behaviour. As Gross (1987: 263) states:

> It is generally agreed that attitudes are only one determinant of behaviour; they represent predispositions to behave but how we actually act in a particular situation will depend on the immediate consequences of our behaviour, how we think others will evaluate our actions, and habitual ways of behaving in those kinds of situations.

Although attitudes do predict behaviour to a limited extent, situational factors often have a stronger influence. It cannot be assumed, for example, that patients who faithfully attend every appointment have a positive attitude towards their treatment; they may simply feel that attendance is expected of them, or have nothing better to do. Similarly health professionals may behave impeccably towards their patients even though their attitudes may not always be positive. Discrimination may also arise from habit, social pressure, or group norms, rather than prejudice. Some people are more inclined to keep consistency between their attitudes and behaviour than others.

A problem when evaluating research which relates attitudes to behaviour, is that *general* attitudes have often been used to predict *specific* behaviour. Atkinson et al. (1993) state that attitudes predict behaviour best when they are strong and consistent, based on the person's direct experience, and specifically related to the behaviour in question. Fishbein and Ajken (1975) agree that general attitudes are poor predictors of specific behaviour, and that to obtain a positive correlation, both the attitude and the behaviour must be specific. Thus in order to infer a health professional's behaviour when confronted with a severely disabled person wishing to live independently, the attitude of the therapist towards that specific issue would be a better predictor than a measure of his or her general attitude towards severely disabled people.

It is also the case that various aspects of our attitudes may be inconsistent. We may, for example, be very attracted to someone yet have serious doubts about his or her integrity. Related attitudes may also conflict – for example, we may be in favour of greater public spending yet object to tax increases. In situations such as these one of the attitudes, or attitude components, may be more related to behaviour than the others.

The function of attitudes

Social psychologists have demonstrated that our attitudes serve many important functions relating to our psychological well-being. For this reason attitudes are often very resistant to change. Below are listed the major functions that attitudes serve (Pennington, 1986; Atkinson et al., 1993).

1 *Adaptive function*: We hold attitudes for practical reasons: to achieve our goals, to increase satisfaction and pleasure, and to avoid punishment. We may develop similar attitudes to those people we like, or to those with whom we work, in order to maintain the pleasure of their company and avoid conflict. In this way our attitudes help us achieve and maintain social adjustment, and avoid social isolation. Those living in isolated areas, where the choice of social contacts is small, would perhaps feel a greater necessity to alter their attitudes in this way than those living in cities with a more diverse population.
2 *Knowledge function*: In order to cope with the complexities of life, we impose a structure on the world making it a simpler and less uncertain place. In this way we may form stereotypes (overgeneralisations) of groups of people to simplify our understanding of them and responses to them. We may believe, for example, that health professionals are outgoing and confident, or that disabled people are in need of care and protection.
3 *Self-expressive function*: Our attitudes give expression to our underlying values and beliefs; by expressing our attitudes we are confirming the positive aspects of our self-concept. We need to tell others about ourselves in order to develop a strong self-identity. The reactions of others may also lead us to modify or strengthen our attitudes.
4 *Ego-defensive function*: Our attitudes give us protection from anxiety and threats to our self-esteem, both from ourselves and from others. If, for example, we value ourselves and believe we are basically good, we are better able to reject or to cope with the criticisms and evaluations of others, and to dismiss or accept our own behaviour when it fails to meet the expectations we have of ourselves. In dealing with threats to our self-esteem we may deny or distort information, or project our conflicts and failings on to other people.

It is clear that in order to change an attitude its function must be known. If, for example, the attitude is serving an ego-defensive function, providing the person with information would be unlikely to bring about change.

Measuring attitudes towards disabled people

There are many ways of measuring attitudes towards disabled people. Most measures focus on disability in general terms, rather than on specific impairments. The survey, using various questionnaires, is by far the most common method, though sociometric measures, to investigate behaviour, and instruments involving video and picture presentation have also been used. The most widely used instrument is the Attitudes Towards Disabled Persons Scale (ATDP) developed by Yuker et al. in 1960. It measures attitudes in terms of perceived differences between groups of disabled and non-disabled people.

The Interaction with Disabled Persons Scale (IDP) is a new instrument which was developed in Australia in the late 1980s and early 1990s (Gething, 1993); it is used to measure community attitudes towards disabled people. The scale explores the motivations and emotions considered to underlie negative attitudes towards disabled people, rather than focusing on the perceived differences between disabled and non-disabled people. Gething (1993) explains that the IDP scale is based upon the notion that negative attitudes reflect strangeness, or lack of familiarity, which creates uncertainty or anxiety.

The Disability Social Distance Scale (DSDS) was developed by Tringo in 1970. It measures how closely people wish to be associated with disabled people with particular impairments. In this way it can be seen to what extent people with particular impairments are viewed as acceptable or unacceptable.

It is not, of course, possible accurately to predict behaviour from any of these attitude measures.

Attitudes of health professionals towards disabled people

Health care professionals share the values and expectations of their society and show the same reactions that unstigmatised individuals have towards those with differences. (Allen and Birse, 1991: 150)

Research evidence regarding whether the attitudes of health professionals are more or less positive than those of the general public tend to conflict (Elston and Snow, 1986; Vargo and Semple, 1988). Studies concerning the change of attitudes of medical students throughout their training, for example, show that they may improve (Mitchell et al., 1984), deteriorate (Rezler, 1974), or remain the same (Duckworth, 1988). Chubon (1982) concludes that after three decades of research regarding the attitudes of health professionals towards disabled people, the evidence is still indeterminate.

Although research findings conflict the weight of the evidence suggests that the attitudes of health professionals are not very different from those of the general public and that they may become more negative as professional education proceeds (Brillhart et al., 1990). Chubon (1982) found the attitudes of occupational therapists to be more negative towards disabled people than those of the general public; Brillhart et al. (1990) found that first-year nursing students had more positive attitudes towards disabled people than graduating nurses; Diseker and Michielutte (1981) showed that empathy towards disabled people decreased during medical training; and Rezler (1974) discovered that medical education tends to increase cynicism. Elston and Snow (1986) used the ATDP scale with rehabilitation counsellors and found no difference between their attitudes towards disabled people and those of other occupational groups.

Duckworth (1988) used the ATDP scale to test the attitudes of first- and fourth-year medical students, house officers, and the general public. He also asked them to agree or disagree with the statement 'Disabled people cause more problems to doctors than non-disabled people'. No significant difference was found among the doctors with regard to age, sex, occupation, intended medical career, length of contact with disabled people, or personal knowledge of a disabled person. Those who agreed with the statement, however, had more negative attitudes.

Lyons (1991) used the ATDP scale to compare undergraduate occupational therapy students with undergraduate business students. No significant difference was found between the two groups or between junior and senior students. There was, however, a significant different ($p = <0.01$) between those students who had experienced close contact with a disabled person and those who had not. Those who had this experience of close contact showed more favourable attitudes. Lyons and Hayes (1993) discovered that the attitudes of occupational therapy students did not change during their professional education, a finding consistent with that of Lyons (1991). De Poy and Merrill (1988) found that occupational therapy students learned to articulate the humanistic values presented to them but did not necessarily apply them; the students, in turn, believed that the faculty did not practice the values it expounded.

Gething (1992) studied undergraduate health professionals. In this study they watched 12 different videotapes of people applying for a job where the use of a wheelchair, the applicant's manner and the applicant's gender were manipulated. The presence of the wheelchair led to a general devaluing by the health professionals of the individual on characteristics having no necessary relationship to disability, for example psychological and social adjustment. Westbrook et al. (1988) found that student health professionals tended to view disability as more tragic and limiting than statistics indicate, and Gething (1993) found that health professionals make negative judgements of personality and adjustment on the basis of disability.

Lyons and Hayes (1993) found that junior and senior occupational therapy students and business students all identified the same most and least preferred disabilities. The most preferred disabilities were: asthma, diabetes, arthritis, ulcer, amputation and heart disease. The least preferred disabilities were: alcoholism, mental illness, mental handicap and hunchback.

Gordon et al. (1990) found that people with epilepsy were preferred by health care students over those with cerebral palsy, blindness and amputation. There seems to be a preference for physical disabilities, those which are not visible, and those which are perceived to be outside the disabled person's control. Sim maintains that ascription of responsibility is a powerful determinant of stigma. He states:

> Any condition encountered in clinical practice liable to be seen as 'self-inflicted' is potentially a target for stigmatisation on the grounds of moral failure. Somewhat less obviously, patients who fail to display appropriate courage or determination in coping with their disability may be regarded as morally deficient in a similar way. (Sim, 1990: 234)

Paris (1993) believes that the negative attitudes of health professionals towards disabled people must be examined for the following reasons:

- Negative attitudes may adversely affect the self-image and recovery of recently injured or disabled people.
- Health professionals may influence the attitudes of the general public towards disabled people.
- Negative attitudes may affect the delivery of services to disabled people.
- Negative attitudes may influence funding decisions.
- Negative attitudes may influence the attitudes of health care students, thus perpetuating a negative image of disabled people.

The attitudes of health professionals are influential in shaping services for disabled people and their life opportunities. Lyons (1991) doubts whether students with anything but highly positive attitudes towards disabled people should be accepted in the health professions. Talking of occupational therapy he states: 'Persons with disabilities have a right to expect that occupational therapy students will receive an education that prepares them to be professionals that are enabling rather than disabling by virtue of their attitudes' (Lyons, 1991: 516).

Other research evidence indicates that the attitudes of health professionals towards disabled people are more positive than those of the general public, and that their attitudes improve during professional education. Huitt and Elston (1991), using the ATDP scale, found attitudes of counsellors more positive than those of the general public, and Gething and Westbrook (1983) found that first-year physiotherapy students had more positive attitudes to disabled people than students of other occupations. Paris (1993), using the ATDP scale, found that fourth-year medical students had more positive attitudes than first-year medical students. Lyons and Hayes (1993) used the DSDS scale to compare the attitudes of occupational therapy students and business students towards disabled people at an Australian University. The occupational therapy students showed much less social distance than the business students although there was no significant difference between the junior and the senior occupational therapy students.

These more positive attitudes may result, to some extent, from the curriculum the students study. Rosswurn (1980) found that the attitudes of a group of nursing students who had received a learning programme planned to promote positive attitudes towards disabled people, had a more positive attitude after the programme, although six months later the improvement was lost. Estes et al. (1991) used the ATDP scale to measure the attitudes of occupational therapy and medical technology students. The occupational therapy curriculum included content related to values and attitudes, contact with disabled people, and information about disability and disabling conditions. The medical technology curriculum did not cover these aspects. Fourth-year occupational therapy students were found to have more positive attitudes than both first-year occupational therapy students and first- and fourth-year medical technology students.

Some of the inconsistencies in the professional literature may be due to the differing nature of professional and personal attitudes. Leonard and Crawford (1989) observed that people's beliefs about the way disabled people should be treated by society, and their own personal reactions to disabled people, were often in conflict. Gordon et al. (1990) found that the attitudes of health professionals varied according to the social context; they were more favourably disposed to working with disabled people than dating or marrying them. Vargo and Semple (1988) studied a cohort of 40 physiotherapy students in their fourth year of study using the ATDP scale. The students were asked to respond first according to their professional reaction and second according to their personal reaction. The students were more positive when they responded professionally ($p = <0.5$).

Health professionals tend to show more positive attitudes when the IDP scale, rather than the ATDP scale, is used. Using the IDP scale, Gething found that nurses and nursing students (Gething, 1992), and physiotherapists (Gething, 1993) had more positive attitudes towards disabled people than the general public. Furthermore those physiotherapists who had daily contact with disabled people had more positive attitudes than those who had less contact.

The fact that the majority of health professionals are women may also be a factor in accounting for their positive attitudes when compared with the general public. Previous research is inconclusive, but many studies show that women have more positive attitudes towards disabled people than men (Furnham and Pendred, 1983; Potts, 1986; Brillhart et al., 1990). Lyons and Hayes (1993) used the DSDS scale to investigate the attitudes of junior and senior occupational therapy students towards disabled people. They found that males chose a far greater social distance from disabled people than females ($p = <0.001$). Similarly, Paris (1993) found that women health professional were more positive towards disabled people than male health professionals. Disabled men tend to be viewed more positively than disabled women by both sexes (Weisel and Florian, 1990).

Attitude change

> The true challenge for rehabilitation in the 1980s is not the development of new technology and miracle drugs but to overcome attitudinal barriers in interaction and relationships through understanding and acceptance. (Rousch, 1986: 1551)

There are many theories of attitude change, but the one which has given rise to the most research is undoubtedly the theory of cognitive dissonance (Festinger 1957). The theory of cognitive dissonance asserts that we seek a state of psychological balance and that our state of mind is negative if our attitudes, or our attitudes and behaviour, are inconsistent. Reber (1985: 129) defines cognitive dissonance as:

> An emotional state set up when two simultaneously held attitudes or cognitions are inconsistent or where there is a conflict between belief and overt behaviour. The resolution of the conflict is assumed to serve as a basis for attitude change in that belief patterns are generally modified so as to be consistent with behaviour.

Thus the health physiotherapist who is expected to carry out treatment procedures with which he or she disagrees, is likely to be in a state of cognitive dissonance. In a situation such as this there may be a shift of attitude to bring it in line with the expected behaviour, or the importance of the discrepancy between the attitude and the behaviour may be minimised by refuting or ignoring it. Alternatively, the health professional may decide to find employment elsewhere or attempt to convert the organisation to his or her way of thinking; these are more difficult options, however, and Baron and Byrne (1991) believe that as human beings we tend to follow the path of least resistance. If there is external justification for our behaviour there is little need for attitude change as we are unlikely to experience cognitive dissonance.

It is necessary to be committed to an attitude or a way of behaving in order to experience cognitive dissonance. The harder someone works towards achieving a goal the more highly that goal is valued and the greater the cognitive dissonance if it turns out to be deficient in some way. Pennington (1986: 74) states: 'any situation in which a person struggles to gain acceptance, is likely to result in the goal when achieved being seen as desirable and worthwhile, regardless of whether it actually is or not'.

The ideas of the growing disability movement, which view disability as a civil rights issue rather than a medical problem, may give rise to cognitive dissonance in those health professionals willing to consider the arguments. Having gone through a long and arduous professional education, and having worked with the best of intentions for many years, it may be difficult to accept that fundamental changes of practice are needed.

Contact with disabled people

Contact with disabled people is an important ingredient in bringing about positive attitude change (McConkey and McCormack, 1983; Berrol, 1984; Sampson, 1991; Lyons and Hayes, 1993). Most people do not get to know about disability at first hand and may avoid disabled people because of feelings of fear and inadequacy. Interacting with a disabled person can place a strain on the encounter and may call into question many taken-for-granted assumptions about the process of communication. It may, for example, be disconcerting when the person with a learning difficulty fails to understand or when the deaf person needs to lip read. Clough (1982) highlights the discomfort of interacting with visually impaired people. He states:

> If someone doesn't look directly at us we feel uncomfortable. If he gazes intently at us we feel equally uncomfortable. If his face and especially his eyes don't immediately respond to what we say we feel slightly deterred, and wonder if he is in any way deficient – so we either speak louder or we get discouraged and turn our attention elsewhere. (Clough, 1982: 34)

Simple contact, or contact on a professional level, does not, however, appear to be enough to bring about positive attitude change (Evans, 1976; Fichten et al., 1985), although the research evidence does, to some extent, conflict (Biori and Oermann, 1993; Paris, 1993). Gething (1993) points out that interaction between the health professional and the disabled person tends to focus on what the disabled person cannot do thereby highlighting the differences between them. Lyons and Hayes, talking of occupational therapy students state: 'In our view much of students' clinical contact with persons with psychiatric disabilities occurs only in situations where, as patients, their problems, deficiencies, or distress are highlighted' (1993: 546).

One factor that consistently seems to promote positive attitudes towards disabled people is equal status contact (Anthony, 1977; Yuker and Block, 1979, McConkey and McCormack, 1983; Mitchell et al., 1984). Contact on an equal level is more likely than professional–client contact to break down stereotypes and promote effective interaction. McConkey and McCormack (1983) found that personal contact on an equal level, where dependence was avoided and where the disabled person could demonstrate competence, was the most successful strategy in bringing about attitude change.

This view is shared by Gething (1992) who believes that effective interaction between disabled and non-disabled people occurs when they are of equal status, where the contact is voluntary and mutually rewarding, and where the context allows the disabled person to present him- or herself as capable and multifaceted. He points out that these features rarely characterise interactions between health professionals and disabled people.

It is important that health professionals, particularly students, have greater equal status contact with disabled people. As well as changing their attitudes through interaction, contact with disabled people outside rehabilitation and other 'special' settings has the potential to change perceptions by drawing attention to the social and physical barriers which disabled people encounter (Allen and Birse, 1991). Gething (1993) believes that it is vitally important to monitor the quality of contact between health professionals and disabled people in order to bring about positive attitude change, and many writers advocate the training and employment of disabled health professionals as a means of changing attitudes within the professions (Turner, 1984; Bennet, 1987; French, 1988; Chinnery, 1991). Positive attitudes would also be promoted by a more equal relationship between health professionals and disabled clients (French, 1994b).

Information about disabled people

Giving information about disability and disabled people is also important in bringing about positive attitude change (McConkey and McCormack, 1983; Berrol, 1984). This may include specific information, such as how to guide a blind person, or broader information concerning the ways disabled people define their situation, and their substantial achievements within the growing disability movement. Duckworth (1988) and Lyons and Hayes (1993) believe that there should be substantial input from disabled people throughout the education of health professionals. This is best achieved by comprehensive disability equality training conducted by qualified disabled trainers.

Some methods of imparting information are more conducive to attitude change than others. McConkey and McCormack (1983) and Dickson et al. (1991) believe that role play is a suitable method for changing attitudes, heightening sensitivity, and familiarising learners with situations they may later encounter. Role playing is perhaps the next best thing to experiencing a genuine event. It does, however, have various advantages over real-life situations in that timing can be made artificially rapid, situations rarely encountered can be enacted, and the learner can receive constructive feedback from supportive colleagues. Mistakes can also be made in a safe environment.

Lyons and Hayes (1993) advocate discussion and reflection of feeling to bring about positive attitude change. According to Beard (1976), attitude change is facilitated by exposure to different points of view and by constructive criticism from other people. Even if attitudes are not changed discussion may help learners to become more tolerant of different viewpoints and perspectives (Curzon, 1990). Discussion does need careful planning, however, or it can degenerate into a forum for the exchange of prejudices.

Social psychologists have discovered, through empirical investigation, many factors which improve the outcome of persuasive communication. These concern the person delivering the message, the message itself, the recipient of the message, and the context in which the message is delivered. It includes such factors as the status and credibility of the communicator, the intensity of the message, whether a one-sided or a two-sided argument is given, and the level of education of the recipients (for a full discussion of persuasive communication see Gross, 1987).

Anthony (1984) concludes that neither information nor contact alone is sufficient to alter attitudes towards disabled people, but that a combination of both factors is required.

A supportive work environment

In order for attitudes and behaviour towards disabled people to change the work environment must be enabling and supportive to health professionals. Marsh and Fisher (1992) believe that managers and practitioners are under enormous pressure to take shortcuts and compromise principles, and that 'user-orientated practice requires user-orientated policies' (Marsh and Fisher, 1992: 38). Chinnery (1990: 53) states that:

> Individual workers may well act in non-disabling ways, but the structure of services which reaches far beyond that which is visible to disabled users, militates actively and very effectively against individual efforts to promote a helpful, non-disabling, client orientated service.

Ellis (1993) notes that advocating for a client can put practitioners into conflict with employers, and Stevenson and Parsloe contend that, 'without a new culture there will be severe limitations on what workers can do' (Stevenson and Parsloe, 1993: 9).

The organisational context and culture should not, however, be used as an excuse for doing nothing, Stevenson and Parsloe (1993) found many examples of excellent practice in the face of organisational opposition. It is also the case that once changes in policy and practice are initiated, shifts in attitude and behaviour are likely to follow (Kilbury et al., 1992).

Conclusion

This chapter has indicated that although research evidence conflicts there is room for improvement in the attitudes of health professionals towards disabled people. In order to promote positive attitudes and behaviour towards disabled people there need to be changes in both professional education and practice. It is important that health professionals receive high-quality disability equality training, that they understand the meaning of disability as disabled people define it, and that they are informed about the important role disabled people have played in the development of services. It is disturbing to note that most research about disabled people has focused on impairment rather than on social and environmental barriers and has been conducted by non-disabled people. Informal, equal status contact with disabled people, and the education and employment of disabled health professionals, would also help promote positive attitudes and improve services to disabled people. As Munro and Elder-Woodward (1992: 41) state: 'The challenge for workers at all levels of community care is to make sure that the service user is in control of his own life style *and* in control of the services surrounding him which are designed to support that life-style.'

Note

Reprinted (with minor alterations) by permission from *Physiotheraphy* (1994), 80(10): 687–93. © The Chartered Society of Physio-Therapy.

SECTION 5: THE WAY FORWARD

The last section of the book contains two chapters which are, in quite different ways, designed to be especially thought-provoking. Dick Leaman shows us the ways in which there is an innate tension in all of our thoughts in this area, between theory and practice, between the seriousness of definitions and the lives of the real people – even between pole-vaulting and the Centre for Integrated Living (you'll see what *that* means when you read the chapter!). Don't be misled by the title – read to the end and find out what it means: and then reflect on the issues it brings to the fore.

Finally, Vic Finkelstein and Ossie Stuart turn our minds to the development of new services. This chapter draws into question many of the assumptions and attitudinal factors that have lain beneath many of the preceding chapters and calls on us all to re-evaluate our approaches to society. They make the point that the unique social contribution disabled people can make to the construction of a more civilised society originates with the insight that there is no causal relation between the possession of a personal deficit and the experience of social incapacity and this fundamentally challenges all prevailing models of disability by replacing them with the social model.

So we have looked at where we started, what we are doing, how it works and how it feels, as well as considering where we should go. The only task remaining to us is to turn it into reality.

16

Four camels of disability

Dick Leaman

Starting from basics

One day in the course of my job as a voluntary sector development worker (disability) in Lambeth, I heard a story about a local disabled woman who had a problem in her accommodation with a door which opened the wrong way around (for her). This caused an enormous difficulty in her daily life and presented a barrier to her activity within her home. When this difficulty so frustrated her that she determined to do something about it she rang for help to Lambeth Social Services Directorate. She spoke to a long-serving and senior social services administrator – a man who was in many ways open to and supportive of progressive ideas although this was buried under deep layers of cynicism and wry protective humour. The disabled woman explained her problem. The social services officer responded that he could not help, because the waiting list for occupational therapy visits was so long that, practically, he could not offer a qualified person to go and do an assessment. He did not say: 'No, social services will not provide the service you are asking for'; the essence of what he said was that access to the service was impossible because there was no effective application procedure. That was the reason the woman could not get the help she needed.

When I heard this story it clattered around in my head and in my imagination I heard the disabled woman saying: 'But I'm not asking you to send a qualified occupational therapist. I just want someone who will come and turn the door.'

A short time before this happened a Health Authority Unit General Manager (Community) had put her head round my open office door on her way past to another meeting, and had said to me: 'If you write a proposal for a CIL in Lambeth, I will fund it'. This relates to the earlier story in that the sort of Centre for Integrated Living (CIL) that I am interested in developing is one that a disabled person can ring up and say: 'I need a door turning', and we will say: 'Right, we will send someone right away to do the job'. We might argue for years afterwards about whose budget or which vote should pay for it, but we will get the thing done in a day or so.

At the new Lambeth CIL we now provide a variety of Independent Living services under the democratic control of local disabled people's own organisations: and these services include a skilled technician who will come and turn a door for you if that is what you say you need.

A straight and sideways look at theory

What is written about above has been called a 'social barriers' model of disability. That is the academic construct which describes our Lambeth CIL Mobile Fix-It Service. One characteristic of both the Lambeth CIL and its political wing, the Lambeth Coalition Of Disabled People (LCODP), is that they have both been very carefully planned; a lot of work in discussions, papers and proposals has laid foundations for our existence and development. The context in which that planning took place was the specific condition prevailing in the inner London borough of Lambeth from the late 1980s. Overall that has been one of financial reduction and crisis in service provision, reflected in the failure of the Welfare State to deal with the management of disability. It also includes the specific structures and bodies which were struggling locally to administer the crisis and the attitudes of key individuals who held positions in the various agencies at the time. Into this unlikely field was brought the seed of ideas which had been produced in collective activity of disabled people, in what is familiarly called the Disability Movement, over the previous 15 or 20 years.

In the early and mid-1970s debates around definitions and terminology had helped (some) disabled people to develop radical new perspectives on the real causes of their problems and thereby on the means and requirements of eliminating them. In the heat and excitement of discovering the tool of theory as if for the first time, 'social' and 'medical' models were compared and contrasted. New ideas and approaches to the control, planning and delivery of services emerged, and the practical expression of these was through the development and work of CILs. In Lambeth, with traditional services facing collapse, some alternative approach was almost dictated – but local politicians, however radical their credentials, were not offering it. The new approach came from disabled people and the issue was whether there was sufficient support and willingness for partnership from the authorities to provide material nourishment for the seed. It began to germinate.

It could be argued whether a 'social' model of disability is the appropriate construct to describe Lambeth CIL. Times have moved on and CILs have changed and model building has taken off as a popular activity. In some places hard-won theory has been reduced to slogans, diverting the challenge to interpret it into a struggle for real social change. In other places the once meaningful debate around terminology and definitions has become the hollow shell of 'political correctness', or else empiricism (anybody should be called whatever they prefer) – that is, it has been totally depoliticised. It should be possible to judge from this chapter whether Lambeth CIL's work is based on a 'social' model. However, this is an individual piece of writing: we all have our own individual model of disability based on our most horrific personal experience. The following is mine.

Case study

I was with a disabled colleague at Heathrow airport and we were sitting, no doubt discussing disability theory, when two porters arrived and started to help us by pushing us in our wheelchairs along the endless passageways to where we needed to go. We were side by side and they were behind us when a friendly conversation was struck up. Unhappily this soon turned into monologue with our porter banging on and on about this wonderful disabled man he had met who rode horses and was a brilliant horserider despite his disability, even flying abroad to ride more horses. Eventually, when this did not stop and more passageways loomed, something had to be done. My colleague and I exchanged glances and one of us spoke from our wheelchair, breaking into the eulogy: 'Yes, I think it's great. I would love to have a go at that, but what I have never understood is how you get the wheelchair on the horse.'

Now, that is not very funny, but what was nightmarish was the man behind going: 'No . . . No . . .' with that tone of voice that means: 'No, that's wrong. I can tell you . . .'. He was still trying to talk again when the other of us carried on: 'What I like is the disabled athletics. My favourite is the wheelchair pole-vaulting . . .' It goes quieter. We could hear imaginations grinding – is this possible? . . . Just, maybe, with the right kind of ramp facing the bar . . . handbrakes on at the top, pole ready across the knees. Then . . . 'It's just like the real thing with able-bodied people. The only difference is you have to mind out for the wheelchair when you are coming down.' That was it. Peace at last.

If we were to develop a 'model' from this experience, would it be a circular one with a large boot attached, and would the construct define successful disability as an able-bodied idiot being stroppily put down by someone in a wheelchair?

Practical development

As a disabled activist in Lambeth since 1984, it was always my agenda to stimulate and support autonomous organisations of disabled people as the means to bringing about social change through empowerment of the oppressed group. Simultaneously with the development of plans for the CIL, I took an initiative to bring together existing organisations in the Borough to unify our activities and provide a forum for collective representation. This became known as the Lambeth Coalition Of Disabled People. There was no possibility of gaining resources for such a body in a climate where funders would only ask: 'What services does it provide?', so we married theory and practice, politics and service delivery. The CIL became the work programme of the LCODP so the two were deliberately and inextricably linked. LCODP became the body which employs workers who develop and run the CIL and in this way it is ensured that the CIL is controlled by disabled people through our representative organisations, and that the Coalition cannot be stopped on the grounds that it does not provide any services. It also ensured that the disabled people involved could not merely complain and criticise the work of professionals but had to develop alternative services and take responsibility for their design and delivery.

It is worth noting that these developments of LCODP and CIL were aided to an extent, though not caused, by the phased implementation of community care legislation, around which the local authority needed to consult with the voluntary sector and service users. This stimulated organisation in the borough and provided an opportunity to present alternative ideas as well as to challenge the principles of failed and inadequate services. The concepts of Independent Living and user-led service are now written in to Lambeth's statutory 'Community Care Plan', and CIL is identified as a priority for support and development. Implementation of the plan is another matter, but at a different political level and possibly involving such bodies as the Social Services Inspectorate.

The primary direction of Lambeth CIL's work is to extend provisions for Independent Living in the Borough and to enable a wider range of disabled people to avail themselves of such opportunities. For this purpose we employ an Independent Living Support Worker. For us this was to a large extent building on the work and experience of another organisation set up around 1985. Lambeth Support and Housing Assistance for Disabled people (SHAD), under the control of local disabled people, had grown to provide integrated housing and 24-hour personal help services for a small number of people who would otherwise be living in institutions or heavily dependent on their families at home. SHAD was a local pioneer of Independent Living, bringing the help that disabled people received (in this case from volunteers) under their full control, and basing the organisation upon the right of that person to lead the life-style of his or her choice from a full range of opportunity.

With community care on the political agenda and resources being directed towards the local authority, but strictly for use in the 'independent' sector, Lambeth CIL in collaboration with the Coalition's members and our close statutory sector colleagues developed further plans to bring Independent Living into the mainstream of provision in the borough. We saw a need for two things. First, an agency which would enable individuals to make more or less direct use of local authority funding to buy in their own personal help arrangements, and which would provide services and/or technical support according to a disabled person's own requirements for Independent Living. Second, training for Independent Living, that is, to raise the expectations and demand of disabled people, acknowledging that the phrase we are using to identify radical new concepts and practices is jargon to most people in the community, who would probably not dare dream beyond the level of obtaining a little more help – and are certainly not out there queuing to apply for an Independent Living situation package.

In 1993 our proposals met with some success, and we now employ a part-time Independent Living Development Worker who has worked to the point where it will soon be a concrete funding proposal and a part-time Independent Living Training Officer who is developing programmes for both disabled people and professionals in the community. This proposal for expanding Independent Living opportunities under the aegis of the CIL would, were it successful, represent a significant devolution of resources (and responsibilities) to organised disabled people in the borough.

Difficulties in real partnership

Much that is inaccurate is spoken about partnership between local authorities and voluntary organisations in service provision. Usually this refers to a relationship where all the power is on one side and ultimately the voluntary sector party is funded by the authority. However, in the Lambeth CIL we have forged a close practical working relationship with the Council's Occupational Therapy department and there is now in operation at the CIL an Equipment Service to which a disabled person can come, see an occupational therapist, and go home with a piece of equipment or specialised aid to meet his or her need. Before this service opened there was no access to such advice or equipment because referrals only went on to a grossly extended waiting list for home visits. We have here an attempt at a practical, working partnership, one which, although very exciting and productive, is constantly challenging and raises all kinds of issues for both parties.

The idea was never that we would simply be two separate operations which just coexist in the same space, but it has to be said that we have not yet fully worked out what our interrelationship is. Real practical difficulties arise because, for example, social services has not yet been able to supply reliable administrative/receptionist support for the service and this affects the CIL's work. Our regular occupational therapist went on maternity leave just as the service was opening, and since then there have been irregular variations in when an occupational therapist is available. Some of us worry about the extent to which CIL is being associated by local disabled people with their unsatisfactory experience of social services. There is an inevitable tendency, until we sort out these problems, for the two to split into 'them' and 'us' but it is very important that we work this through.

Recently, after a lot of intense discussion, we adopted an operational policy. The key to it is the statement 'It is not just that we do different things: the point is that we do things differently'. I suspect that this indicates where we have to examine for a resolution to our problem. It is not just about our manner and being nice and caring to people. We in CIL have no monopoly on that. It has to do with how we are able to manage our services, whom we are accountable to, what powers we have, and the constraints under which we work.

This section has focused on difficulty, but I do not want to end here on a negative note. These practical difficulties are exactly the issues we have to deal with and these are the issues which will show us who are our real friends and supporters, whether or not they are disabled or able-bodied professional people.

The CIL must never be seen as an end in itself, nor as a final solution to our problems. It is a step on the way. It is a tool we can use. Similarly, models of this or that kind of disability have to be challenged to show how they help us not merely (academically) to describe our struggle, but to help us to bring it to unification and to a better collective understanding of the powers which obstruct our liberation. It is only by understanding those powers that we will be able to oppose them.

Lambeth ACCORD

Lambeth ACCORD is the disability organisation that I have worked for since the middle of 1984, when it was being set up; it is a unique and hybrid organisation by Lambeth out of Brussels. Largely oriented towards vocational assessment and training, it nevertheless manages to maintain a comprehensive approach to disability and to the empowerment of all kinds of disabled people in the local community.

All the work and development that I have described in Lambeth has been brought about and facilitated by ACCORD, a voluntary organisation with a principled and consistently non-sectarian approach to supporting disabled people's activity. Mine is not the only work of this kind which has been accomplished by ACCORD employees, and notably we have been leading agents in development work with local people with learning difficulties. In the last 10 or 15 years there has been a great increase in the numbers of disabled people who have been able to find paid employment in the 'disability' field. We are disability professionals. Some work for statutory authorities, others in the voluntary sector; many have simply set up in business as consultants, trainers, and freelance 'experts'. The outcomes of our work will probably demonstrate the principles and 'models' we are working to and how these are constrained or enhanced by our employment or income-generating conditions. ACCORD has been unique in this respect. It is not an organisation that could ever be replicated but it should be significant in any study of disability professionalism in our time, and its relation to the Disability Movement in this country and abroad.

Note

The author apologises for the chapter title, which should of course be 'Four Cameos of Disability': but it has all been done in a bit of a rush and there are bound to be typing errors. So, reader, enjoy the chapter and remember the title! Our struggle is without doubt very hard, but that does not mean that we cannot have fun with it, nor that we theorists and activists are sad and miserable people. See you at the pole-vaulting – or at Lambeth CIL.

17

Developing new services

Vic Finkelstein and Ossie Stuart

In the 1970s a small group of dissatisfied disabled people began to question prevailing beliefs about the causes of their dependency on welfare and the care of voluntary and statutory services. They regarded themselves as perfectly capable of controlling their own lives and concluded that their dependency was the result of disabling barriers created by a world designed for able-bodied living, rather than the result of any personal impairments (physical or mental defects). This interpretation involved a clear distinction between the conditions of 'impairment' and 'disability'. The meaning of 'disability' was radically redefined and it was recognised that this had fundamental implications for the development of new approaches to support systems (UPIAS, 1972). However, the deficit interpretation of disability was so absolutely unquestioned at that time that there was little prospect of promoting new approaches for services until the social interpretation of disability was at least recognised as a legitimate alternative. All attention, therefore, was given to promoting the argument that disability can be interpreted, just as well and most fruitfully, as being socially created. When this group published its views (UPIAS, 1976) Mike Oliver identified this interpretation as a 'social model of disability' and contrasted this with what he called the dominant 'medical model' (Oliver, 1983).

The social model of disability incorporates a holistic interpretation of the situation facing disabled people. It suggests that people with physical and mental impairments can have satisfying life-styles *as disabled people* if the focus of attention is shifted towards the removal of disabling barriers rather than concentrating only on the rehabilitation of disabled individuals (over-coming the effects of personal impairments). It is only recently, however, that the growing acceptance of this model has made it possible to turn attention to furthering the analysis and to providing an expanded view of the type of services that might be needed to assist disabled people remove the social and personal disabling barriers.

It is still at the earliest stage of speculation to consider what will be the future of services for disabled people when informed by the social model of disability. This is when the untravelled road from fantasy to reality is at its most confusing and daunting but also, nevertheless, challenging, stimulating and exciting. This is particularly so when we realise that for the first time in human history it has become possible for disabled people to achieve equal citizenship with their able-bodied peers and to play a corresponding role in the development of society. For the present generation, however, the challenge is to identify the effective route to emancipation and to set in motion those changes to the services and their structure which will lead to an appropriate community-based support system. For this we need not only a sound and detailed theory but also good information about all the relevant facts (see, for example, Cale and McCahan, 1993; Nelson, 1994). Unfortunately, disabled people and their organisations are still almost completely absent from any real decision-making in the planning and delivery of services and public utilities which they may use. This includes the welfare system, housing, state benefits, education, transport, access to public buildings and, perhaps most important of all, employment. Information about appropriate services, then, arising out of the experience and perspectives of disabled people's life-styles is very limited.

Given the limitations in our knowledge, in this chapter we can only speculate about the kind of services that might be established if the social model were to provide the principles underlying support systems for disabled people in the United Kingdom. Despite this limitation the discussion about what are appropriate services for disabled people provides us with an opportunity to explore what we hope are both radical ideas and realistic end goals. In challenging the image of what having an impairment might be in one possible future, of necessity we also use the opportunity to re-imagine the boundaries of health and welfare provision.

A frequent complaint made by more active members of the 'disability movement' is that despite stated intentions the approach to welfare provision in 'Care in the Community' legislation both limits the opportunity for disabled people to control their own lives and at the same time maintains their dependency on others. In other words this policy is accused of adding yet another set of disabling barriers to confront the life-styles of all disabled people. A future system underwritten by the social model of disability would need, therefore, to have as its fundamental principle only the provision of support for disabled people which is at the same time empowering. The purpose would be to recognise the right of disabled people to their own forms of social responsibility which enable them to control their own lives.

The term 'services for disabled people' in our proposed world of the future has a particular meaning. We believe that this can no longer be accepted as involving variations in the 'cure' or 'care' management of disabled individuals. In the new world, we believe, services for disabled people should be conceived in terms of 'support' and would acquire an enabling role in the same way that public utilities (for example, postal services, railways, water and electricity supplies, and so on) are created by able-bodied people for able-bodied people to enable more satisfying life-styles. As such, they form part of the necessary public support network which enables both full participation in society and citizenship rights.

In the current service structures the resources provided to disabled people for transport, education, leisure, child support and employment all fall under the umbrella of 'special' provision and the philosophy of caring for the 'unable'. If the reality of the life experience of disabled people is to inform seriously the development of new support systems then it will be necessary to create these outside a caring paradigm which classifies all interventions in relation to disabled people within a culture of 'special' needs. The appearance of the term 'special' in the vocabulary of professional and voluntary workers with disabled people in the health, welfare, education, housing, leisure, transport and employment fields is the most public expression of a 'disabling culture' that maintains a distance between disabled people and their non-disabled peers.

Albrecht (1992: 20) tells us that:

> disability is strongly influenced by cultural and economic factors . . . persons with disabilities are found in societies across all cultures and throughout history, yet their identification and adaptive patterns vary markedly by culture, political economy, and environment. Therefore any analysis of impairment, disability and handicap in a society requires that persons with disabilities be studied in their cultural and political economic context.

And

> The climate of persons with disabilities is shaped by the culture, values, and institutions that produce, define, and respond to disability. In our society, social problems have become the objects of massive human services that drive our economic system. These businesses identify social problems embedded in individuals and their social relationships, reify them, and make them and their solutions commodities to be bought and sold in the marketplace. In this context, disability is a reified concept abstracted from a set of social relationships and constructed into a social problem. (Albrecht, 1992: 27)

Despite its support for the greater employment of disabled people, the International Labour Organisation still locates the source of unemployment among disabled people within individuals with impairments: 'for the purposes of this Convention, the term 'disabled person' means an individual whose prospects of securing, retaining and advancing in suitable employment are substantially reduced as a result of a duly recognised physical or mental impairment' (quoted in Gaff, 1994: 69).

What is commonplace to non-disabled people is 'special' to disabled people because of its unfamiliarity and limited relevance. That the *common* in the lives of disabled people is perceived as *special* in the lives of non-disabled people, especially service providers, reflects the absence of disabled people's real impact on the way society is structured. When ramps, British Sign Language and bleeping zebra crossings, for example, are commonplace and disabled people have a direct impact on the structures of society then able-bodied people will find their life-styles being influenced by disabled people in the same way that disabled people presently find their lives being shaped by non-disabled people. In such a dynamic interrelationship of equals it would no longer make sense to identify disabled people's needs as special any more than, for example, to regard a stand-up urinal as a provision for the special needs of able-bodied men! The idea that disabled people's needs are special has become part of the uncritical dogma that informs service provision in Britain. This dogma is supported by a well-established, extremely pervasive, 'disabling culture'. However, before discussing the impact of this disabling culture in preventing any significant changes to the way services for disabled people are visualised and implemented we need at least to question the relevance and success of other struggles against entrenched discriminatory cultures (such as racism and sexism) where examples of good practice might be expected to be found.

Sharing lessons

Despite the promotion of 'collaboration' and emphasis on 'consultation' the relationship between service professionals and users often involves inequality and dependency. Power, responsibility and authority reside with the professional and not with the user. Users have a limited and mostly perfunctory role in the assessment for community support that they might require. Until very recently they have had no role in shaping the services and in creating the professions to run those services. We believe that there is growing evidence that service structures and the way they are currently maintained prevents disabled service user autonomy and responsibility even when there are attempts at re-negotiating the relationship between professional and user. This is exemplified in the lengthy discussion in a book by Davis and Mullender (1993: 70) in which they say: 'The "co-equal" basis of the relationship between the Coalition and the County Council, was clearly shown by the events of this time to be easier to write into the DCIL constitution, than to put into practice in the real world' (see also Davis and Mullender, 1993, especially Chapters 9, 12 and 15). Services of the future, then, must ensure that users and their organisations play a central and decisive role in any assessment and goal setting process. The role of the service provider should be just that – to *provide* services and allocate resources which would enable the attainment of life-style goals which the user has identified as most appropriate to his or her personal circumstances. We will suggest one way in which users and their organisations can exercise this responsibility below.

For inspiration about changing social relationships and the discriminatory cultures that feed prejudice many people have turned to the strategy of the civil rights movements of the United States and the United Kingdom as useful models to copy. In this model a civil rights bill would include the formation of a commission, like the Commission for Racial Equality, to provide expert advice on disability issues and investigate cases. Applying the lessons from the civil rights movement of black Americans and the political tactics of the British anti-racist movement, it is believed, ought to bring positive results. The demand for the same concessions conceded to the British anti-racist movement should provide clear objectives and justification for legislation to prevent discrimination. To many people black political organisations are believed to have achieved nothing but good for the people they fought for.

Yet, we need to ask, has this hard-earned legislation transformed the lives of black people for the better? The singular success of the anti-racist legislation means that the ethnic minority population now have legal redress if they are racially discriminated against in employment or receive discriminatory services. For example, under this legislation workers of ethnic minority origin can obtain legal redress if they are discriminated against on grounds of race. Public employees will face severe disciplinary action for behaviour considered racially motivated. All publicly funded organisations are obliged to apply equal opportunities criteria to their employment practices when dealing with customers.

Such legislation is quite unique in Europe. Few countries in the world have sought to create comprehensive legislation to protect their minority population. The importance of British anti-discriminatory legislation should not be underestimated. Yet, this legislation has obviously not removed discrimination from the day-to-day experience of the ethnic minority population. This conclusion highlights limits to the gains that are possible through civil rights legislation. In other words anti-racist legislation cannot be an end in itself but only a beginning.

We do not simply reject the views of disabled people who advocate the adoption of black civil rights strategies when we suggest that they may be too uncritical in adopting what has only led to a relative achievement for black people. However, the comparative failure of this legislation to transform the lives of the ethnic minority population in Britain ought not to be ignored. The legislation has singularly failed Asian youths caught up in vicious racially motivated gang warfare across both North and East London. It has failed those murdered and maimed in race attacks. It has failed in preventing cases of racially motivated injustice by the police. It has failed black youth caught in pockets of grinding poverty, unable to obtain decent education or employment. It has also failed the victims of immigration laws which allow for the wholesale criminalisation and eventual expulsion of Jamaicans seeking to visit this country to spend Christmas with their relatives. Similar legislation in the United States has failed to prevent the impoverishment of generations of African Americans.

Few can disagree with the view that it is far better for Britain's ethnic minority population to have some form of protective legal framework in place than to have nothing at all. However, this comforting thought fails to address the whole question. Why are people only perceptibly better off under what is still quite radical and unprecedented legislation? The answer to this question provides the fundamental prerequisite without which any civil rights legislation cannot be meaningful.

In our view the reason for the relative failure of such legislation can be found in the absence of fundamental changes in the value placed upon human beings, regardless of ethnic origin (or, for that matter, whether they have an impairment). Put simply, attitudes towards black people embedded in British culture mean that racist assumptions about black and Asian culture continue to set the boundaries of the black British experience for the foreseeable future. Without cultural change legislation of the kind championed by ethnic minorities will remain restricted and of limited value. Cultures (in this case a racist culture) are far too entrenched to be simply changed through a process of introducing new laws.

Lasting change requires more than merely winning the battle for civil rights for disabled people. It requires more than just the support of a benign government. It requires more than a disability commission with a key 'policing' role over the delivery of services and responsibility for the representation of impairment in popular culture and the media. The engine of change requires the sum of these things but more. It requires all these things within a context of a fundamental transformation of the restricted cultural view of disability in the United Kingdom. We have called this cultural barrier a 'disabling culture' and it stands in contrast and in opposition to the development of a 'disability culture' being created by the movement of disabled people in the UK.

A disabling culture

At this moment services for disabled people are framed by a 'disabling culture' which assumes that certain negative social consequences are bound to arise out of the possession of an impairment; disability is an individual experience; it is an experience of deprivation and disadvantage. From this perspective, it also logically assumes that the welfare state is the primary vehicle with which to meet the needs of disabled people. Here, the problem of disability is seen as one of a relationship between an individual and welfare state services. These 'problems' are peculiar to each individual and thought to be quite separate from prevailing political and social structures (Shakespeare, 1993).

The dominant cultural view of disability is bound very closely to the idea that disabled people's needs are separate from the political economy. Disability itself is perceived as being neutral (or apolitical). As Shakespeare (1993) reminds us, disabled people are seen not as a collective, but rather as a series of individuals with specific medical problems. The rhetoric of user empowerment, typified by the introduction of the 1990 Community Care Act, does not disguise the fact that services delivered to disabled people are still informed by administrative concerns (what to do about the 'needy') rather than civil rights. In the light of the current emphasis on community care it seems strange that this model of intervention is dismissed so extensively: 'The "community care" framework, which for 30 years between 1960 and 1990 provided model problems and model solutions, has become obsolete in the design, planning, implementation of evaluation of human services' (Baldwin, 1993: 17). Despite the claims of social policy research, which influences policy makers in this field, that the social model of disability has been taken on board their aim, to improve *current* policies and to introduce new ones through empirical investigation and the persuasive power of case studies in the individual experience of disability, counters their claim. We agree with

Shakespeare when he argues that social policy has progressed no further than rhetoric in adopting the social model of disability.

It is easy to criticise such non-progressive assumptions. However, those who campaign for a radical adoption of the social model of disability face a real dilemma. The reality is that their constituency, the vast majority of disabled people are non-politicised, are marinated in a disabling culture and identify themselves with a repressive, rather than a progressive, model of disability. There is a real danger that, as with both the equal opportunities campaign in the UK and the civil rights movement in the USA, the 'freedoms' and 'rights' which are won for this group of people will be of no real material benefit to them. In other words, the structures and culture which create disabling barriers will remain largely untouched. Disability will continue to be perceived as a problem carried within the individual. The state will continue to tinker and improve the welfare system to compensate individuals for their impairments. The power over resources will remain with health professionals. Finally, disability will continue to reside outside the political sphere.

The counter to this gloomy disabling culture is relatively straightforward although obviously no easy practical task for those wishing to implement change. It requires the transformation of a disabling culture, which is captured and entrenched in a health and welfare approach to disability, into an egalitarian culture which celebrates the validity of differing life-styles. It is precisely this need to counter the prevailing culture that has motivated the UK disability movement to create its own celebration of difference in the form of a 'disability culture'. This growing disability culture represents a tentative, but nevertheless very real, practical challenge to the fundamental cultural misconception that a health service in a welfare state can properly intervene to reduce the effects of disablement.

From the beginning

In a future where a disabling culture is no longer an obstacle to service development for disabled people we can expect the introduction of two principles to guide the way social support is made available. First, given that a social model of disability would now inform practice, the disadvantages that disabled people face would be recognised much more as a consequence of barriers to accessing public utilities and services concerned with the general quality of social life. The first principle, then, would be that all utilities and services which are regarded as important to the well-being of the country's citizenship must also be accessible to all disabled people as of right. In addition, since the social model informs us that the disadvantages to a disabled life-style are related to the way society is designed for able-bodied living, the second principle states that disability-specific services should be located within those sectors of social management (national and local voluntary or government administration) which are concerned with the development and maintenance of a favourable environment. This suggests that the removal of disabling barriers should be a concern of all government departments rather than the special responsibility of the health and welfare sector. At the social level, then, it would make sense to assign coordination of the disability specific services to the Department of the Environment. We will return to the radical consequences of applying these two principles, derived from the social model of disability, in concluding this chapter.

Since the social approach to disability involves the reduction of disabling cultural and environmental barriers in all areas of life this has implications for all situations and stages in a person's life. The first service concern, then, starts in the beginning, with the conception of a foetus with impairments. The absence of a disabling culture among medical and health workers would mean that prejudice towards the possessor of an 'impairment' is reduced. To put a simple example, the question of abortion would arise not in relation to preventing 'disability' but only out of a woman's 'right to choose' or medical concerns about the mother or baby. The cultural value placed on an impaired child which does not endanger its mother while pregnant or at birth would differ little from that of any other newborn baby. It would be quite improper for medical intervention to be offered on the basis of an assumed future poor quality of life *because of disability*. This, it is worth repeating, is a quite separate matter to those medical interventions which are rightly concerned with reducing the effects of impairments.

Disability-related service interventions after the birth of a child with impairments would have two concerns. First, to target those barriers which might impede the baby's development in exploring, manipulating and knowing the world in which it is developing its own personal life-style. Second, to provide support so that the disabled child's parents are able to establish and maintain a parental relationship with their disabled child unhindered by the need to protect the child from a hostile world which is mainly designed for the convenience of those who conform to cultural expectations of able-bodied standards. Meeting the latter concern means also that parents do not have to give up their jobs or substantially change their life-styles because a disabled child has joined the family. The focus of attention, however, must be concerned with assisting the development of the child's life-style rather than the needs of the carers. It is our contention that providing appropriate support to the disabled person is not only the proper way of responding to the central concerns of that person's development but also the most effective way of ensuring that carers do not enter life-styles in which their own wishes and goals are neglected.

Supporting a disabled child so that it develops into an active, confident and knowledgeable citizen also depends upon the degree of responsibility afforded to it as it grows. Any child with an impairment must enjoy the same opportunities to learn social skills as its able-bodied peers. Shifting the responsibility for barrier removal to the Department of Environment should ensure that disabled children of school age are no longer smothered by a welfare service that is so concerned with care and protection that it loses sight of disabled people's citizenship rights to make their own (risky if necessary) choices and have an active influence on the world in which they live: 'Independent living is about access; access to schools, jobs, transport, houses, public buildings and leisure etc. – all the things that non-disabled people take for granted – and about disabled people having control of the services they need' (Bracking, 1993: 14).

All too often both professionals and parents unthinkingly collaborate in protecting disabled children from risk taking and personal responsibility. A consequence is that disabled children can grow into adulthood poorly equipped with the social skills necessary to form meaningful relationships, to compete for jobs and to sustain their own independent households. This completes the 'vicious circle' – disabled people need to be protected because they lack the social skills for running their own lives. The welfare mentality rooted in a disabling culture with a passion for 'special' provision animates what amounts to a conspiracy of protection between legislators, government, service providers, carers and sometimes, guardians or parents. One devastating consequence has been segregation in special schools where the curriculum and preparation for adulthood are guided by a perspective of long-term dependency on carers, permanent unemployability compensated for by a holy quest for meaningful leisure activities, and an end goal of isolation from public view. Not infrequently even this limited programme is interrupted for medical interventions: 'Some American laws, for example, define disability as "an inability to engage in substantial gainful activity", a definition that identifies disability with unemployability' (Albrecht, 1992: 21). Morris (1994: 61) puts it this way: 'Disabled people are not normal in the eyes of non-disabled people. Our physical and intellectual characteristics are not "right" or "admirable" and we do not "belong".'

The demise of the special school in response to the adoption of the social model means that disabled people must have the educational opportunity to learn the skills necessary for them to become socially responsible people. Disabled children would enter mainstream schools not only as a route to future employment.

> It is widely accepted that the best way of preventing discrimination against disabled people in education is to ensure that mainstream facilities are accessible and that disabled people can, as far as possible, be integrated into them. (Foley and Pratt, 1994: 42)

Social skills are part of cultural life and if the disabling culture is to be challenged effectively then disabled children must, too, have a stimulating presence in the schools where the important building blocks of culture are learnt. Skills, such as interacting with peer groups, learning respect for authority, the management of personal hygiene, even the management of time has to be taught to every child. The presence of disabled children in such a learning environment, supported by a curriculum which responds to the messages signalled by a disability culture, will ensure that these skills are not one-sided – disabled children assimilating the values and culture of the able-bodied world – but multifaceted skills where able-bodied children as well as their disabled peers learn the advantages of a different time scale in carrying out activities, the excitement of being skilled in multimedia forms of communication, the benefits of multifarious approaches to mobility, and the advantages of collateral thinking that is necessary for the removal of barriers to different life-style experiences. It is in this sense, in sharing experiences and the lessons of different life-styles, that the education system in our new world would become an integrated system.

To guarantee that there is indeed an equal participation and contribution between disabled and non-disabled people to the culture of the educational system in a school we believe that the board of governors should be legally bound to include representative members of the local disabled people's organisation. Their task would be to ensure that the advantages of a disability culture, celebrating the value of diverse life experiences, drives into obscurity the disabling culture which maintains integration is best advanced through dealing with the special educational needs of individual disabled pupils. This task would include monitoring the training of both able-bodied and disabled teachers and lecturers. The expectation is that these employees would be informed about, and sensitive to, the educational implications of schooling in a world shaped by multicultural influences. By this we mean that a disability culture will be accepted as legitimately standing alongside the cultures of ethnic groups and the different viewpoints of feminism.

We acknowledge, of course, that there are difficulties in ensuring true representation:

> There is considerable disagreement between the more traditional organisations of disabled people in the voluntary sector and the newer organisations of disabled people about how to give users a voice. (Hoyes et al., 1993: 39)

The local disability organisations would also have a role in the identification and removal of educational and classroom barriers which might limit possibilities for integration. The curriculum, for example, would include as a matter of course the perspectives of different social groups when presenting educational exercises. Just as girls and not only boys need to be seen in active roles in English storybooks, so disabled people need to be seen participating in social events in their own inimitable style. Sentences which refer to 'walking' and 'running' need to be balanced from time to time with sentences referring to 'wheeling' and 'pushing'. Similarly 'signing' can be placed on an equal footing with 'talking'. The intention is to give equivalence to different forms of mobility and communication, and so on.

Classroom barriers, such as reading from a blackboard, would be monitored to ensure that students with visual impairments are not provided with alternatives which are regarded as 'special' provision to compensate for disability. The natural approach cultivated would be multimedia communication for all and, as such, this would include forms of communication accessible to students with and without impairments. Similarly, the classroom architecture would need to be monitored to ensure that no one group of students is put at a disadvantage in negotiating movement through this environment. A disabled child sitting at a desk involving craft work, for example, should not be confronted by any barriers which prevent access to materials so that he or she has to ask others for help. Barriers of this kind not only covertly encourage passivity among disabled students but ensure that, in addition to the craft work skills, they are also learning skills in managing dependency on others. At the same time fellow students are learning that disabled people are dependent people. While support would be on hand to ensure that all children can meet the school's routine, including matters of health, this would not take priority over a child's curriculum. Morris (1993: 173) makes a related point to the provision of assistance in the home situation: 'Those who need help with daily living activities cannot be treated with respect, their autonomy cannot be promoted, if their physical require-ments are assumed to turn them into "dependent people".'

Good-quality access, small class size, well-trained support workers and personal assistance can all contribute to the move away from a problem-oriented approach which pays too much attention to what disabled children cannot do rather than the disabling barriers which may prevent success in achieving the goals which they have set for themselves. For example, learning to write with a pen or pencil should not become an imperative which then denies the acceptability of other forms of record keeping and communication, such as using a cassette recorder or portable word processor. Another example might involve school sports and recreation, particularly where team games are part of the curriculum. These would have to include a contribution from all pupils. So, alongside sports normally associated with school activities, such as soccer, netball and athletics, opportunity for participating in archery, basketball and table tennis should also be possible at most primary and secondary schools. Integration raises the possibility of not only replicating each sporting event with an equivalent form accessible to disabled students – for example, the 100 metre sprint is mirrored by the 100 metre wheelchair dash – but also innovating exciting new sports such as a 100 metre wheelchair run with an able-bodied person pushing a wheelchair steered by a disabled user over an obstacle course, or more simply, a relay race with mixed participants.

The view that there are 'special needs children' not only reflects the extent to which the disabling culture has pervaded the education service but confirms the almost total absence of disabled adults in shaping the world in which we learn and pass on values from one generation to another. Unlike the world where able-bodied adults have a decisive say in the shape of educational provision for able-bodied children, disabled adults have no recognised right to influence the education of disabled children. On the contrary, the disabling culture assigns this right to able-bodied people who then, in contrast to their own education, see the education of disabled children in terms of 'special' provision. The disabling culture transforms ordinary human needs into special needs and corrupts the identity of disabled children into special needs children.

In concluding our argument in this section that services for disabled children must abandon the disabling culture as its source of inspiration we need to ask whether the development of future services for disabled adults based upon the social model of disability faces the same challenge. In other words if there are 'special needs children' does the disabling culture also identify 'special needs adults'? Do 'special needs children' grow into 'special needs adults'?

Towards an end

While adults in general are expected to manage their own life-styles, the disabling culture sees no autonomous social functioning in the mainstream of social life for disabled people outside the network of 'care'. Until recently the overwhelming disabling barriers have prevented disabled adults from countering this view and this, together with the absence of champions in the same way that able-bodied parents championed the welfare of their disabled children, has contributed to unimaginative and limited services. The dominant perspective for those disabled people unable to negotiate the disabling barriers in the community has been a future in a residential institution. Closing down these institutions has only meant that the institutional approach to care has moved into the community under the 'community care' fiat.

When services are developed for disabled adults with the same assumptions underlying the concept of 'special needs children' there can be little opportunity for practitioners, who are often poorly trained, to solicit a valid and central input from the users or their representatives in the process of identifying appropriate interventions. The social model of disability, on the other hand, turns this on its head and makes the disabled person the provocateur of change in determining his or her own life-style. The service provider, then, is assigned the role of providing encouragement and support in this process. Disabled people cease to be 'special needs people' and start to become citizens with all the rights of consumer choice in what products they wish to purchase and use in making their own lives.

The thrust of intervention, therefore, settles on the provision of support. This includes providing resources to assist disabled individuals identify the personal and social barriers that they face and helping them to devise ways of overcoming these barriers. The overwhelming emphasis in this approach is that the disabled person has to have a deciding 'vote' in the decision making which affects his or her life-style. This not only goes further than current concessions on 'consultation' with disabled people but effectively challenges the validity of community *care* as an approach to the support systems needed for independent life in the community.

In our fantasy of a non-disabling future, precisely because this is a new world where the disabling culture is extinct, the close involvement of disabled people both individually and collectively in the planning, establishment, delivery and evaluation of services will be paramount. This will go a long way in ensuring that any proposed new service does not suffer the same fate as its predecessors based on the individual (or medical or administrative) model of disability – start with great hope and end discredited as yet another barrier laid on the shoulders of disabled people. A non-disabling future should not be seen as resting solely on the action of individuals. We see this as of necessity involving the scrutiny of designated organisations of disabled people structured into the support system at all levels.

This viewpoint gives us the main criteria for the future development of community-based support services for disabled adults based upon the social interpretation of disability – the target is the dismantling of disabling barriers and the management of this process is vested in the democratic control of disabled adults. In practice this means that the removal of disabling barriers is relegated to a practical and technical, rather than a clinical, task and its control becomes a socio-political issue involving citizenship rights. This would immediately re-align the power relationship between those who provide services and those who use them. It would do this because it replaces the dependency-making 'care' package with its emphasis on assessment of 'needs' and the inevitable dominance of the professional practitioner's viewpoint over that of the service user 'client'. This change would place disabled adults in a key position to provide role models for disabled children, undermine the philosophy of provision based upon special needs, counter the public image of disability meaning inadequacy and dependency, provide extra legitimacy and interest in a disability culture which reflects the life experiences of disabled people, and create a framework for disability-related support networks which impact positively on the quality of life of all citizens.

Designing accessible buildings, public transport systems, comfortable and efficient mobility aids such as wheelchairs, visual and hearing aids, readily accessible multimedia communication systems, and so on, as well as providing appropriate personal help, teaching disabled people how to manage personal assistance and financial arrangements, and so on, are enormous tasks involving many people and relying on access to many skills. In this context it should be clear that what we have said here, and elsewhere in this chapter, should not be interpreted as meaning we see no role or future for able-bodied professionals in the management and delivery of support systems. We do feel, however, that the application of the social model implies a change in the location of service providers. We feel that it will no longer make sense for community-based support services to be developed, staffed and maintained from the health and welfare setting. The provision of technical assistance in adapting a home for a disabled person, for example, seems more logically coordinated from housing departments than social services and the underlying knowledge base for the assessment and design of such adaptations seems most appropriately located in the architectural and engineering sciences. We can envisage the training of experts in housing adaptations for disabled people obtaining their qualifications in schools of architecture where not only the lessons of mainstream design informs disability design but standards set by disabled people (for example, wider doorways for wheelchair access, or greater variety in the location of lighting for flexible use by people with visual impairments) can impact on building codes that are set for all people.

Many services, of course, could be effectively transferred to Centres for Integrated (or Independent) Living (CILs) where disabled people have a direct management role. This is already strenuously advocated by those setting up CILs in the UK. Seconding, or locating, professional practitioners currently employed by the statutory services in the CILs under the management of disabled people would be an important development on the road to new service provision. Coordinating direct payment and contracts with employees for personal assistance could, for example, also be facilitated through CILs where disabled people are taught the skills of personal financial management and have access to assistance when needed. This could also have the two-fold function of ensuring that all responsibility for using social provision does not fall solely on the shoulders of hard-pressed disabled individuals. At the same time the CIL management structure (with representatives from local govern- ment) could provide a means of monitoring the expenditure of socially provided funding for personal services.

In market economies adulthood and status are endorsed by access to employment. Disabling barriers to employment, however, have proved to be the most resistant to change and the disabling culture, which all too often concedes that impairment leads to unemployability, makes advances in this area very difficult to progress. This, of course, is one reason why so many disabled people have turned to 'disability awareness' or 'equal opportunities' training as a way of influencing access to employment. Foley and Pratt draw attention to this difficulty in changing discrimination in employment:

> The government's continued and exclusive reliance on 'education and persuasion' to overcome the disadvantages faced by disabled people is difficult to understand when its own research so conclusively demonstrates that it has been ineffective in eradicating prejudice and discrimination in employment. (Foley and Pratt, 1994: 36)

It is folly to assume, however, that the removal of barriers to the employment of disabled people will not increase the costs of production or the costs of marketing and selling products and services. If one company, or the business enterprises in one country, include disabled employees while others do not this can influence the balance of competition. We are all aware of how access to 'cheap' labour can give industry in one country an edge in the international competition war. This has two implications. First, encourag- ing the employment of disabled people only makes sense when all competitors in the market are faced with the same, or similar costs – in other words the removal of disabling barriers to the employment of disabled people is an international civil rights issue and involves the establishment of a level ground in the international market. Clearly, this becomes an issue for the United Nations organisation in promoting international agreements and in ensuring international policing. Second, just as the international proscription against 'cheap' child labour represents an advance in the civilised state of all humanity we would argue that removing disabling barriers to the employment of disabled people at the international level reflects another gain for all human beings. This is no less than recognising the need for a world-wide campaign against a disabling culture that is sustained by the international market system. The adoption of a social approach to disability by organisations such as the Disabled Peoples International marks an important development in understanding the way forward in addressing the practical needs of disabled people within the employment setting. There is an interesting discussion on the role played by the Disabled Peoples International in this context in Lewis (1994).

And, finally . . .

If the social model of disability is to inform general service provision it must have a universally accepted reference point. The medical model, for example, acquired its status and reference point not through the effort of scientific endeavour establishing the supremacy of this approach over other models but organically over a long historical period of neglect, the professionalisation of help and piecemeal legislation. In this process the medical profession gained dominance over the services administered to disabled people. In other words medical interpretations of disability have been given outstanding prominence in the administration of interventions to cater for 'the incapable disabled'. This has resulted in the medical model overshadowing the significance of the administrative model in shaping interventions to alleviate the situation of disabled people. Over time the medical model crystallised in the philosophy of 'rehabilitation' and its enabling legislation and this still remains one of the key reference points for current services. See, for example, Oliver (1990) for further discussion on the medical model.

Albrecht links the relation between medicine, disability and rehabilitation in this way: 'The social meanings given to impairment and disability shape public and institutional responses to these conditions and lay the foundation for the construction of a rehabilitation industry' (Albrecht, 1992: 67). If, on the other hand, applying the social model to practice means, as we argued earlier, 'that the removal of disabling barriers is relegated to a practical and technical, rather than a clinical, task and its control becomes a socio-political issue involving citizenship rights', then it seems clear that anti-discrimination legislation (ADL) can provide just such a reference point for the social model (see Chapter 12). However, if this is not to end in farce (or to result in no more gains than have been achieved with similar legislation on gender and race) ADL needs to be shaped by informed opinion. Knowledge of the Americans With Disabilities Act (put into force in 1992), at least, would be important in forming an opinion about the significance of ADL and its focus as a reference point in removing discrimination. The Act, for example, says

> The Act declares that no institution covered by law . . ., 'shall discriminate against a qualified individual in regard to job application procedures, the hiring, advancement, or discharge of employees, employee compensation, job training, and other terms, conditions, and privileges of employment.' Apart from employment it

covers public services, including transport, public accommodation, and telecommunications. (Banton, 1994: 50)

All the evidence at this point in time, however, is that current intentions are to introduce such legislation in response to agitation from a very disparate pressure lobby with very little real agreement about the social model of disability and its relation to the development of appropriate services. Indeed, apart from agreeing about the need for ADL we see no concrete signs of these issues even debated, let alone elaborated, among the collective ADL lobby.

In our view ADL legislation should not only set out the conditions for ensuring that disabled people attain their citizenship rights but it should also redefine the parameters for the support systems which they are expected to use into the next century. This goes well beyond accepting access rights to public buildings, transport, education and employment. It provides a mechanism for structuring disabled people's control over the way that they are treated by publicly funded service providers. In doing this it puts in place an important lever for shifting the British disabling culture into a more amenable frame of mind towards the disability culture that is being developed by people who have impairments.

There are two components to this proposal. First, 'disability equality training' should help service providers shift from being *providers* to *support* workers. This means a major shift in ethos from *care* to *resource* provision. Support system workers, then, become a key resource (not just the managers of resources) to be tapped by disabled people as they negotiate the complexities of barrier removal when they control the route to their personal life-style goals. The importance of control in the lives of disabled people has been emphasised repeatedly by disabled people. For example:

> Disabled people define independence, not in physical terms, but in terms of control. People who are almost totally dependent on others, in a physical sense, can still have independence of thought and action, enabling them to take full and active charge of their lives. (French, 1994a: 49)

Second, control is not only implied at the personal level as disabled individuals take an active role in realising their own goals but also at the social level when national and, most importantly, local representative organisations of disabled people have a statutory role in supervising the collective services. We believe that such a democratic approach is likely to be more effective than a 'Commission'. We do not support a Disabled Persons' Commission along the lines of the Commission on Racial Equality.

Where advocates are recruited they would be responsible to the local organisations of disabled people and would be mandated to design 'empowerment' packages to enable disabled individuals live according to their own chosen life-style. Resource workers in the support system should be directly accessible to disabled people, or their advocates when these are appointed, to obtain any necessary provision, such as wheelchairs, or services, such as home help, when these are identified in each individual's goal plans. The relation between personal barriers, such as an inaccessible toilet or inaccessible information in visual form, and social barriers, such as inaccessible television programming can be addressed by ensuring that those working with individuals and those working at the social policy level share the same reference point set by anti-discrimination legislation – both identify barriers in terms of the social model rather than ascribe problems to the consequence of individual deficits.

The introduction of ADL should be seen as essentially another historical stage in the development of greater understanding. If disability is indeed socially constructed by the way society is organised then changing the structure of society is not only the route to bettering the lives of disabled people but will also have a fundamental impact on the lives of all citizens. This makes it even more essential that the struggles of disabled people should be socialised, or 'mainstreamed'. Removing the barriers that contribute to the social construction of disablement cannot be the unique concern of only a minority social group and their supporters guided only by the 'special' needs of this group. In this respect, improving the quality of life of disabled people not only inextricably links the provision of new (Department of the Environment rather than health and welfare) services with the goal of emancipation but bonds these objectives to the same national goals of all citizens.

In our view it would be a gross mistake to address the problems of disablement as if this was the 'special' problem of unique individuals or, at best, the problem of a unique vulnerable and dependent minority group. In arguing that the most effective way of improving the lot of individual disabled people is by altering the life-styles of all UK citizens we are saying that the welfare of disabled people can best be improved by changing the British disabling culture. This, paradoxically, means that the focus of attention must not only move from the individual to the social group (as argued by many supporters of the social model in opposition to the medical model) but needs also to shift from the narrow concerns of the disabled population to the wider concerns of the national population! In this respect the single most important lesson from the life experiences of disabled people can be exported to the social arena where it can have a lasting effect on society as a whole.

The unique social contribution disabled people can make to the construction of a more civilised society originates with the insight that there is no causal relation between the possession of a personal deficit (impairment) and the experience of social incapacity (disability). This fundamentally challenges all prevailing models of disability (medical, administrative, individual, deficit, and so on) by replacing them with the so-called social model. In practice separating the experiences of impairment from the experiences of disability finds its most dynamic expression in a service separation between medical interventions and the broader concerns currently defined under the 'health' construct. What this means is that the service interests of disabled people cannot be met without changing society and this change of necessity involves the separation of the 'illness' services from the 'health' services. Indeed, it can be argued that just as medical dominance emerged when the medical profession gained administrative control over the lives of disabled people, medical dominance over health emerged when this profession was given administrative control over the 'health' service. Furthermore, the disability experience teaches us that once medical needs are separated from general life-style needs then social coordination between these concerns (at the government level) is best separated between a national medical service (an illness service) and the environment department. There remains no place, in a world reformed under the interests of disabled people, for a National Health Service.

Such is our fantasy for the 'brave new world'.

References

Albrecht, G.L. (1992) *The Disability Business: Rehabilitation in America*. London: Sage.

Allen, M. and Birse, E. (1991) Stigma and Blindness. *Ophthalmic Nursing and Technology*, 10(4), 147–51.

Americans with Disabilities Act (ADA) (1990) Public Law 101–336, 104 State. 327, US Congress.

Anthony, W.A. (1977) Social Rehabilitation: changing society's attitude towards the physically and mentally Disabled. In J. Stubbins (ed.) *Social and Psychological Aspects of Disability*. Baltimore: University Park.

Anthony, W.A. (1984) Societal Rehabilitation: changing society's attitudes towards the physically and mentally disabled. In R.P. Marinelli and L.E. Dell Orto (eds) *The Psychological and Social Impact of Physical Disability*. Springer: New York

Assistance and Disabled People. London: British Council of Disabled People.

Atkinson, R.L., Atkinson, R.C., Smith, E.E. and Bem, D.J. (1993) *Introduction to Psychology* (11th edn). London: Harcourt Brace Johanovich.

Baldwin, S. (1993) *The Myth of Community Care: An Alternative Neighbourhood Model of Care*. London: Chapman and Hall.

Banton, M. (1994) *Discrimination*. Buckingham: Open University Press.

Barnes, C. (1990) *Cabbage Syndrome: The Social Construction of Dependence*. Lewes: Falmer.

Barnes, C. (1991) *Disabled People in Britain and Discrimination: A Case for Anti-Discrimination Legislation*, London: Hurst, in association with The British Council of Organisations of Disabled People, Belper, Derbyshire.

Barnes, C. (1992) *Disabling Imagery and the Media*. Belper: The British Council of Organisations of Disabled People.

Barnes, C. (ed.) (1993) *Making our own Choices: Independent Living, Personal Assistance and Disabled People*. Derby: The British Council of Organisations of Disabled People.

Barnes, C. (1995) *From National to Local: An Evaluation of National Disablement Information Providers' Services to Local Disability Organisations*. Derby: The British Council of Organisations of Disabled People.

Baron, R.A. and Byrne, D. (1991) *Social Psychology* (6th edn). London: Allyn and Bacon.

Beard, R. (1976) *Teaching and Learning in Higher Education* (3rd edn). Harmondsworth: Penguin Books.

Bennet, G. (1987) *The Wound of the Doctor*. London: Secker and Warburg.

Berrol, C. (1984) Trainee Attitudes Towards Disabled Persons: effect of a special education program. *Archives of Physical Medicine and Rehabilitation*, 65, 760–5.

Biori, B. and Oermann, M.H. (1993) The Effect of Prior Experience in a Rehabilitation Setting on Students' Attitudes Towards the Disabled. *Rehabilitation Nursing*, 18(2), 95–8.

Bolderson, H. (1991) *Social Security, Disability and Rehabilitation*. London: Jessica Kingsley.

Bowlby, J. (1981) *Attachment: Separation and Loss*. London: Penguin Education.

Bracking, S. (1993) An introduction to the idea of independent/integrated living. In C. Barnes (ed.) *Making our own Choices: Independent Living, Personal Assistance and Disabled People*. Belper: The British Council of Organisations of Disabled People.

Brillhart, B.A., Jay, H. and Wyers, M.E. (1990) Attitudes towards people with disabilities. *Rehabilitation Nursing*, 15(2), 80–2, 85.

Brisenden, S. (1986) Independent living and the medical model of disability. *Disability, Handicap and Society*, 1(2), 173–8.

British Association for Counselling (1985) *Definition of Terms in Use with Expansion and Rationale*. Rugby: BAC.

Brown, R. (1986) *Social Psychology* (2nd edn). New York: Free Press.

Cale, L. and McCahan, D. (1993) Information: the tool that enables. In Policy Studies Institute, *Information Enables: Improving Access to Information Services for Disabled People*. Papers presented at the National Disability Information Project's 1993 Conference. London: Policy Studies Institute.

Campling, J. (1981) *Images of Ourselves*. London: Routledge and Kegan Paul.

Cassell, J. (1985) Disabled humour: origin and impact. In M. Magler (1990) *Perspectives on Disability*. Palo Alto, CA: Health Markets Research.

Chaffin, P.C. and Peipher, R.A. (1979) Simulated hearing loss: an aid to in-service education. *American Annals of the Deaf*, 124, 455–71.

Channel Four television (1994) *Sign On*. November.

Chinnery, B. (1990) Disabled people get the message: non-verbal clues to the nature of social work. *Practice*, 4(1), 49–55.

Chinnery, B. (1991) Equal opportunities for disabled people in the caring professions: window dressing or commitment? *Disability, Handicap and Society*, 6(3), 253–8.

Chubon, R.A. (1982) An analysis of research dealing with the attitudes of professionals towards disability. *Journal of Rehabilitation*, 48, 25–9.

Clare, M. (1990) *Developing Self-Advocacy Skills with People with Disabilities and Learning Difficulties*. London: FEU.

Clare, M. (1991) *Parents in Partnership: Setting up Parents' Support Groups*. London: Skill.

Clore, G. and Jeffrey, J. (1972) Emotional role playing, attitude change and attraction towards a disabled person. *Journal of Personality and Social Psychology*, 23, 105–11.

Clough, E. (1982) Attitudes. *Inter-regional Review*, Summer, 71, 34–7.

Codes of Practice for Counsellors, Trainers and Supervisors. Rugby: British Association for Counselling.

Corker, M.E.M. (1989) Deaf–hearing integration: A personal view. *Deafness*, 3(5), 4–5.

Cowie, R. and Douglas-Cowie, E. (1992) *Postlingually Acquired Deafness: Speech Deterioration and the Wider Consequences*. Berlin: Mouton de Gruyter.

Craft, A. (1992) *Aspects of Adulthood: Sex Education in Further Education for Learners with Severe Learning Difficulties*. London: FEU.

Culley, S. (1991) *Integrative Counselling Skills in Action*. London: Sage.

Curzon, L.B. (1990) *Teaching in Further Education: An Outline of Principles and Practice* (4th edn). London: Cassell.

Dalgleish, M. (1994). Countering the Labour Market Disadvantage of Disability. In Michael White (ed.) *Unemployment, Public Policy and the Changing Labour Market*. London: Policy Studies Institute Report 188.

Dart, J. (1990) Editorial. *Congressional Task Force on the Rights and Empowerment of Americans with Disabilities*, Library 7, Rights and Legislation, Disabilities Forum, Compuserve.

Davis, K. (1986) Equal opportunities and people who are disabled. UPIAS New Circular No.1, June.

Davis, K. (1993) On the movement. In J. Swain, V. Finkelstein, S. French and M. Oliver (eds) *Disabling Barriers – Enabling Environments*. London: Sage

Davis, K. (1994) Disability and legislation. In S. French (ed.) *On Equal Terms: Working with Disabled People*. London: Butterworth-Heinemann.

Davis, K. and Mullender, A. (1993) *Ten Turbulent Years. A Review of the Work of the Derbyshire Coalition of Disabled People*. Nottingham: Centre for Social Action, School of Social Studies, University of Nottingham.

Davis, M. (1993) Personal Assistance: Notes on the historical context in Making our own Choices. In C. Barnes (ed.) *Making our own Choices*. Derby: The British Council of Organisations of Disabled People.

Davis, M. and Wallbridge, D. (1981) *Boundary and Space: An Introduction to the Work of D.W. Winicott*. London, Karnac Books and New York, Brunner Mozel.

De Poy, E. and Merrill, S. (1988) Value acquisition in an occupational therapy curriculum. *Occupational Therapy Journal of Research*, 8, 259–74.

Department for Education Circular 93/01 (1993) The Further and Higher Education Act 1992.

Department of Health Circular (1984) HC(84)9/LAC(84)8.

Department of Health and Social Security Circular LAC(88)2 (1988) Disabled Persons (Services, Consultation and Representation) Act 1986, Implementation of Sections 5 and 6.

Department of Health Circular LAC(92)15 (1992) *Social Care for Adults with Learning Disabilities*.

Department of Health Circular LAC(93)12 (1993) Disabled Persons (Services, Consultation and Representation) Act 1986, Implications for Sections 5 and 6.

Derbyshire Coalition of Disabled People (DCDP) (1993) Editorial. *INFO*, 10, Clay Cross, Derbyshire: DCDP.

Dickson, D.A., Maxwell, A. and Saunders, C. (1991) Using role play with physiotherapy students. *Physiotherapy*, 77(2), 145–53.

Dimmock, A.F. (1993) *Cruel Legacy: An Introduction to the Record of Deaf People in History*. Edinburgh: Scottish Workshop Publications.

Disability Challenge (1981) May, 1.

Disability Discrimination Act (DDA) (1992) No. 135 of 1992, The Parliament of Australia.

Diseker, R.A. and Michielutte, R. (1981) An analysis of empathy in medical students before and following clinical experience. *Journal of Medical Education*, 56, 1004–10.

Duckworth, D. (1991) Personal communication by telephone.

Duckworth, S. (1988) The effect of medical education on the attitudes of medical students towards disabled people. *Journal of Medical Education*, 22, 1023–30.

Egan, G. (1993) *The Skilled Helper*. Pacific Grove, CA: Brooks Cole.

Ellis, K. (1993) *Squaring the Circle: User and Carer Participation in Needs Assessment*. London: Joseph Rowntree Foundation.

Elston, R.R. and Snow, B.M. (1986) Attitudes towards people with disabilities as expressed by rehabilitation professionals. *Rehabilitation Counselling Bulletin*, 29(4), 284–6.

Employment Department (1990) *Employment and Training for People with Disabilities*. London: Employment Department Group.

Estes, J., Deyer, C., Hansen, R. and Russell, J. (1991) Influence of occupational therapy curricula on students' attitudes towards persons with disabilities. *American Journal of Occupational Therapy*, 45, 156–9.

Evans, J.H. (1976) Changing attitudes towards disabled persons: an experimental study. *Rehabilitation Counselling Bulletin*, June, 172–9.

Festinger, L. (1957) *A Theory of Cognitive Dissonance*. California: Stanford University Press.

FEU (1989) *Towards a Framework for Curriculum Entitlement*. London: FEU.

FEU (1992) *A New Life*. London: FEU.

Fichten, C., Hines, J. and Amsel, R. (1985) Public awareness of physically disabled persons. *International Journal of Rehabilitation Research*, 8(4), 407–13.

Finkelstein, V. (1990) *Disability: Changing Practice*. Disability Awareness Training Pack. Milton Keynes: Open University.

Finkelstein, V. (1991a) Disability: an administrative challenge? (The Health and Welfare Heritage). In: M. Oliver (ed.) *Social Work: disabled people and disabling environments*. London: Jessica Kingsley.

Finkelstein, V. (1991b) It is insulting to trivialise disability. *Therapy Weekly*, 17(25), 5.

Finkelstein, V. (1991c) *Disability: Identity, Sexuality and Relationships*. Disability Awareness Training Pack. Milton Keynes: Open University.

Fishbein, M. and Ajken, I. (1975) *Belief, Attitude, Intention and Behaviour*. Reading, MA: Addison-Wesley.

Fisher, H.E.S. and Jurica, A.R.J. (eds) (1977) 14 Elizabeth, c. 5, Statutes of the Realm, IV, Part I. In *Documents in English Economic History: England from 1000 to 1760*. London: G. Bell.

Foley, C. and Pratt, S. (1994) *Access Denied: Human Rights and Disabled People*. London: National Council for Civil Liberties.

Foreman, C. (1985) *Where are We Going? If the Cap fits Wear it*. UPIAS Circular 58.

Fraser, D. (1984) *The Evolution of the British Welfare State*. London: Macmillan.

French, S. (1988) The experiences of disabled health professionals. *Sociology of Health and Illness*, 10(2), 70–88.

French, S. (1994a) The disabled role. In S. French (ed.) *On Equal Terms: Working with Disabled People*. Oxford: Butterworth-Heinemann.

French, S. (1994b) Disabled people and professional practice. In S. French (ed.) *On Equal Terms: Working with Disabled People*. Oxford: Butterworth-Heinemann.

Funk, R. (1986) Self-advocates push beyond civil rights. *Independent Living Forum*, 4(1), 3–5. The Research and Training Center on Independent Living, Kansas University.

Furnham, A. and Pendred, J. (1983) Attitudes towards the mentally and physically disabled. *British Journal of Medical Psychology*, 56, 179–87.

Further Education Funding Council Circular 92/06 (1992) *Students with Learning Difficulties and Disabilities*.

Further Education Funding Council Circular 93/05 (1993) *Students with Learning Difficulties and Disabilities*.

Further Education Funding Council Circular 94/03 (1994) *Students with Learning Difficulties and Disabilities*.

Further Education Funding Council Circular 95/07 (1995) *Students with Learning Difficulties and Disabilities*.

Gaff, A. (1994) *The Human Rights of Persons with Disabilities*. Ramallah, West Bank: Al-Haq.

Galloway, T. (1987) I'm listening as hard as I can! In M. Saxton and F. Howe (eds) *With Wings: An Anthology of Literature by Women with Disabilities*. London: Virago.

Gething, L. (1992) Nurse practitioners' and students' attitudes towards people with disabilities. *Australian Journal of Advanced Nursing*, 9(3), 25–30.

Gething, L. (1993) Attitudes towards people with disabilities of physiotherapists and members of the general public. *Australian Journal of Physiotherapy*, 39(4), 291–5.

Gething, L. and Westbrook, M. (1983) Enhancing physiotherapy students' attitudes towards disabled people. *Australian Journal of Physiotherapy*, 29, 48–52.

Glendenning, C. and Bewley, C. (1992) *Involving Disabled People in Community Care Planning – The First Steps*. Manchester: University of Manchester.

Goffman, E. (1968) *Stigma: Notes on the Management of a Spoiled Identity*. London: Penguin Books.

Gordon, E., Minnes, P. and Holden, R. (1990) The structure of attitudes towards persons with a disability, when specific disability and context are considered. *Rehabilitation Psychology*, 35, 79–90.

Gregory, S. (1993) The language and culture of deaf people: Implications for education. *Deafness*, 3(9), 4–11.

Griffiths, Matthew (1989) *Working Together? Enabled to Work. Support into Employment for Young People with Disabilities*. London: FEU.

Gross, R.D. (1987) *Psychology: The Science of Mind and Behaviour*. London: Edward Arnold.

Hansard (1993) *Parliamentary Debates*, 26 February. London: HMSO.

Harris, P. and Rayment, S. (1994) Article in the *Daily Mail*, Friday 25 July 1994. London: Down's Syndrome Association.

Hillman, J. (undated) *Cataract: A Guide for the Patient*. Leeds: St James's University Trust Hospital.

HMSO (1981) *Education Act*. London: HMSO.

HMSO (1990) *NHS and Community Care Act*. London: HMSO.

Holmes, G.E. and Karst, R.H. (1990) The institutionalisation of disability myths: impact on vocational rehabilitation services. *Journal of Rehabilitation*, 56, 20–7.

Honey, S., Meager, N. and Williams, M. (1993) *Employers' Attitudes to People with Disabilities*. London: Institute of Manpower Studies, Report 245.

Hoyes, L., Jeffers, S., Lart, R., Means, R. and Taylor, M. (1993) *User Empowerment and the Reform of Community Care: A Study of Early Implementation in Four Localities*. School for Advanced Urban Studies, University of Bristol.

Huitt, K. and Elston, R.R. (1991) Attitudes towards persons with disabilities expressed by professional counsellors. *Journal of Applied Rehabilitation Counselling*, 22(2), 42–3.

Hull, J. (1991) *Touching the Rock: An Experience of Blindness*. London: Arrow Books.

Human Rights Act (1994) 1993, No. 82, Parliament of New Zealand.

Hunt, J. (1988) UPIAS Internal Circular (February).

Hunt, J. (1992) *The Disabled People's Movement Between 1960–1986 and its Effect upon the Development of Community Support Services*. Unpublished MA dissertation, The Polytechnic of East London.

International Labour Organisation (1983) International Labour Organisation Convention No. 159 concerning vocational rehabilitation and employment (disabled persons). Quoted in A. Gaff (1994) *The Human Rights of Persons with Disabilities*. Ramallah, West Bank: Al-Haq.

Jacobs, M. (1988) *Psychodynamic Counselling in Action*. London: Sage.

Keay, D., McKay, J., Took, M. and Stables, C. (1994) Some personal experiences. In M. Floyd, M. Povall and G. Watson (eds) *Mental Health at Work*. London: Jessica Kingsley.

Kettle, M. (1986) *The Employment of Disabled Teachers*. London: The Royal Association for Disability and Rehabilitation.

Kilbury, R.F., Bensoff, J.J. and Rubin, S.E. (1992) The interaction of legislation, public attitudes, and access to opportunities for persons with disabilities. *Journal of Rehabilitation*, 58(4), 6–9.

Kirklees Metropolitan Borough Council (1992) Level Best Conference report.

Kirklees Metropolitan Borough Council (1993) *Targeting for Diversity in Employment. Guidelines for Managers*.

Kirklees Metropolitan Borough Council (1993–94) Wordlink Annual Report.

Kubler-Ross, E. (1989) *Death and Dying*. London: Routledge.

Kyle, J.G., Jones, L.G. and Wood, P.L. (1985) Adjustment to acquired hearing loss: a working model. In H. Orlans (ed.) *Adjustment to Adult Hearing Loss*. San Diego, CA: College-Hill Press.

Kyle, J.G., Jones, L.G. and Wood, P.L. (1987) *Words Apart: Losing your Hearing as an Adult*. London: Tavistock Publications.

Ladd, P. (1988) The modern deaf community. In D. Miles (ed.) *British Sign Language: A Beginner's Guide*. London: BBC Books.

Ladd, P. (1993) *See Hear!* Debate on Deaf and disabled people. BBC Television.

Lambert, M.J., Shapiro, D.A. and Bergin, A.E. (1986) The effectiveness of psychotherapy. In S.L. Garfield and A.E. Bergin (eds) *Handbook of Psychotherapy and Behavior Change*. New York: John Wiley.

Lane, H. (1993) *The Mask of Benevolence*. New York: Alfred A. Knopf.

Large, P. (1982) *Report of the Committee on Restrictions Against Disabled People*. London: HMSO.

Leonard, R. and Crawford, J. (1989) Two approaches to seeing people with disabilities. *Australian Journal of Social Issues*, 24, 112–25.

Levine, E.S. (1981) *The Ecology of Early Deafness: Guides to Fashioning Environments and Psychological Assessments*. New York: Columbia University Press.

Lewis, C.S. (1994) International aspects of the disability issue. In J.A. Nelson (ed.) *The Disabled, the Media, and the Information Age*. Westport, CT: Greenwood Press.

Lewis, V. (1987) *Development and Handicap*. Oxford: Basil Blackwell.

London Boroughs Disability Resource Team (1991) *Disability Equality Training Trainers Guide*. London: CCETSW.

Lumb, K. (1994) The ramp. *Coalition* (magazine of GMCDP), June.

Luterman, D. (1987) *Deafness in the Family*. Boston: College-Hill Press.

Lyons, M. (1991) Enabling or disabling? Students' attitudes towards persons with disabilities. *American Journal of Occupational Therapy*, 45, 311–16.

Lyons, M. and Hayes, R. (1993) Student perceptions of persons with psychiatric and other disorders. *The American Journal of Occupational Therapy*, 47(6), 541–8.

McAnaney, D. (1994) The development of social enterprises in Ireland. In M. Floyd, M. Povall and G. Watson (eds) *Mental Health at Work*. London: Jessica Kingsley.

McConkey, R. and McCormack, B. (1983) *Breaking Barriers: Educating People about Disability*. London: Souvenir Press.

Macfarlane, A. (1994) Subtle forms of abuse and their long term effects. *Disability & Society*, 9.

Macfarlane, A. and Hassan, A. (1994) *A Report on a Survey of Domiciliary and Respite Care*

Services in the London Borough of Merton. MAFIA, Vestry Hall, London Road, Mitcham, Surrey.

Manchester City Council (1986) (Aug.) *Disabled Policy: Services Suffer*. Social Services Insight.

Manchester City Council (1987) *Population Sample Survey*. Planning Department.

Manchester City Council (1989) (Feb.) *Changing the Composition of the Workforce*. Report to Policy and Resources Committee.

Manchester City Council (1990) *Equal Matters in Manchester*.

Manchester City Council (1991) *Report to the Disabled People's Sub-committee*. Chief Executive's Department.

Manchester City Council (1992) (July) *Disabled People's Equality Targets – the Way Forward*. Report to Policy and Resources Committee.

Manchester City Council (1993) (Nov.) *Progress on Extension of the Targetted Recruitment Scheme Across Council Departments*. Report to Equal Opportunities and Anti-Discrimination Sub-committee.

Manchester City Council (1994a) (Sept.) *Briefing Note on 'Umbrella' Voluntary Organisations*. Grant Aid Panel.

Manchester City Council (1994b) (Dec.) *Manchester City Council and Manchester Disability Forum Service Specification Agreement*.

Manifesto, K.D. (1986) (June) *Equal Opportunities and People who are Disabled*. UPIAS New Circular No. 1.

Mansfield, J. (1980) *The Adventures of Jill, or the Ups and Downs of Being Hard of Hearing*. London: RNID.

Marsh, P. and Fisher, M. (1992) *Good Intentions: Developing Partnership in Social Services*. London: Joseph Rowntree Foundation.

Marte, A.L. (1988) How does it feel to be old? Simulation game provides 'into aging' experience. *Journal of Continuing Nursing Education*, 14, 166–8.

Martin, J. & White, A. (1988) *OPCS Report 2. The Financial Circumstances of Disabled Adults in Private Households*. London: HMSO.

Martin, J., White, A. and Meltzer, H. (1989) OPCS Report 4. *Disabled Adults: Services, Transport and Employment*. London: HMSO.

Maslow, A.H. (1962) *Towards a Psychology of Being*. Princeton, NJ: Van Nostrand.

Maychell, K. and Bradley, J. (1991) *Preparing for Partnership. Multi-agency Support for Special Needs*. National Foundation for Educational Research in England and Wales (NFER).

Mearns, D. and Thorne, B. (1988) *Person-Centred Counselling in Action*. London: Sage.

Mitchell, K.R., Hayes, M., Gordon, J. and Wallis, B. (1984) An investigation of the attitudes of medical students to physically disabled people. *Journal of Medical Education*, 18, 21–3.

Montgomery, G. and Laidlaw, K. (1993) *Occupational Dissonance and Discrimination in the Employment of Deaf People*. Edinburgh: Scottish Workshop Publications.

Morris, J. (1987) Progress with humanity? The experience of a disabled lecturer. In T. Booth and W. Swann (eds) *Including Pupils with Disabilities*. Milton Keynes: Open University Press.

Morris, J. (1993) *Independent Lives: Community Care and Disabled People*. London: Macmillan.

Morris, J. (1994) Prejudice. In S. French (1994) *On Equal Terms: Working with Disabled People*. London: Butterworth-Heinemann.

Morris, O.F. (1976) Simulation of visual impairments as a training technique. *New Outlook for the Blind*, 70, 417–19.

Munro, K. and Elder-Woodward, J. (1992) *Independent Living*. Edinburgh: Churchill Livingstone.

National League of the Blind and Disabled (1988) *A Brief History of the National League of the Blind and Disabled 1899–1987* (Year Book 1988). Manchester: NLBD.

Nelson, J.A. (1994) *The Disabled, the Media, and the Information Age*. Westport, CT: Greenwood Press.

NFER/FEU (1988) *New Directions: A Curriculum Framework for Students with Severe Learning Difficulties*.

Oliver, M. (1978) Disability, adjustment and family life . . . some theoretical considerations. In A. Brechin, P. Liddiard and J. Swain (eds) *Handicap in the Social World*. Sevenoaks: Hodder and Stoughton.

Oliver, M. (1983) *Social Work with Disabled People*. Basingstoke: Macmillan.

Oliver, M. (1990) *The Politics of Disablement*. London: Macmillan.

Oliver, M. (1994) Moving on: from welfare paternalism to welfare citizenship. *Journal of the Centre for Social Action*, 2(1).

Open University (1989) *P555 Patterns for Living: Working Together*. A course for people with learning difficulties. Milton Keynes: Open University.

Padden, C. and Humphries, T. (1988) *Deaf in America: Voices from a Culture*. Cambridge, MA: Harvard University Press.

Pagel, M. (1988) *On Our Own Behalf – An Introduction to the Self Organisation of Disabled People*. Manchester: Greater Manchester Coalition of Disabled People.

Palmer, I. (1993) *Training in Counselling and Psychotherapy – A Directory*. Rugby: British Association for Counselling.

Paris, M.J. (1993) Attitudes of medical students and health care professionals towards people with disabilities. *Archives of Physical Medicine and Rehabilitation*, 74, 818–25.

Pennington, D.C. (1986) *Essential Social Psychology*. London: Edward Arnold.

Philpot, T. (1994) *Search 20*. London: Joseph Rowntree Foundation.

Pockney, R. (1989) Personal communication by letter.

Pockney, R. (1991) Personal communication by letter.

Potts, M.J. (1986) Sex differences in medical students and house staff attitudes towards the handicapped. *Journal of the American Women's Association*, 41, 156–9.

Prescott-Clarke, P. (1990) *Employment and Handicap*. London: Social and Community Planning Research.

Rae, A. (1985) *For, not of*. UPIAS (July).

Ramsdell, D.A. (1978) The psychology of the hard of hearing and deafened adult. In H. Davis and S.R. Silverman (eds) *Hearing and Deafness* (4th edn). New York: Holt, Rinehart and Winston.

Reber, A.S. (1985) *Dictionary of Psychology*. London: Penguin Books.

Redfern, P. (1991) Can deaf people make decisions? *Deafness*, 2(7), 11–12.

Reid, C. (1994) Voice-over training needed. *British Deaf News*, February, 19.

Reynolds, R. (1991) Revenge of the wheelchair users. *Disability Now*, August, 9.

Rezler, A.G. (1974) Attitude changes during medical school. *Journal of Medical Education*. 49, 1023–30.

Richardson, M. (1990) Disabled for a day. *Nursing Times*, 86(21), 66–9.

RNIB (1991) *Finding Out About Blindness*, Training Pack. London: Royal National Institute for the Blind.

Rogers, C.R. (1951) *Client Centred Therapy*. London: Constable.

Rogers, C.R. (1961) *On Becoming a Person*. London: Constable.

Rosswurm, M. (1980) Changing nursing students' attitudes towards persons with physical disabilities. *Journal of American Registered Nurses*, 5, 12–14.

Rousch, S.E. (1986) Health professionals as contributors to attitudes towards persons with disabilities. *Physical Therapy*, 66, 1551–4.

Sampson, D.E. (1991) Changing attitudes towards persons with cerebral palsy through contact and information. *Rehabilitation Education*, 5(2), 87–92.

Schlesinger, H.S. (1985) The psychology of hearing loss. In H. Orlans (ed.) *Adjustment to Adult Hearing Loss*. San Diego, CA: College-Hill Press.

Semple, J.E., Vargo, J.W. and Vargo, F.A. (1980) Disability simulation and its effect on changing the attitudes of physical therapy students towards disabled persons: some preliminary experimental results. *New Zealand Journal of Physiotherapy*, 8(2), 6–8.

Shakespeare, T. (1993) Disabled people's self organisation: a new social movement? *Disability, Handicap and Society*, 8(3) 249–64.

Sim, J. (1990) Physical disability, stigma, and rehabilitation. *Canadian Journal of Physiotherapy*, 42(5), 232–8.

Smith, B. and Povall, M. (1994) Overcoming barriers to employment. In M. Floyd, M. Povall and G. Watson (eds) *Mental Health at Work*. London: Jessica Kingsley.

Smith, B., Povall, M. and Floyd, M. (1991) *Managing Disability at Work*. London: Jessica Kingsley.

SSI Department of Health Social Services Inspectorate, SWST Scottish Office Social Work Services Group (1991) *Care Management and Assessment: Practitioners' Guide*. London: HMSO.

Staffordshire Social Services Department (1994) *Building for the Future*. Learning Disabilities Day Service Review.

Stevenson, O. and Parsloe, P. (1993) *Community Care and Empowerment*. London: Joseph Rowntree Foundation.

Stowell, R. (1987) *Catching Up: Provision for Students with Special Educational Needs in Further and Higher Education*. London: Skill.

Sutcliffe, J. (1990) *Adults with Learning Difficulties: Education for Choice and Empowerment*. National Institute of Adult Continuing Education (NIACE) in association with The Open University Press.

Sutcliffe, J. and Simons, K. (1993) *Self-Advocacy and Adults with Learning Difficulties*. Leicester: NIACE.

Swain, J. and Lawrence, P. (1994) Learning about disability: changing attitudes or challenging understanding? In S. French (ed.) *On Equal Terms: Working with Disabled People*. Oxford: Butterworth-Heinemann.

Therapy Weekly (1991) Children experience dilemma of disabled. 17(21), 3.

Thornburgh, D. (1990) *The promise of the Americans with Disabilities Act*. Speech at the Office of Personnel Management Eighth Annual Government-wide Conference on the Employment of Persons with Disabilities, Library 7, Rights and Legislation, Disabilities Forum, Compuserve.

Touching the Rock (1991) BBC2, 2 June.

Tringo, J.L. (1970) The hierarchy of preference towards disability groups. *The Journal of Special Education*. 4, 295–305.

Troyna, B. and Siraj-Blatchford, I. (1993) Providing support or denying access? The experiences of students designated as 'ESL' and 'SN' in a multi-ethnic secondary school. *Education Review*, 45(1), 14–21.

Turner, C. (1984) Who Cares? *Occupational Health*, 36(10), 4494–552.

Understanding Disabilities Educational Trust. Promotional literature. Farnham: Understanding Disabilities Educational Trust.

Union of the Physically Impaired Against Segregation (1972) *Policy Statement*. UPIAS.

Union of the Physically Impaired Against Segregation (1976) *Fundamental Principles of Disability*. UPIAS.

UPIAS (1990) (Nov.) *UPIAS is Dead*. Final UPIAS internal circular. [The UPIAS was dissolved in October 1990.]

Vargo, J.W. and Semple, J.E. (1988) Professional and personal attitudes of physiotherapy students towards disabled persons. *Australian Journal of Physiotherapy*, 34(1), 23–6.

Vostanis, P. (1990) The role of work in psychiatric rehabilitation: a review of the literature. *British Journal of Occupational Therapy*, 53(1), 24–7.

Warr, P. (1987) *Work, Unemployment and Mental Health*. Oxford: Clarendon Press.

Warr, P. and Wall, T. (1975) *Work and Wellbeing*. Harmondsworth: Penguin.

Weisel, A. and Florian, V. (1990) Same and cross-gender attitudes towards persons with physical disabilities. *Rehabilitation Psychology*, 35(4), 229–38.

Wertheimer, A. (1989) *Self-Advocacy and Parents: the Impact of Self-Advocacy on the Parents of Young People with Disabilities*. Part of the Working Together Series. London: FEU.

West Midlands Regional Health Authority (1993) *Action for Health*. Report of the Regional Director of Public Health.

Westbrook, M., Adamson, B.J. and Westbrook, J.I. (1988) Health science students' images of disabled people. *Community Health Studies*, 12(3), 304–11.

Wicker, A.W. (1969) Attitudes versus actions: the relationship of verbal and overt behavior responses to attitude objects. *Journal of Social Issues*, 25, 41–78.

Wilson, E. and Alcorn, D. (1969) Disability simulation and the development of attitudes towards the exceptional. *Journal of Special Education*, 3, 303–7.

Wood, J. (1990) Children discover how it feels to be disabled. *Therapy Weekly*, 16(40), 10.

Yuker, H.E. and Block, J.R. (1979) *Challenging Barriers to Change: Attitudes Towards the Disabled*. Albertson, NY: Human Resources Center.

Yuker, H., Block, J. and Campbell, W. (1960) *A Scale to Measure Attitudes Towards Disabled Persons*. Albertson, NY: Human Resources Center.

Index